T0195728

CULTIVATING A NEW GENERATION

CULTIVATING A NEW GENERATION:

THE POWER OF BEING A COUPLE

DAVID ORTEGA B.

To order additional copies of this book, contact:
Xlibris
1-888-795-4274
www.Xlibris.com
Orders@Xlibris.com
810930

Contents

Introduction xi

Chapter 1   Waking Up to a Whole New World 1

   The Actors of the Movie 1

   Your Parents' Contribution 5

   Emotional Wounds Colliding 8

   The Memory in Your Body 17

   Thought Takeaways 18

Chapter 2   Seeing the Choices of Life 43

   Is It Really Somebody's Fault? 44

   Owning Your Role 56

   Finding a Common Ground 59

   Thought Takeaways 65

Chapter 3   Building a Healthy Ground 81

   Creating Opportunities 82

   Empowered Women 85

   Toxic Environments 92

   Thought Takeaways 106

Chapter 4   The Snowball of Self-Sabotage... 115

Your Actions Dictate Your Consequences 116

Breaking the Trust... 127

Being Responsible to Start Healing.. 130

Thought Takeaways 133

Chapter 5   The Healing Journey.. 148

Owning Your Life... 149

External Slavery vs. Inner Freedom 155

Living with Resentment or Forgiveness.. 159

Thought Takeaways 173

Chapter 6   A New Member Brings Peace and Wisdom............................... 190

Going Deep in Your Relationship.. 191

Your Reset Point... 199

A New Fresh Start.. 211

Thought Takeaways 219

Chapter 7   The Clearest and Toughest Mirror: Your Child....................... 239

Focusing on Parenting without Forgetting Your Partner.......................... 239

Political Family Interference... 242

Childhood Awareness and Smoothing Couple's Interaction.................. 246

Thought Takeaways 264

Chapter 8   Building Your Relationship Day by Day........................ 288

    The Hamster Wheel Effects 289

    A Social-Supported Life Model.. 292

    Your Five-Core Inner Healing to Save Your Relationship...................... 300

    Thought Takeaways 313

Final Remarks: A New Generation to Heal Our Earth.................................. 343

Endnotes 345

Index 355

For my mother, my father, my brother. My beautiful daughter, Valerie,

and my wife, Mary, who are among the most valuable influences in

my life and who without question have shaped me, empowered me,

and allowed me to find my own inner journey with all the interactions,

insights, teachings, and love that they have given me!

INTRODUCTION

WE COME HERE to this earth, to this reality, to enjoy it, to make the most of it and soon in life, we start questioning what is our purpose here.

However, we shouldn't be as arrogant as we have been for several decades, thinking that the world is only the human species, being insensitive to all that is around us, becoming oblivious to the fact that we are just one more species in this rich diversity where we coexist with a million other living organisms.

If we soon cultivate and realize we are not only humans but also a huge ecosystem that needs and works together to allow life to be experienced in such a rich way, then we might be able to turn around all the damage that we have been performing on this beautiful planet.

To do that, we must be able to experience at the fullest our senses and hear all the broad variety of sounds we are surrounded with, how each of the languages spoken by species has a purpose and can have an effect as well on us—the touch that enable us to perceive the magical variety of weather, which is coupled with nature changes that in some extent produces an internal change in us, in a hug felt as a gentle expression of our parents' love for us. Witness the majestic expression of nature creations with awe, with curiosity, with wonder, and let that visual scenery inspire reflection within us, pay attention to all the amazing examples of wisdom that other species express to us, but we are too busy to see them, savoring earth's gifts that allow us to nurture our physical bodies and becoming more mindful of eating what our bodies enjoy and not the artificial food that creates disease in our bodies.

We are created with a perfect team of cells, of little fabrics that work together to cooperate and to create from within a perfect balance, without recognizing that it is easy to fall in the automatic behavior of just surviving without even being humble enough to read our own manual, knowing what happens inside us, understanding how we perform wonders within every minute of our existence, building proteins, repairing and healing tissues, interconnecting chemicals that light up and embellish our interior to perform a perfect symphony of our life!

We possess a brain capacity that separate us from all other species, waves that start developing and acquiring more connections, knowledge of every sensed stimuli, that bit by bit start building experiences that we start to enjoy, to avoid, to become familiar with pain to learn how to protect us, to interact with other humans or living beings, allowing us to feel connected. Step by step, a story of our lives starts being written inside of us and being projected into our realities.

This is the story that each of us get for a certain time frame that nobody knows how much will last, that might feel like an enigma, but that is supposed to awaken your curiosity to be able to experience it with gratitude, with a humble outlook, with a sense of accountability to do your best efforts in discovering your own path.

Is there a destiny for each of us? Do we really have a path already marked, already drawn, by a higher self?

Where is that "higher self," how do you interact more with that divine wisdom?

Is this path a straight line, or would you find or create detours from it?

How and what do we have to learn from that tortuous journey?

What is the message that we need to pass along or help others with, so that they can encounter their own path?

Are people that we find in our path supposed to give us feedback, clues, or are they supposed to point us in some direction that we need to take?

Why are we resistant to take advice from people, even if we clearly know many times that their advice can save us some turns, bumps, and falls?

I believe that as human beings, our inherent right is always being a better version than before. We only have this present moment in our hands, yet we waste our precious time by either thinking about the past or wondering about the future, knowing that any of those actions will lead us anywhere but to experience anguish, melancholy, sadness, anxiety, and many other toxic emotions, which we ourselves are choosing to feel.

Then how do we achieve that better version?

How do we understand more and more the right choices for our path and the best impact that we can leave for the people around us?

I believe in my opinion those are the ultimate questions for most of us.

We should learn how to take those choices without complicating our lives, letting life unfold to us and allowing us to discover step by step, committing ourselves with the present process and not with the goal, igniting our spark for life as we move forward, maintaining our inner self to be awake and enhanced to guide us throughout the road.

If you relate and resonate with this brief reflection, that this moment is all we have, that committing to the process and not with the goal is the answer, that every day you have a new opportunity to course correctly and do it better, acting on your life, moving the needle with a better understanding than yesterday, discovering more who you are and what you want, what you need, and what is the impact that you are willing to leave in this life experience, THEN THIS BOOK IS FOR YOU!

Knowing that you are engaged in it already, I am grateful and I can assure you that by choosing to read it, you will enroll and commit in your own journey within you; experience every major emotion and feeling with more consciousness of the present moment; understand why your emotions or feelings are triggered by your thoughts; be able to see you launch your actions with more wisdom; be able to let your programmed experiences behind to stop the influence of your culture, society, and family; and arrive at the freedom that you deserve.

Hopefully, you will also find more answers and probably questions of what happens inside of you, but also you will be able to awaken again that curiosity that will allow you to find your own path, first on a thought level, then emotionally, then enhancing your feelings, enlightening your behaviors, and finally engaging yourself and accepting the challenge that will come from reading this book.

You will generate more awareness and accountability to finally use your tools as well as the book tools provided in each chapter so that you understand your own inner energy, your reactions, your biochemistry, the interactions that happen internally within you and with your environment, your emotions without giving them power to screw your life or take you completely out of your road.

So, tighten your seat belts because you are about to enjoy the ride.

CHAPTER 1

Waking Up to a Whole New World

The Actors of the Movie

VILMA WAS HER name, or at least that's the name her parents chose for her.

She was a beautiful little girl, one that you could describe as a drop of perfection from a couple that could be seen as the perfect match for certain people that have a wider point of view.

As an infant and a story of a little child, we're going to be centered more on the environment where she grew up and how, as little as she was, she already had an influence of her parents' way, a relation that can seem magical at the beginning when you witness certain reactions or patterns from each other and how this kind of influence can already have a huge impact on her years to come and her future life.

Thus, let's start talking about the influencers in her environment with the main actors, her parents: Mario and Betty.

Mario was a corpulent man. He came from a family with several issues regarding overprotection, not giving him a sense of responsibility of what he had to do, how to take his own choices, and sometimes even how to be able to be self-sufficient.

He didn't even finish high school due to a lot of problems to stay focused. He was pretty much surrounded by a very toxic environment of alcohol, drugs, and taking the "easy" way to obtain things, meaning just extending a hand for what he wanted or sometimes having the habit of stealing from others, not in the literal way but by playing his charismatic personality traits.

With an opinionated character, not used to being responsible at all, spoiled by his parents who allowed him to always get out with his way in terms of material stuff, he was bored with his life and always looking for adrenaline and danger to make up for his lack of emotional attention that he rarely fulfilled because in spite of all the "overprotection" for material things that his parents gave him, he never really had the attention that he needed in terms of how he felt and so many questions that he had, most of all during his puberty and transition to being an adult. His life was pretty much full of reckless decisions until he turned twenty-one years old when something striking was going to happen in his life. A very special person was going to be a part of the transformation.

He worked in a sports store, in a fancy neighborhood in Mexico City known as Mazaryk. He was a simple employee who pretty much sat in his chair to play video games in his cell phone and check social media for about eight hours until he could finally go home and engage in another stupid adventure-seeking passion, adrenaline, and some kind of "meaning" or emotion for his life. Even though he didn't finish high school, he was pretty good with technology and had a very charismatic personality to engage people in false stories, amusing them to the point where they got interested and bought whatever he offered, meaning he was good with words as well; he had sales skills, using his ability to perform storytelling adventures.

Betty, on the other hand, had apparently a pretty opposite background to Mario's. She was a simple girl who already graduated from the Autonomous Metropolitan University, with a business administration degree. She worked at a very well-known tech company, Epson, formerly known as IBM, in Mexico City as well. She was just in a starting position as client support, dealing with technical issues regarding software. She was pretty good at her job, and her boss saw her as a young promising girl although she didn't have a clue about it.

She was a chubby girl, not worried about her physical appearance, which sadly also included a dose of having a very poor eating behavior. She had a pretty simple and lonely life, mostly dedicated to her work. She was a little bit workaholic and mostly shy to talk about her too much. Therefore, she didn't have many friends, but the ones she had were similar to her in her drive, discipline, and way in leading their lives pretty much in a healthier way.

She had a different story in the parent setting as that of Mario's but in a strange way; they could be complemented with some inner feelings that they had about themselves. Her father was a very strict, cold male chauvinist that treated her very poorly in spite of her academic achievements and all the independence that she showed since she was a little girl. Her mother was very house oriented who just dedicated her life to house chores, pleasing the husband, and being interested in pleasing her family, but not paying attention to her daughter. Therefore, she also lacked a lot of attention and guidance through her childhood and puberty years, which forged a strong character in her, allowing her to develop a strong sense of independent, self-driven achievement as well as being able to handle very well any struggle or hardship in terms of professional development.

However, her skills in relating to people, self-esteem, and care for her outlook and appearance were not a priority for her and absorbed that lack of attention that she didn't receive as a child. Since she was a teenager, she picked up jobs to be self-reliable economically and not have the necessity of asking anything from her father because she didn't like his manners or the way he always tried to diminish her.

She performed several roles as a clerk in a clothing store and as a waitress, and when she was studying her career, she also learned English and finished a teacher's course program that allowed her to teach English while she finished her degree. She cared a lot in developing several skills in order to be able to survive without the help of her parents and also courage for the way her father treated her mom and her. She was determined to eliminate that pattern in her life and not be an image of her mom with any of her male partners.

That made very complicated her emotional relationships with the opposite sex, but up to now, that was not something she cared about, at least in a superficial sense of feeling.

Your Parents' Contribution

Betty and Mario were not the exception but the rule in terms of the damage that they both suffered in terms of attention, guidance, and a reliable example to follow. That being said, their emotional deficiencies or holes were profound and deep as we can see from their personality traits.

But what was the contribution to those wounds, or what were the examples they received from their caregivers? Let's meet the parents and some of their background!

Let's begin with Betty's father, which as you could see was quite an influence on her life and personality. He was a very common guy in terms of culture traits, beliefs, and clichés that a Mexican society and some others have been dragging for several years—strong in character; emotionally detached from his feelings; cold, of course, in expressing any kind of affection and much less any kind of appreciation of what he received or how he was treated by his wife.

With a strong history of pain due to his father and grandfather who used to beat him for pretty much everything, both of them alcoholic, and lacking every sense of consciousness in treating a child, he was raised just to be able to survive, have an offspring, and work. Pretty much every opportunity he had, he used to take out all of his pain with her daughter and his wife by diminishing both just for the fact that they were women and they had to follow the model of serving the husband and father in order to keep things calm and quiet. One good trait that he didn't repeat from his own story was that at least he didn't beat Betty at any stage of her life although he was very rude, strong, and strict to make things happen.

He was absent most of the time, as his job used to be very demanding and he was good at avoiding any kind of emotional or relationship time. He was a retired worker from one of the biggest energy companies in Mexico CFE (Federal Commission of Electricity). He used to drink although not to the point of his inherited history; he had a strong will, and he could stop right before he did something stupid.

Betty's mom was a "simple" woman in terms of not being a rebel or being able to provoke any kind of problems. She followed the simple style of "how a woman should be" and provided his husband with everything he needed and wanted. Although she also had a dark and more painful story in terms of her mother and grandmother, which marked Betty's mom personality for her whole life without of course knowing what happened before, the only thing that Betty knew about her mother was that his grandmother committed suicide and left her mom and her uncle alone, and they managed to survive and grow up. Due to that pain and hardship that she experienced in her past, the easiest way to cover it up was to develop a pleasing and submissive personality that was very strong and reflected on her way to be "the perfect host" with her family and not being able to deal with rejection, being wrong, or going against what everyone else expected from her. In fewer words, she developed a people-pleaser personality to avoid being "abandoned."

On the other hand, Mario's father was a very successful businessman who didn't care about anything but money, appearance, and showing off of all his achievements, material assets, and framing a perfect family picture for everyone else. Very selfish in showing also any kind of affection, appreciation, or gratitude for many of the things that happened in his life, he was strongly disappointed of Mario's attitude of being able to have a strong character, finish a business career as he would have wanted, and inherit a position in his father's company to continue the legacy.

He was also a ghost in terms of being present with his family unless it was related to a social event where he could display "the perfect family" image that he needed to be able to be supported in many of his endeavors and successes.

That, of course, brought a lack of presence as a father or husband, which would have consequences on Mario and his wife.

Mario's mom, on the other hand, was an affectionate woman when she was sober because she used to have a very unhealthy relationship with alcohol and other men that paid some attention to her. When she was drunk, she was not able to show affection or pay attention to Mario, as everything she wanted was to feel seen, desired enough by his husband, which was something that also never happened.

She used to spend all of her time with her friends in social events and in the gym, and the little time she spent in her house and the little time she was sober was when Mario could enjoy her presence. That's why Mario developed a storyteller ability to engage her mom in a talk, to appear interesting to her, and to be able to have some attention at least for the moments that she was sober.

It was harder for Mario to discover something about his parents' pain as both of them played a very good role at disguising all that emotional damage with money and alcohol, and they both became very good actors for "the perfect family" appearance.

Emotional Wounds Colliding

As every story in humanity, everything happens for a reason, and people's encounters are the most synchronic way to show us the wounds, the voids, and sometimes if we are lucky and awake, the way to follow to recover from our past stories.

Therefore, Mario's and Betty's story was not going to be the exception.

One Friday afternoon, Mario was having one of his worst days due to failing his final exam in chemistry, which was the last subject he was missing in order to finish all of his high school subjects and be able to finally obtain his high school degree. He was pretty upset with himself, playing again and again a self-pity story in his head of how stupid and irresponsible he was for not taking seriously that test once again, listening to his friends who lured him to get high and play some more hours of video games. In addition to being scolded by his boss at the sports store for losing so much time attached to the phone and engaging in talks with beautiful strangers who enter the store to buy and then return to the store looking for him due to some stupid promises of love or issues that he managed to engage them in, basically making a scene at the store and scaring off clients due to the noisy behavior of the hurt women who came looking for him and for answers about his disappearing behavior.

One of his "only good habits" that he had was that sometimes he visited the gym that his parents paid him, where he also sometimes engaged in "fantasy talks" with women just to flirt and make a quick getaway from his boring and monotonous life.

Who would've known that his worst day could turn around and be one of his best days by having the opportunity to meet that "special person"? As the day couldn't get any worse, he thought that the only responsible thing that made him feel better (stressing the word *responsible* because drugs and alcohol were not at all a responsible choice) was going to the gym and taking a swim, which he loved to do and made him feel calm, stopping some of his toxic thoughts and the self-pity voice that kept playing inside his head. After swimming almost three kilometers with a lot of anger and stress having been released in the water in every stroke he gave, he was able to release some of that toxic tension and stress (by naturally releasing dopamine, serotonin, and some endorphins).

Having highlighted that, we can just assume he was already filled with a nice mix of positive and powerful chemicals, this natural mix that allowed his body and mind to feel a "good vibe" again to end an uphill and disappointing day with a different mind-set, instead of continuing with his "fatal day" as we described it earlier.

Just when he was going out of the reception of the gym, one of his "secret admirers," according to his best friend in the gym, was outside talking over the phone; so when he saw her, he felt that nothing worse could happen in that lousy day and thought inside his head, "What the hell," and dared to approach the girl. He sat right beside her and waited until she finished her call, as he was a little rushed and feeling confident by all the natural mix of chemicals generated through the swim. He just grabbed her phone and spoke with her friend. Apparently, she already had a plan for them according to her friend, and they were going to shop some stuff for a baby shower that they were going to throw for another college friend on Sunday, which in that moment obviously didn't seem important at all for Mario. Thus, he told her friend that she was going to call her back after and hung up the call.

After hanging up and not even waiting for Betty's shocked face, he asked her name, "After all this show, what's your name?"

Partly mumbling due to the unexpected surprise and kind of rude behavior, she said, "Betty." She was thinking in her mind what a jackass turned out to be this guy, but at the same time she also had a crush on him and didn't pay too much attention to the first thought.

Betty's background in terms of relationships was not her strong skill; therefore, she didn't know how to react and much less what to expect from that. She just tried to relax and see what was going to happen after that abrupt introduction. The first impression that was building in Betty's head of Mario was (in addition to the attraction), he unconsciously reminded her of her father in regard to his attitude toward her mother, bossing her around and not letting her decide. But at that moment, obviously nothing could appear to be "wrong" or dysfunctional. Actually, everything was fitting up for these two "strangers" as they both had a deficit of emotional attention, and they were both starving for recognition in pretty much the same extent and apparently with some interests in common.

The night continued with the abrupt encounter although it is worth to mention that Mario already knew some basic things about Betty (that he found out from his best friend at the gym). Betty also knew some basic stuff about Mario although a little enhanced on the "positive side" by his friend Louis from the gym too.

Thus, after they introduced themselves, Betty agreed to continue the night according to Mario's plan and just let herself flow with her crush, so we can officially say that their first date unfolded in a "perfect way" to end a lousy Friday for Mario and a surprising, unexpected night for Betty.

As Mario didn't expect anything from that day, but to arrive at his place and just let it end, he had a very lousy outfit that didn't fit with the plans he now had in his head. Mario wanted to go to a nightclub, but of course, he would have to change his saggy gym clothes that made him look like a gang fella.

At the club, they started to exchange stories, mostly about their family background, occupation, and basic information that allowed them to start knowing each other. Counting that it was a first-impression kind of way, they had to be both careful with the kind of "personality" they were going to show, as we all know first dates are pretty much a makeup story with the best qualities enhanced and the dark stories left behind.

As we mentioned earlier about Mario's personality traits, he had a pretty good way of engaging and impressing women with some fake hero talk or interesting storytelling kind of way to the point that many of his previous conquers were brokenhearted after two or three dates, which by the way was his personal record, sort of saying.

What he didn't know was that Betty was a more clever prey than the ones before, so she was not buying the whole story as easily as Mario could have thought, but she was smart enough to allow him to think that everything was fine. Anyway, that night unfolded pretty easily as it should, mostly due to the fact that the two of them did not allow expectations to come in the way. They danced, drank, and exchanged some kisses to begin their dating journey.

After that "magical Friday," they started a straight frequent set of dates (more or less seeing each other even twice or three times per week). Suddenly and as time flies, Mario and Betty became pretty much more engaged in a more formal relationship, where more danger and hurt or pain could be developed, taking into account that these young couple had some childhood wounds and some past that both of them were trying to forget or maybe as many people they were not even aware of. These two didn't have a clue of the journey that was going to unfold for them; neither do they have any idea of how their destiny path was beginning to be shaped!

In just of a blink of the eye, six months had passed. Mario and Betty were both surprised as this was an unexpected turn of events, more because everything began as an adventure that they let themselves get into. Taking into account Mario's background and "personal record," this was unprecedented, but it was also building up a pretty good dosage of guilt, pain, jealousy, and resentment that was growing like a snowball toward them, either to break them up or to embark them on a "last chance" to regain confidence and continue with their journey.

As a way to celebrate their anniversary day, Betty and Mario decided to make a trip to boost their relationship. In Betty's mind, it was an opportunity to see if the relationship had any future or if it was just about time to end it!

They decided to go to Mazatlán (a beautiful Mexican spot with amazing sunsets and a pretty good nightclub life that made them forget any kind of problems). The trip was going well between day trips knowing some little towns or tourist spots and mixed with reckless nights full of music, dance, and of course, a side dish of booze. With that said, everything seemed to fit, even if it was disguised by the place and fun they had. For that reason, Betty was more secure that the relationship had some future and they could be able to save it after all the hurt, fights, and disrespect exchanged by both of them due to the opposite ways they were cared for during their childhood, but sharing a lack of attention and recognition that they both needed. After that summer adventure where they renewed their trust, they both had to take a deep breath and some impulse for it to be transformed into a more serious relationship, but not without a huge surprise for both of them.

After a month and a half from their trip to Mazatlán, Betty was pretty cranky, angry, and feeling weird, physically as well as emotionally confused.

She started to experience some morning sickness, vomiting, and nausea, which made her suspicious that she might be pregnant as her period was also late.

Mario, on the other hand, was trying to shift his life from being an irresponsible teenager to a more responsible adult by finishing high school and enrolling himself in college, so everything for him seemed finally on track. He was very excited, even thinking about future plans with Betty, but just for the two of them, of course. He was almost twenty-two years old; thus, the idea of being responsible for another human being was not even a remote possibility in his head. However, as we all know, life throws us some surprises, obstacles, or detours whenever we least expect them to happen, and they were not going to be the exception for any one of them.

Consequently, in another Friday afternoon, approaching the end of July, Betty asked Mario to meet her at a cafe near her parents' place to talk about some "stuff," according to Betty's words. As we all know, usually when a woman expresses in that "I want to talk" way, men usually think that is not something good. However, Mario didn't predispose himself and, of course, didn't even suspect anything, as all the complaints and "symptoms" of Betty were only seen by him as part of her apprehensive personality and hypochondriac character.

Mario arrived at the coffee place happy to tell Betty that he had enrolled in a bachelor's degree in systems engineering at the National Autonomous University, in addition to finally receiving his high school diploma, so he was in the mood to celebrate such a huge step toward an "adultlike" behavior. After a pretty good streak of childish behavior, he finally was feeling proud of himself, as he was straightening his life into a much more responsible path. Without knowing it or recognizing it, Betty's influence was permeating his sense of accountability.

When he was just opening his mouth to tell Betty that he had great news, Betty didn't let him finish the news and delivered him a blood test and pregnancy test result.

Mario saw the paper; his hands were shaking and sweating, and after just reading the important information that said "pregnant," he was shocked for about five minutes. He continued to review the paper at least five more times; he even Googled some technical terms to verify that it was true.

In his mind, there was a storm of chemical reactions leading to a repetitive cycle of anger, confusion, disappointment, and a great amount of fear. After he recovered from the shock of that "disappointing news" for him and this new turn of events in his life, he was thinking that he didn't even have the chance to tell her anything about his "progress." The only words he could produce were "Betty, do you really want to continue with this pregnancy?" As soon as Betty heard those words, she was filled with pain, hurt, self-pity, and a huge amount of self-diminishing words that both her parents had continuously repeated to her throughout her childhood. She was devastated with Mario's reaction, so she just stood up and left the coffee place with tears in her eyes. Mario took at least three minutes to react and go after her, so by the time he approached the parking lot to her car, she was already starting the engine filled with tears, sobbing, and in that moment also inundated with rage and disappointment, mostly due to the programmed words of her parents.

She turned down the window and just told him "I don't want to see you right now. Goodbye."

Mario was speechless. He was confused, angry, and afraid; and with a mixed cocktail of neurotransmitters and hormones in his head and body (insulin, cortisol, and a rush of adrenaline), he really didn't know what to do. He just wanted to punch anything that crossed his way.

The Memory in Your Body

Mario on his side and Betty with her emotions have showed us how our internal wounds, the emotional need to crave love, acceptance, and the predisposition to react in certain ways is just a reflection of something deeper that at plain sight is not perceived by many of us.

Plenty of their discussions, disagreements, and of course, the behavior of building everything inside is what led them to eventually boil the chemical cocktail of emotions, which were also mixed with their past story. This is what is called memory of your body, the assembly of all your experiences that were programmed, the unconscious repetition of events, and a replay of a movie that sometimes you witnessed since you were a child or that your brain just constructs with the poor messages received and the lack of a different setting where you could be more aware of many of those toxic behaviors.

Many, if not all, of couple's discussions are just a collision of the egos, patterns, and learned behaviors that are ingrained in every one of us, more in the ones that don't even pay attention to the way they react, express, and interact with others. Moreover, all of this story will allow us to set the stage to go deeper into what Mario and Betty have experienced due to all the turmoil of emotions, unexpected events, and of course, the painful past that they shared without being aware of how it was affecting them.

Thought Takeaways

What are some key events and messages that this love story can show us? Paying more attention to the story setting, background information, and development of events, we can extract powerful insights and go deeper, so let's dive in them!

I.   What are some of the personality traits that Betty and Mario developed to cope with their emotional pain?

II. How does your parents' behavior reflect the way you repeat patterns or create discussions?

III. What is happening inside you that ignites your reactions and leads you to burst or become hurt during those arguments, discussions, or fights?

IV. Why did Betty and Mario fail to boost their relationship during that trip?

V. How does the "Memory of Your Body" work against you?

I. What are some of the personality traits that Betty and Mario developed to cope with their emotional pain?

Taking some of the insights and traits from Betty that can be analyzed to clearly see how we tend to develop shields and protection from pain, we can bring the most evident.

A shy personality

There's nothing wrong with being shy or introvert. However, if we paid attention to the lack of awareness in terms of Betty's external appearance, we can infer that this characteristic is usually showed by people who had been emotionally neglected, had poor examples, of course, of a healthier life, and it is also a protection from lack of emotional attention.

Many people don't realize yet that having a healthier outlook and taking some time to look different is not only about aesthetic value, but more about caring for your internal health and about the way you look and that you deserve and can achieve a much better internal health than the one that you have been having. That, of course, will have an effect in the way you look, in your physical appearance, which doesn't have to be shallow or superficial if you gain it through worrying and acting on your health!

Workaholic and obsessed with her professional performance

We would think that this is a trait that many people would see as positive and as a leverage. In some cases, it is, but when you relegate all the other aspects of your life to immersing yourself in work, whatever this kind of work may be, then as any other kind of addiction, it becomes unhealthy.

Moreover, in Betty's case, we're seeing also a trait that was developed to cope with the pain of rejection or abandonment, which was developed due to the fact that her father most of the times was completely absent or, when present, just didn't even care about her or her mom. Because he was not displaying affection or even attention for them, consequently, Betty "had to" find something that was rewarding and that gave her recognition. Luckily, she acquired a workaholic personality that kept her safe at least from other more harmful addictions.

Nevertheless, this trait was also affecting her inner health as she usually had big amounts of stress hormones. She developed very poor eating habits as well as a sedentary lifestyle which all of this eventually can lead and trigger some internal genes to develop chronic diseases such as hypertension, diabetes, obesity, anxiety, and depression.

Let's move on to Mario's traits that helped him cope with his childhood pain.

Reckless attitude toward life

Mario, as we could witness from many of his background and past and current behavior, was a young man that developed a "rebel" attitude toward his life in order to take off the lack of attention that their parents covered up with material stuff.

He behaved like a brat in order to make his parents disappointed, to let some steam off his inner body and of course inflict some pain in them. We certainly could also witness that he developed several addiction to drugs, alcohol, and toxic friendships that just lured him to disconnect from his painful reality that he was just creating to cope with the emotional neglected life that he had, to cope with the pain that his parents inflicted in him through also reckless behavior in terms of the paternity obligations that they had with him.

The only healthy behavior we could perceive through his story was his affection for swimming, which will eventually help him find another kind of life.

Psychopathic lying skills

As harsh as it may sound, his skills developed to lie to women and sometimes to everyone. Inventing clever and engaging stories was a mechanism that he developed to cope mostly with the pain inflicted by his mother whenever he saw her drunk and flirting with younger men just to raise her ego and feed also the lack of emotional support and attention that she had from her husband.

Thus, in this case, Mario developed the ability to tell stories, to invent a fake life, just like his parents also showed him that he could do it; and he also released some of the pain with the silly idea of making women suffer through the image of a "dreamy guy," only to play with their feelings, just like his mother played with his, to then provoke emotional pain and make them feel worthless, also just like how his mother made him feel.

In the end, this mechanism to cope with his childhood pain would also have the reward of making him feel secure, needed, and worthy of even the most appealing woman just to obtain a rush of adrenaline, reinforce his ego, and of course, superficially and momentarily fill his emotional deficit of attention and affection.

II. How does your parents' behavior reflect the way you repeat patterns or create discussions?

As we just went deeper into some of the personality traits that many of us have developed to cope with certain emotional pain during our childhood experiences, we can easily now slide into the most intense damage that our caregivers/parents unconsciously inflicted on us and how this programmed setting and behaviors produce a deep pain within us that we often carry on to the adult stage and replay in our relationships or in some sabotaging behaviors that we don't want to see or we are too busy and immersed in a victim-mode lifestyle to even pay attention to them.

In Betty and Mario's story, we can clearly see that both of their parents had very toxic behaviors, which happened to be also strongly influenced by their upbringing. So the most important message that we should take on from this bullet thought is to realize that programmed behavior, pain, and poor messages and/or examples become ingrained in our psyche. Just like some viruses or bacteria, they get stuck in our "emotional" DNA (deoxyribonucleic acid) or internal hardware and just stay dormant until some similar situation or past memory is triggered, causing more pain and awakening a chain reaction of emotional events that will lead us to repeat patterns, to create defense mechanisms, to sabotage ourselves, or worse, to even inflict pain in others just to many times unconsciously find some relief.

It may sound coarse, but it is just like when you have one of these diseases that ingrains in your DNA such as salmonella or herpes and some contact through interaction with something in the environment triggers it to wake up and make you ill. Then you will have to take some medication to fight the infection, but the virus or bacteria will be there dormant until you find again circumstances that wake it up.

The same happens with this emotional pain; it becomes ingrained in your DNA since childhood until you find a similar circumstance, a triggering event, a person that reminds you of any of your parents, or you simply develop a personality that helps you cope with the pain and that allows to carry on with your life in a more or less unconscious but "kind of healthy" way but mostly lets you live with the pain inside of you because that was what you learn, that was what you witnessed, and also that is the easier road to travel for many.

It also happens with your genes in terms of a disease or unhealthy habits that start creating stains in your DNA, your emotional marks, events, and of course, traumas, which become strongly attached to your psyche and little by little starts infecting and creating a way of being that can turn out to be toxic and capable of being triggered afterward in your adult relationships.

> How you bond with caregivers during early childhood affects how you behave in relationships and friendships, how in touch you are with your emotions and how much you will allow yourself to love others on a conscious level. When adequate attachment between child and caregiver is lacking, the child grows up with an impaired ability to trust that the world is a safe place, and that others will take good care of her/him. As a consequence, the neglected child develops an insecure attachment style. This style can lead to serious difficulties handling romantic relationships, work relationships and friendship later on in life. (Ainsworth 1969)

Many of us have seen this kind of stories, and of course, when we are the observer, we are keen to see the "mistakes" or toxic behaviors that we wouldn't like to be associated with. Those arguments and discussions that are just created from minor circumstances are more grounded in a deeper pain, in an emotionally malnourished childhood that is now looking for an outlet and sometimes is so strong that it is capable of producing outrageous reactions that will just feed the toxic loop, recycle negative emotions, and start creating resentment in couples that, of course, after is just like the dust that you put under the rug! It will start to create an unhealthy environment, fungus, bacteria, and in this case, a mindless game of doing things to compete, humiliate, or prove that you're the one that has the reason or the one wiser in the relationship. Even worse, it will start to feed your ego until you are just making the snowball bigger!

It is just amazing how these dark emotions stay within you when you're not able to take action and you're just unconsciously and selfishly believing that you're a healthy individual that just happens to have bad luck in terms of the people that you have met throughout your life, instead of being more accountable in recognizing that you are the common denominator in all the failed relationships or you're the one afraid to have a relationship because it will occupy time in your life that is dedicated to work, without seeing that it is just another way of avoiding facing the fear factor that you developed due to a toxic example or poor marital behaviors from your parents/caregivers.

The solution here to stop repeating these patterns and examples is by first recognizing that you have a problem, whether it is that you spoil your relationships, you're afraid of commitment, or you don't even dare to initiate a relationship because of the big fear of being hurt.

Easing your way to see things as they are, being humble to accept that you need some help to dissolve and face the pain that you have from your childhood, is something worthy, not something that you should be ashamed of. Pretty much more than 80 percent of people suffered from some type of emotional neglect or poor example that stayed in their memory but does not show up until they face some kind of resemblance or trigger that activates it. Moreover, you become aware, conscious, and accept that you're now on the path to break the cycle and avoid replaying the movie of your parents or just create a new version with updated characters.

III. What is happening inside you that ignites your reactions and leads you to burst or become hurt during those arguments, discussions, or fights?

Many times we just think that bursts or reactions such as the ones that you have during a discussion or something minor that trigger you is the normal way to act when, in fact, it isn't; however, these kind of events also have a biological and physiological cause that can help you see more clearly what is going on inside your body and mind. Therefore, let's break down some of the emotions or behaviors that we witness from Betty and Mario's discussion regarding the pregnancy news.

Prior to revealing such an impactful news, Betty and Mario had several issues, arguments, and discussions that they tried to fix by taking a trip and supposedly in Betty's head just to try to reignite the relationship and amend things. However, that is exactly what we discussed previously, trying to fake that nothing happens. Thinking that doing something fun will make underlying problems disappear and give you again that confidence, trust, and emotionally stable relationship is just acting irresponsibly and putting the dust under the rug.

Why? Just because all those discussion, problems, and apparently minor details that any of you "let pass" is something important that was not said, that was not taken care of, that is building up, and that will certainly come out and not in the best time. Our emotions that are kept inside our body and do not find an outlet produce several chemical substances that with time start creating bigger issues. For instance, during a heated argument or discussion, your body starts to generate high amounts of cortisol, adrenaline, and noradrenaline.

In a deep discussion and as impactful as the one depicted in our story and that already has a little individual forming inside the mother's womb, strong discussions and fights should be tried to be softened and handled with more tolerance, compassion, and consciousness that there's a growing life inside. There's no point to overreact or generate toxic emotions that will eventually affect the development of the fetus.

Therefore, let's find out what is happening inside Betty's body.

First of all, a deep sense of low self-worth, anger, and frustration is being produced; all of these emotions will detonate a cascade of high amounts of cortisol, adrenaline, and noradrenaline.

What does cortisol do to our body?

- ⊙ It increases the production of glucose through the breakdown of glycogen. (This molecule is like a tangerine made of small sugars subunits, and it's the main storage form of glucose in our body.) In addition to this effect, it inhibits the production of insulin; therefore, in the long term, being exposed to high levels of stress-released cortisol could make our cells become insulin resistant.

- ⊙ It increases the production of adrenaline, which activates the fight-or-flight response by flooding the blood with glucose, as previously mentioned, supplying an immediate energy source to large muscles. This response is what makes you feel angry, overwhelmed, and with the intense feeling of taking out all that steam pressure that in those moments is also due to brain confusion and the inability to think clearly. You naively think that hitting something, breaking things, yelling, or just running away from the place/person or situation is going to help you when, in fact, the best antidote in those moments to reduce that hormone is breathing, calming your mind, and allowing yourself to detach from the situation to see it as an observer and make a better decision.

- ⊙ It lowers your immune system when you are frequently exposed to high quantities of it, triggering a cascade of effects, such as increased colds or illnesses, increased tendency to develop food allergies, increased risk to develop an assortment of gastrointestinal issues (because a healthy intestine is dependent on a healthy immune system), and in extreme situations, as it has been shown, increased risk of cancer and possibly increased risk of autoimmune diseases.

What does adrenaline do to our body?

Physiologic effects. It activates the fight-or-flight response, increasing the heart rate, blood pressure, and dilation of respiratory passages (meaning that breathing and oxygenation become more efficient as the lungs expand and allow more oxygen to flow). All these changes, if they are maintained for a long period of time (more than an hour), produce indirect effects, such as increasing the amount of cortisol and promoting the release of glucose, which will give the signal to increase fat as storage. These factors are known to predispose people to develop obesity and type 2 diabetes.

Metabolic effects. It increases the amount of glucagon (a hormone opposite to insulin), which will in turn break down glycogen storage, producing higher amounts of blood glucose ready to be used to fight or flight, also increasing the availability of fatty acids that will work also to increase energy fuel if needed. Unfortunately, our brain doesn't distinguish if this response was triggered because you really had to run or fight or if it was just turned on due to an emotional problem, thereby making you feel angrier and predispose you to hurt someone due to the high amounts of this hormone.

Finally, what does noradrenaline do in your body?

As it is a very close "brother" hormone/neurotransmitter of adrenaline, it can cause the same reactions, such as an increment of blood pressure; induced breakdown of glycogen, releasing more glucose to the blood and increasing heart rate and muscle contraction; and of course, it can also cause the same effects in terms of predisposing you to develop type 2 diabetes and obesity.

The main difference in this hormone is that it can lead you to hypotension, increased headaches, lack of attention, and if it is continually produced or triggered, can predispose you to develop ADHD (attention deficit hyperactive disorder), as well as depression.

All these pools of chemicals generated as a consequence of a heated discussion or little by little building up in your body are going to start generating a toxic environment for the unborn child, which eventually can lead to epigenetic consequences that will interfere with the healthy and normal development of the baby.

What is epigenetics?

To define it in a more amicable way, it is all the changes produced in our genes through the environment, meaning pretty much all that we do, perceive, or feel; everything has an effect in our genes that is cumulative and eventually can lead to "turn on" genes, allowing disruptive changes in what information is being read and codified for your proteins. If they are toxic substances, accumulation of this will lead incrementally to making you more prone to developing a chronic disease.

For example, let's say that I'm reading a book, and I leave it on the table right next to a glass of wine. Suddenly, my child stumbles on my glass of wine and throws the wine on my book, leaving at least two to three pages wet and unable to being read. This will probably affect the meaning and understanding of the whole chapter, leaving me with a poor message and some havoc that I will eventually have to fill out with suppositions or assumptions, but they will not be accurate.

If you imagine that the pages of the book are the different sequence of your genes, that it was not changed or replaced after being stained by the wine, that they're still there but they are not readable, just damaged, tainted, or marked and as a result of those stains, when they're read, the message can generate a defective protein, then if this same phenomena is repeated, that would lead to an accumulation of defective proteins that will lead to the development of a disease.

Going back to our story, and having said that Betty will have an overflow of chemicals inside her body, if this situation continues and she keeps having arguments and problems in her relationship with Mario, these events will most likely produce a sea of stress hormones that will eventually taint, mark, or damage some of the genes in her child, predisposing or leading her/him to the production of defective proteins that will in turn affect somehow the development of a healthy child.

This does not mean that he/she will have a disease as soon as he/she is born; it only means that the effect of those substances for a prolonged time will start diminishing the whole capacity to make a perfectly healthy protein.

IV. Why did Betty and Mario fail to boost their relationship during that trip?

Every relationship will have its bumps and ups and downs; however, as depicted in our story, when you begin a relationship from a place of unconsciousness, a random encounter that is led just by the rush of feeling accepted or flashed with something that you have desired for so long, which by the way more than 80 percent of relationships begin that way, it is easy to fall into the trap of thinking that the person that you found is going to fill your voids, or the other common thinking that you're going to be able to fix him or her. Whichever of these foundations you choose, it is very likely that you will encounter obstacles raised by your ego, ignited by the fact that you are the healthy one and your partner is the one that has to be fixed. Those beliefs will, of course, start generating emotional triggers that will develop a battle between egos, a fight from emotional wounds, an environment that sooner rather than later will be filled with grudge, resentment, and hurt.

All in this boiling pot will keep growing, cooking, and heating until some minor or heavier disagreement turns on the valve and provokes an explosion of all those chemicals that have been accumulating for weeks, months, or even years that will depend, of course, on your level of tolerance and awareness that something is not right and needs to be fixed from the ground up.

As we were never cultivated, educated, or raised with an awareness of first taking care of ourselves, filling up our emotional cup, and then starting an intimate relationships, and we were just programmed or "educated" to believe in fairy tales and soap operas full of imaginary situations, a blue gentleman and a princess that will make a story worthy of a happy castle, then we think that real life is about finding half of a person to fill, repair, or, even worse, satisfy every need that we crave or have in spite of the amount of emotional pain that we have suffered or accumulated usually throughout our childhood.

That is the main mistake that usually happens in relationships, a very high expectation that the other person that we will find will be able to solve every emotional need, be able to make us feel "complete," make us feel "worthy," and also be able to withstand every abuse, irrational behavior, or emotional manipulation that we have developed as part of our damaged past and history.

Those facts are the ones that little by little start contributing to an unconscious way of constructing healthy relationships, tolerating or inflicting emotional pain, subconsciously projecting and replaying the same old movie that we witness as children, repeating toxic patterns, and becoming another statistic in the huge amount of failed relationships, breakups, or divorces. And without leaving a very huge important fact, this also includes engaging in casual, unprotected sex and causing unwanted pregnancies that will just end up either in abortions or irresponsible parenting that will start a story of another damaged child that will grow up repeating the same pattern. All these relationship stories will just become an endless cycle of damaged people and families that deserves to be healed, that deserves to be stopped, and that can be rewired if we just accept one simple fact: owning our emotional wounds and repairing them.

This is exactly what happened in our story. Neither Betty nor Mario were accountable in resolving what they had tolerated, discussed, or fought about; they just pretended that a trip, a distraction, would make things better and would allow them to move on, when in fact they never shared their emotions and how they felt, designed some space to talk about the important issues, and solved them or agreed upon them. They should have planned a trip to reset and allow them to generate a healthier environment, but at least with a clear compromise to be able to open up and discuss some of the relevant issues that were already affecting their relationship.

Even this kind of strategy or approach would be temporary because they would still have a lot of unresolved emotional pain within them, but at least it will show a disposition from both of them to have a more conscious and mindful relationship. This is hard to imagine, as we just plotted out the way we're deeply bombarded and programmed with messages of fake relationships, false concepts of love, and unconscious parenting examples from which many people suffered.

Hence, a healthier approach for them, in terms of the development of the story, would have been to compromise, to find some space to talk, even if it was during the trip; that would have been even helpful for them as it would have been in a completely different environment, which would have helped them to be more relaxed, more conscious, and able to lay out their thoughts and arguments in terms of the fights, discussions, or misunderstandings that they have already accumulated.

Temporary solutions, just as the shortcuts offered in many media platforms, have the consequence of producing a rebound effect. Why? Simply because they are not dealing with the root problem; they're just trying to put the dust under the rug so you won't be able to see it clearly. In the end, these types of solutions will produce more pain or reckless behavior that can lead to bigger discussions or more pain generated due to resentment of not being able to let it all out and fix the real cause.

V. How does the memory of your body works against you?

Our body possesses the capacity to store a lot of information, to record events that we're not even aware of or wouldn't even think about, but if we try to see our DNA as a huge library of information that can help you be more aware that you at least have stored information of seven generations within you, therefore—and this is not meant to stress you more—it has just the purpose to inform you and make you more aware and mindful of how can you start repairing your present story because even if you have this kind of information stored, that just means that it is in your past, which is not even from you or your parents, grandparents, and so on!

Having said that, we can create more consciousness or awareness and heal plenty of that pain by becoming accountable for our own emotional voids, needs, and wounds, learning from childhood to be more awake to our emotions, identifying and recognizing what we are feeling, being able to express in a healthy manner, as well as learning to meditate and have more control of our thoughts and their pattern. In addition, we should be able to detach from them because we are not them, because we have been trained and "educated" to think that our thoughts are our reality when, in fact, our reality is just our present moment and is not dictated by our past and much less by the past of many unconscious generations that left in us a dent that now we have to repair. However, without being overwhelmed by that, we can deal with that fact in a simpler and more powerful way if we just let ourselves be focused in every moment in time, in every answer that we want to produce, if we somehow detach from the concept of time, which has a very heavy weight because it leads us to think that we are a result of our past and a visualization of the future, when in fact we are energy that is available just in this moment, just in this vertical line. That way of thinking gives you leverage to imagine that you're a particle of energy that can change this moment, that can act differently, that can become healed by synchronizing your heart and your brain.

Develop the ability to focus on your present moment, an ability to concentrate, relax, and let the train of thought pass. But be able to create a space of awareness, a space of connection with your higher power, and get to know yourself better in order to be able to handle more wisely your emotions and, of course, your actions.

That is pretty much the best tool that we can develop to become a healthier version and start dissolving the memory of pain, the memory of emotional wounds, and leave behind messages or beliefs that are just floating there to find an outlet, a recognition, and of course to be able to comfort yourself before you generate the anxiety of looking someone else to fix you.

How can you be able to produce a different outcome from the one that you were trained or you witnessed?

Let's start with the kind of behaviors or emotions that usually are felt or produced under an environment of emotional pain.

Feeling apprehensive or anxious. We create a physiological, psychological, and emotional state of being anxious when we behave in an apprehensive manner, such as being worried, fretful, and/or concerned.

Anxiety occurs when we worry that something is dangerous or has the potential to harm us.

Behaving overly apprehensively, such as worrying too much, can have an adverse and profound effect in the body, which can cause it to exhibit a wide range of unusual and debilitating symptoms. As cortisol and adrenaline levels are raised, you are set in a state of emergency, which, as pointed out earlier, if this behavior is repetitive, your immune system declines, your metabolism slows down, important hormones such as insulin stop working properly, predisposing yourself to diabetes. Due to this glucose regulation dysfunction, your fat synthesis is activated, releasing leptin, which will block your satiety centers and which will start a toxic cycle that will disrupt your weight balance, predisposing you to develop obesity, cardiovascular diseases, not to mention a few other symptoms.

Solution. Try these five simple steps to reduce anxiety:

- Take a deep breath. (Oxygen reduces stress.)
- Accept you're anxious. (Feel the feeling.)
- Realize your brain is playing some tricks on you. (If we allow it, our brain will make every challenge or difficult situation into a much bigger threat than it is.)
- Question your thoughts. (Is this worry realistic? Is this really likely to happen? What might I do to prepare for whatever may happen?)
- Use a calming visualization. (Close your eyes if you can; visualize a place where you've had a very nice experience and a feeling of peace such as a beach, river, or wood.) (Anxiety Centre & Tartakovsky M. 2018)

Negative bias of the brain. The adaptive and evolutionary advantages of this bias are obvious: the consequences of a dangerous or injurious event is often much more dramatic than the consequences of ignoring or reacting slowly to neutral or even appetitive stimuli. The emotional reaction that probably affects the negativity bias is the attention to affective stimuli (L. Carretié et al., 2001). We are wired to see the negative first due to the danger that it represents to our well-being, but this is just a primitive reaction that can be diluted with some practical exercises.

Solution. Try these three steps whenever you have a negative-biased thought:

- ⊙ Look for good facts and turn them into good experiences. Make a conscious effort on seeing the positive side of the situation even though it may seem as if it doesn't have anything positive. Identify any resistant thought, and if you're able to do it, write it down in a note on your phone and set it as a reminder every three to four hours.

- ⊙ Savor the experience. Concentrate all your attention into positive experiences. Give yourself ample time (at least twenty to thirty seconds) to fully enjoy that moment. By elongating our positive sensations, we allow more neurons to fire and wire together in response to the stimulus. This solidifies the experience in our memory.

- ⊙ Intend and sense that the good experience is sinking into you, becoming aware of the different ways in which a positive experience affects you. Identify the emotions involved. Visualize the positivity spreading throughout your body. Consider the brain's plasticity as neurons fire and wire together. When we consciously interact with our positive experiences, we can strengthen their neurological presence. (Hanson 2016; Vaish 2008)

Attachment to parental issues. How you bond with caregivers during early childhood affects how you behave in relationships and friendships, how in touch you are with your emotions, and how much you will allow yourself to love others on a conscious level. When adequate attachment between child and caregiver is lacking, the child grows up with an impaired ability to trust that the world is a safe place and that others will take good care of her/him. As a consequence, the neglected child develops an insecure attachment style. This style can lead to serious difficulties, handling romantic relationships, work relationships, and friendship later on in life (Ainsworth 1969). We all have seen and experienced some sort of emotional issues from our parents as it is a behavior usually passed on from generation to generation, and if it is not consciously recognized and identified, the damage can go on.

Solution. Apply these powerful strategies that will help you recognize and work with emotional attachment issues:

⊙ Create a coherent narrative. Research tells us that to break free of a cycle of strained attachments, we must make sense of it and feel the full pain of our past. This means that we should be able to recreate a coherent story of what happened to us when we were children. It is well known that by simply asking certain kinds of autobiographical questions, we can discover how people have made sense of their past— how their minds have shaped their memories of the past to explain who they are in the present (Siegel 2010).

⊙ Rely on your social circle. When we feel insecure, we often play over and over again diminishing thoughts or create fictitious scenarios that drive us to more sad feelings until we are immersed into a feeling state of sadness, depression, or anxiety. To break this kind of toxic cycles, it has been proven that calling your best friend that has good vibes or just having a cup of coffee with someone that has a stronger confidence on herself or himself will help you feel much better. It is important to note that the person you look for should make you feel secure and he/she preferentially should be a confidant for you. Why? Simply because talking with him/her about your confidence issue will most likely make you feel better, and he/she will probably help you see things from another perspective.

⊙ Find a therapist or emotional coach. A good therapy relationship allows a person to form a secure attachment with the therapist. Having a corrective emotional experience with someone who can consistently provide a secure base and allows us to feel and make sense of our story is a gift that can benefit us in every area of our lives. Many times, therapy is seen as something that just "unbalanced" people look for, but it is many times the opposite. It has been proven that most successful people have had in their life a therapist or emotional coach to guide them through difficult times and decisions. So, leave the prejudices and word of mouth out of the question (Firestone, L., 2018).

All of these strategies, kind of simple set of steps, will allow you to start owning your present journey, healing that emotional memory, and being able to generate a different result in your current or future relationships.

CHAPTER 2

Seeing the Choices of Life

D OING A QUICK recap of Betty and Mario's story, we left off with the sudden departure of Betty when she told Mario she was pregnant and the confusion/shock that Mario had after that. Betty managed to get away from Mario at least for two weeks by shutting off her cell phone and telling her mother to tell Mario that she was on a job trip.

Mario, on the other hand, made many efforts to try to contact her, but he was not successful; plus, he also needed some "thinking" to do—about what road to take or the different circumstances and consequences of going through with the pregnancy.

What was going on in Betty's mind during those weeks "off" and away from Mario? Well, we know her background, and we know she's the more mature in the relationship. Therefore, during those weeks, Betty talked with a very good friend, Karen, who was five years older than her and already a mother, so she understood what it was to be pregnant and knows about the incredible joy and happiness that a child can give you as well as all the responsibility involved in the upbringing of a child. Hence, she was her best choice to go for advice. Once they got together, they talked for several hours during different days as Betty was coming out with more and more questions and scenarios to face what was about to come.

Is It Really Somebody's Fault?

Karen showed Betty a very clear picture of what could happen in either scenario, starting with the joy, happiness, fulfillment, and compassion that she felt when her child was born. Karen also had a pretty rough start during her pregnancy as her husband also had a panic attack when he found out about their baby. She was a very mature woman who knew how to handle his husband's jitters and fear when he faced the news of an unexpected child. Therefore, she knew about the perception of men in terms of responsibility and avoiding having children, more when it happens unexpectedly and, of course, they are not prepared to be fathers. She began by saying, "Men are by nature more task focused and usually plan ahead or see the future easier than women. Therefore, they seem to have (at least the ones that know what they want) a very straight path for their life, and when something or someone gets in the way unexpectedly, they turn on the fight-or-flight response, which triggers a behavior to run away or get angry with them, making it impossible for them to see other scenarios or benefits from having a child even when they are supposedly 'prepared.'"

Karen loved to talk about men's way of thinking because she found it very interesting and different from women's, and in order to understand her husband and be empathic with him, she had to become almost an expert in the way men think and feel. Betty was amazed and grateful that she picked the right friend and person to talk about the topic. Let's get a little deeper into Karen's way of describing how men think and feel.

Karen started explaining to Betty that men's brain is designed to focus more on danger, on possibilities, on threats, and seeing the whole pros and cons of almost every situation because as we know by history and evolution, men almost in every season had to be the ones that needed to provide food, shelter, and protection for their family. That way of thinking didn't leave too much space for feelings or sometimes empathy toward any situation different from having resources, food, or commodities for the family. Although nowadays this role is changing, feelings are not the strong side of most men due to patterns, beliefs and traditions. Even when a modern man can take care of children or the household, it is still not common for them to talk about their feelings as they were not encouraged to do it since they were children.

Actually, this clearly explains why Karen's husband and Mario, along with many other men, when they find out about an unplanned pregnancy start to feel anxious, threatened, and literally in danger–their mind is not prepared for that scenario, they don't feel that they have the tools to deal with such a responsibility, and they most of the times are not taught to recognize feelings or empathy toward any kind of situation that requires them to show their emotions. Thus, they are pretty much trapped and driven toward triggering the fight-or-flight response, filling their heads with stress hormones, which in turn makes them prone to do any kind of reckless or stupid behavior.

As soon as Betty heard that explanation, she suddenly realized that Mario wasn't rejecting her or the baby. Listening to that explanation allowed her to feel more empathic with him and even feel bad for not knowing how to handle the situation at that time, and let's be honest here, many times when men are faced with this kind of situations, where they feel threatened or afraid, the worst thing to do is force them to ease those feelings and try to make them understand because in those moments it is just not biologically possible. The best thing a woman can do in this situation is to take some space, let things cool off, and approach her partner from a more relaxed angle in order to help him come back to a state where they can think clearer and probably show them the "future" of the situation, the advantages that having a kid might have, starting to lower the "danger" and discomfort that the situation might bring.

What happened to Mario's side of the story?

Let's move to Mario's way of facing the challenge.

First of all, Mario, as we know by the background, didn't have too much tools to deal with the situation. In terms of emotional intelligence or problem-solving experience, he had grown as a spoiled child, having access to many material things, not being pushed to earn almost anything in his life, being ignored on what he felt almost in every stage of his life and also being minimized for not knowing what he wanted, leading him to throw his life into drugs, lousy jobs that didn't require mental effort, and developing a storytelling ability to attract women without compromising with them but just growing his ego to feel he was worthy. Additionally, he had an attitude of not worrying about "social approval" for anything he was doing. All these behaviors triggered inside him a desire to have an escape of such a burden and buildup of emotions that nobody cared about.

Can you imagine all that emotional baggage? On top of it all, just when he was finally feeling that he could take care of his life, a "threatening" news hits him right in the face.

Therefore, he was just feeling overwhelmed, confused, and didn't know what to do with all those feelings. Mario really needed to get away at least for two to three days in order to shut down the huge anxiety, guilt, anger, and powerless feelings that he was experiencing, as he was also starting to fill his head with multiples stories, explanations, "what if" scenarios at least for the first couple of days. After that exhausting internal battle in his head about what could be the best thing to do, if he should stay with Betty and support her and go on with the pregnancy or ask her to terminate the pregnancy and then disappear from Betty's life, he decided that he needed a lot of help. He realized he only really had one choice in terms of who he could approach to discuss these emotional issues, his more stable and mature cousin (who was his only sane option, sort of saying). He was his only chance to ask for help, to be listened to, and to try to figure out the best way out of this dilemma.

Liam, Mario's cousin, turned out to be just what Mario needed in terms of advice. He was a successful entrepreneur; he designed a car wash service made for every busy individual. His business practically solved every issue about not having time or luck to find a decent car wash service nearby, as he had several employees that worked for him; they worked on call from every major company when needed. He was also married and had a beautiful young daughter of around three years old; therefore, he knew the responsibility of having to provide for a family. He owned his apartment, and his wife was a schoolteacher that dedicated most of the afternoon to their child. At least we can say that Mario was smart enough to approach this kind of man in order for him to receive some good advice. Having said some small details about Liam's background, let's continue with Mario's side of the story.

Mario told Liam that he was very worried, anxious, angry, and with a really bad insomnia problem since Betty dropped the news on him. He explained that he loved Betty very much and valued her for the stability and drive that she brought to his life. However, he explained that everything was turning out great for him; he was finally even taking back his academic background, finishing high school and applying for a major in systems engineering. Unfortunately, the news about having a baby threw him on the floor for his dreams. In addition to not feeling capable, responsible, and mature enough to face this kind of responsibility, he thought that this kind of major event was not the best timing in terms of how his life was developing. As explained before, all these reactions were triggered due to a poor and self-depreciating upbringing that he had suffered from his parents in terms of love, attention, and understanding; therefore, one might think that his behavior and reactions could be "justified."

Liam listened to him closely, as he was just so eager to spit everything out from his mouth and express the most terrifying and incredible scenarios from the news. After he finished all the "tragic scenarios" and let his feelings out, Liam began to talk.

"Look, Mario, I understand your situation. I also know my uncle; therefore, I think I know your story and maybe I can even understand some of your fear, anxiety, frustration, and anger. However, let me show you a more real scenario in my view, as well as what could happen, but first I want you to help me answer these questions: What do you want in terms of your relation with Betty? What do you see in her that helps you feel more secure about you? What are the things you don't like in her? Are they tolerable? Do you know her family? What about your in-laws? Do you think they will accept you, or will they make your life miserable?"

After hearing those questions, Mario started to feel more nervous and anxious. He even tried again to get out of the room and leave Liam with unanswered questions. As soon as Liam noticed his reaction, he grabbed him by the shoulders and said to him, "Calm down, man. Breathe . . . Everything is safe and fine. It's just you and me here, nothing will happen. We are just trying to figure out the best solution for this situation."

Mario started taking some deep breaths. He even closed his eyes for a moment, and after doing those breathing exercises, he could begin answering Liam's questions: "Okay, Liam, first question. Betty has been a lifesaver for me. I was at the point of my life where I practically fell like rock bottom. I was consuming more and more drugs, didn't see anything worthy in my life. My parents, as you know, have always been self-absorbed and never paid attention to me. My job was boring and monotonous, and I just failed again in my last missing subject, to be able to obtain my high school diploma. So that night, I just felt empty, lost, and I just felt that every attempt to get out from the emotional hole was a failure. My father's words resonated in my head again and again, calling me an emotional wreck, a shame for his name, etc. In addition to that, I started to have suicidal thoughts because from every angle I wanted to see in my life, I couldn't justify my existence or if I have something to thrive for. My social circle was very toxic—they were friends that also consumed drugs. I felt that they were friends with me because of my parents and all the material stuff I had, but not one of them really valued me for who I was. The only good thing in my life was the exercise, swimming. It was the only place, moment, and time where I really felt good and worthy, but I was even beginning to leave this practice forgotten and was performing it less and less frequently due to my toxic friends and the peer pressure of being high in order to 'enjoy' life. Plus, it was also a quicker way to feel something, literally speaking.

"Therefore, when I met Betty that tragic day, and the way I met her, it was just as if someone high above me (God or the universe) had given me a chance to get out of the dump where I was stuck. When we first started dating, I didn't realize that the relationship was going to last because I felt so insignificant and not worthy of her, but she was and has been up to now very patient and understanding with me, my issues, and my background. Therefore, that made me believe in myself again. Each day, I was able to quit the drugs more and more although I have to confess that even with her, I sometimes smoked, but when I saw her, and I was able to appreciate the way she cared about me, that sensation of being accepted and protected made me feel that I didn't need to experience the high of the drugs. It also made me feel stupid because you should know that she's a very smart girl that has worked her ass off to get to where she is in her life now.

"Thus, there's no doubt I want to continue with her all the way through. I even want to marry her; I want to have children. Nevertheless, I felt that was not ready right now. All of my doubts, fears, and anxiety are not because of her or the baby—they are more about me. I don't feel worthy, capable, responsible, even intelligent enough to sustain a much more complicated and compromised relationship. Moreover, I don't really know or have an idea if my parents are going to accept her or like her. Even though she seems like the right girl for me, they won't think that because she comes from a lower social class than us. Does that answer the question, Liam?"

"Pretty much," he said. "This gives me a clear picture of your feelings toward her and sets the stage for the second question. Okay, Liam, the second question. I see in her genuine love, true caring, and a very responsible, smart, and mature way of acting and handling her life. She is very aggressive in terms of achieving things. She has a self-drive built in herself, a very analytic way of seeing things even though she's also very emotional and moody sometimes in her own tender way. She has solid values, which allowed her to accomplish many things professionally. She has faced many situations where she was undermined. She comes from a hardworking family that never had luxuries. She knows how to solve problems bigger than what shoes to wear or what kind of dress she could use for a stupid social event. In fewer words, she is not shallow as many other women that I met before.

"She's practically everything I would ever want in a woman without knowing it because as I told you, I was in a very, very low point in my life when she arrived. Thus, when I'm with her, I feel valued, cared, understood, and as ironically as it may seem, that was what I always wanted from my own family. Therefore when I feel it with her, I can see myself in that kind of relationship for a very long time, and I also can see myself having a family, something that just a few months back I could never have imagined I could have or didn't even felt that I wanted in my future."

"Wow, Mario, that's pretty good to hear! Did you just listen to yourself? Do you realize what you have just said to me?"

"Yes! I never thought I was feeling like that. Underneath all this anxiety, fear, and anger; I think, deep inside of me I have always known or been sure that with Betty's help and her strong character I could be able to be a different man.

"Perfect, Mario. You see, there's nothing to be afraid of. We are just peeling off the layers of negative thoughts, emotions, and feelings that you have built pretty much your whole life, and I can understand that is not easy to take away the masks and shields that not only you but also many people have developed to protect themselves from pain and vulnerability."

"Okay, Liam, it's time for the third question. What do I don't like about her?

"Sometimes she's very stubborn and rejects every opinion I have about some things that I notice she could improve from, like her appearance or the way she takes care of herself. I believe she rejects them because she might think I want to change or control her, but in fact, it is not at all like that. I just simply want to see her healthier and more concerned about her health and her outlook.

"Another thing that is difficult for me to deal with is the excess of responsibility from her regarding her job and work stuff, as she very easily falls in the workaholic mode and I feel her boss manipulates her every time he wants, to the extent that she answers his calls pretty much at any time during the night, weekends, or even on her vacation or holidays.

"Lastly, her family sometimes is suffocating in terms of the amount of compromises, parties, and family reunions they have and that they demand her to attend, leaving her with not much choices to decide what to do with her life or making her feel guilty about any decision different from assisting with the reunion or staying until they want, which can stretch to really long hours. Apart from that, I believe I like pretty much everything about her."

Liam replied, "Okay, that just leaves me with a doubt. I also ask you if those things are tolerable. Can you live with them?" Mario's face said everything; it was a forced yes. Liam said, "Okay, Mario, I guess that by the look on your face, you told me everything I needed to know. I should ask you; Do you really think you can mediate or negotiate a medium point for these complaints or observations that you have?"

"Yes, of course!" Mario answered promptly.

"Well, that sounds good for me then."

"Moving on to the next question, number four, I do know her family.

However, I really haven't had too much contact with all of them. Although she tells me everything about them, as I told you, they always have some kind of gathering, event, or self-invitation from her uncles or aunts.

"What I can say about them? Hmm, I can just say they are too much into appearances or well-behaved manners. They are sometimes too religious on the surface. Their behaviors are guided by the Catholic church's beliefs, but when you hear some stories about them, it doesn't make any sense that they believe and predicate those principles, but in real actions many times they are not congruent with them. This is just my point of view as an observer that thinks that if you go to church, you are truly a believer of something, and the least you should be doing is being more congruent with your actions. If you're going to judge and criticize almost every different way of thinking or behaving, that is just contradictory with the respect and compassion that supposedly Catholic religious principles are guiding you. Anyway, you perfectly know what I mean, don't you?"

"Yes, of course, our grandparents lived like that, and fortunately, not all of our descendants picked up that way of thinking."

"And finally, we get to question five. I believe, they can 'accept' me although I know that they might not respect a lot of my thoughts, and I just hope Betty hasn't mentioned to them anything about my addiction to drugs because then, I think they will definitely make my life miserable with open or probably 'hidden' judgments at their 'family talks,' and they won't allow me to be near their daughter, or they will try to make her more dependent on them.

"If she hasn't mentioned any stuff related to drugs, then I think I have a pretty good chance to get them to like me although you know I'm not good at faking any kind of behavior, but I can tolerate and adapt to some of their behavior or way of thinking."

Owning Your Role

"Okay, Mario, that sums up everything I needed to hear about your relationship with Betty. Now, I don't think I have to tell you where are the answers to your main concerns, do I? Mario, hmm I think it would help me a lot to hear your point of view or any kind of advice that you can give me, please."

Liam said, "Okay, well, you made it pretty clear that you're completely in love with her and you see her as your support, your complement, sort of saying in terms of the attention and care she shows to you, but most of all, there was one particular thing that you mention about her, which I really think is the strongest argument to make your decision easier. You said you saw her as a mature, responsible, and caring woman. Those three words together, I believe, is all you need to get the strength, security, and courage to go on with her and support her in every decision she wants to make.

"And more importantly, you said that you picture yourself with her for a very long time, having a family, and that's exactly what is going to happen, just not in the ideal times that you might want it. With that regard, I can add that many times in our life we won't have the exact timing or the things exactly as we picture them. We might have sometimes some different timing, or things can be presented to us in a different wrapping. But believe me, God or the universe doesn't make mistakes. You have been given those gifts at the time you needed them, and many times that also means that you should work something within you to be up to the situation.

"Thus, I can say that because I have known you from a long time ago, you're now a whole different man, and I can really say that word because before her. You were just a teenager, so I recommend you to not overthink or make any pessimistic scenarios in your head. Be more realistic with your life. If you think about it, there's no big difference if you already had in your mind plans about having a family with her. What is really happening is that it will be a little or some time before the time you wanted it, but you can always rearrange your life to the events that sometimes happen sooner than you expected.

"What I've learned more since I'm a father is that you can plan pretty much your whole life ahead of you, but there are going to be times or moments where things won't go your way, and that doesn't necessarily mean that you have to reject them or run away from them. That just means you have to look for the best message or purpose that they will have in your life, identify the good spot, the opportunity that is being presented to you, by arriving earlier or simply by not being exactly as you wanted them. Look, Mario, to close it up, it's easier to understand everything if I make this analogy for you.

"Let's say that you're driving in your favorite road. Everything is fine–the sun, the landscape, the music, the weather. Suddenly, there's a huge hole on the road that makes you deviate. Therefore, you have to turn abruptly from the road, and as a result, you get a flat tire and end up hitting a tree. Obviously, that scares you and probably leaves you with some scratches and your bumped car, but if you are able to remain positive and objective, you'd think nothing major happened, either to you or to the car. You got stopped, and of course, you're angry about your car. Although it is just a small bruise and a scratch, you had to call a tow service to help you change the tire and check the car. Nonetheless, right after the insurance and the tow company finish everything, you find out after chatting with the mechanic that just a mile from where you deviated there was a terrible accident, where some people died and it was very close to the time you had your flat tire. Therefore, that hole on the road, your flat tire, and even the bump in your car literally saved your life because otherwise, you would have been moving toward the big accident, which probably would have left you severely injured or maybe even dead.

"The lesson here is that many times in our life we will have holes, bumps, detours, and hopefully some minor accidents, but every stone or obstacle in our ideal apparent or desired perfect road has a meaning, carries a purpose, a lesson, and maybe it also contains a life-changing experience, such as the one you're going to live with Betty in just a few months from now.

"So, buck it up, man. Be grateful for your own momentum that you're having and embrace this 'beautiful bump' that life is throwing at you. See it as an opportunity to drastically prove to yourself that you're up to the task, and please be humble, be self-critical because we both know that this woman has put off with more than you could ever ask, and she even though before you did it that you could be a good father. Otherwise, she wouldn't have told you anything about the pregnancy, and probably she could have stepped away from you."

Mario was really grateful and overwhelmed, so he said, "Thank you, Liam. I really appreciate your time, the questions, and the deep reasoning and reflection that we did. You really helped me go inside of me, directed me toward all the answers that ironically, I already had inside, but I didn't know how to find. That different perspective from you and seeing things as if I were an observer of my own life helped me see the decision that I now have to take."

Liam said, "You're welcome, Mario, you know you can always count on me and tell me everything you need or would like to now. After all, in just a few months, we'll be sharing the same parent boat, haha."

Finding a Common Ground

Mario left Liam's place excited, full of hope, and eager to see Betty and tell her that he will be with her, that he wants to have the baby, and that they can just forget and let go of the previous discussion and panic scene they had both created.

Betty, on the other hand, was also more calm, peaceful, and she was missing Mario after she spoke with Karen.

After this brief separation and sharing their emotions with their own confidants, Mario called Betty and made an appointment with her to talk and have a reconciliation. As previously mentioned, Mario was so excited that he reserved a table in a very nice restaurant for dinner. It was a place where they used to enjoy nice and memorable moments, so it was also a special environment to help them create a more loving atmosphere. Their table was by the terrace, the night was clear, some stars could even be seen. There was a perfect weather, kind of warm, and why not a glass of wine to celebrate? It was not a bad way to rekindle their relationship and take a deep breath toward whatever life could yield for them.

Betty groomed herself up; she looked very beautiful and already had that amazing glow by which pregnant women shine.

When they arrived at the restaurant, they acted as if they had just met in terms of the way they were seated, Mario's gestures and Betty's way of moving and seeing him after a while.

Mario asked Betty if she wanted to start talking. Betty said, "Okay, I will start. Thanks!" Betty began by saying that she apologized for having run away from the coffee place the last time they talked and saw each other. "You just have to understand that at the moment, I felt devastated by your reaction. I could hardly think of any other reaction."

Mario just nodded his head as a kind gesture of understanding her and, of course, accepting her apology and the way things happened. "Well, Mario, after this time, it's clearer for me, and now I understand more why you reacted in that way because during these few weeks that we've been apart, I spoke with a very close friend, Karen, which by the way, I think has a very mature and objective way of seeing things. We discussed what happened, so she explained to me why men sometimes react in an abrupt, heartless way when they feel threatened by some unplanned event in their life, which was exactly what happened with us.

"I can now understand that you felt threatened and disappointed by the fact that you were having a better outlook in your life. You were excited about being enrolled in a bachelor's degree, finally being able to start a new career, and of course, a new life. And with regard to this topic, I want to be very clear–I need you to know that I want to be completely supportive on that– I think this unplanned pregnancy might change the way things will unfold, but for sure it won't be an impediment for you to finish your career or cut your wings in any way you might have thought.

"However, I understand that if you are not ready for this kind of commitment, I just want to tell you that my decision in terms of the pregnancy is to continue with it no matter if you decide to be with me or not. I was raised with religious values and more than that with a value for life that is very important for me. Besides, I feel confident that I can keep my job until I have to go for maternity leave and then look for a school or nursery where they can help me take care of the baby while I'm working.

"You might not understand what I'm feeling and it's obvious because you're not carrying a new life inside of you, but finding out that I was pregnant and knowing that it was yours made me feel stronger and full of hope that things will work out for us. You know that we had a rough start, and our last trip helped me in particular to define my future with you, but this gift from heaven is for sure the lead to a road with you. I really believe we can be good parents and, of course, be a healthy couple."

Mario began to have watery eyes, and some tears even dropped from his eyes, sliding through his cheeks. He also looked eager to start talking and interrupt Betty, but he held his breath and let Betty finish her point of view.

Betty just added that she understood his reaction, that she was going to be supportive of his decision, and that if he decided to stay with them (she and the baby, of course), she was going to be supportive in every decision or new endeavor that he might have in mind and support his every new challenge and effort to become a new person.

Mario began by saying, "Thank you very much, Betty. Thanks for your kindness, your mature and understanding words you just said to me. If there was still any doubt in me that this situation was going to be threatening or difficult, now you have helped to dissipate more all my fears.

"Well, Betty, just as you needed to speak with someone to be able to clarify the way you felt, and luckily you found Karen, I just want you to know that I also had a hard time finding someone to talk with because as you know, my 'friends' are not very mature or reliable for any kind of deep conversation such as this one, and usually we (men) have a hard time finding someone reliable to whom we can speak in terms of important or deep life conversations. But after suffering from repetitive thoughts of fear, being angry more at myself for the time wasted with my life and for being so self-destructive, I finally realized that I do have a person with whom to speak about the topic, and he was my cousin Liam. So, I went to his place, and we had a very productive and revealing conversation about the topic. He made me some questions, where I realized almost by myself the answers I needed, and I was also surprised by them because of the way I discovered I felt about you, which was completely different from what I thought at the beginning of this issue.

"Okay, Betty, my conclusions from that talk and what I want to tell you is that I love you so much. You have been an angel sent from God to me. You are, even though not many times I have said this to you, exactly what I needed and what I expected from a couple, and you arrived into my life in my worst dark moments to save me and help me see that life in general is worth living. I never told you this before, but just before I met you, I was already giving up on living. I even had an attempt of suicide, which was not successful due to my mom, who took me to the hospital right away and they cleaned out all the poison (drugs and alcohol) that I had taken to finish my life. Therefore, I'm very grateful to you for being in my life, and I want you to know that I will be here with you and our baby all the way through." Betty's face started to get flooded with tears. Some of her makeup began to dissolve, but she took a deep breath and let Mario continue.

Mario continued by saying, "Betty, I want you to know that I admire the way you have overcome every obstacle in your life, how you're a strong, independent woman that has made her way in a very difficult male environment and has pushed through every challenge you have faced. Seeing you, hearing your story of how you overcame your obstacles in your job and all the humiliations, the stupid rejections, or struggles that you had with your boss and coworkers long ago, made me realize that you're made of steel. Any obstacle that presents to you, you will be able to solve it, and this situation, even if it is not an obstacle as we agree now, it's one of the most challenging endeavor for both of us because we're going to have to mediate a lot of things. We'll have to grow and mature faster in order to give this baby a very different future from the one we had.

"I have no doubt that you will support me and that you will be able to handle your mom role with your professional career as well. I also know more than ever that your vision of yourself has brought the attention of your boss, and I believe that in just a few years, you will have a leading position in your company, even with that male-biased approach that your boss has many times.

"This might come as a surprise to you, but I even see your family as a nice complement of bonding sometimes to what I never had in terms of warm reunions or showing affection as you do, even if sometimes I think is too much from your side." Betty started to laugh with some tears, and she agreed that sometimes is even overwhelming for her too.

Finally, Mario said, "I think, Betty, I'm sure now that we can be together, we can be successful as parents, we can succeed as professionals, and if we let our egos out of the picture, we can heal each one for its path and start joining one new story together to be a healthier couple than the examples we had, than the scars we still have.

"No one thinks or says it's easy, but we're obviously not the first ones that have passed through this kind of situation so let's give the best of each other, to do it in a very different way of how we were raised."

Betty was completely in tears; they hugged for a long time. They were both excited, compromising and bringing all the love that they should've had before, in addition to passing many of those positive emotions and vibrations of love to their baby.

Thought Takeaways

Let's take a plunge into the lessons of this chapter and separate the takeaways from each side:

I. How did Betty and Mario's time off allow them to process the emotions?

II. What's happening inside many of us as women and men in terms of our biology?

III. How do men and women process emotionally a difficult situation or discussion, and how does the social environment affect each of the gender in terms of dealing with emotional and couple issues?

IV. What kind of agreements and strategies could be helpful to deal with those kinds of situations?

←――――――――――――――――――――――――――――――→

I. How did Betty and Mario's time off allow them to process the emotions?

⊙ <u>Let's start with women and dealing with time off</u>

Women, as we have heard, based on history and evolution, usually process their pain or emotional issues in a more personal way. However, in general, as every event of life, it will all depend on the maturity level and emotional pain that they have within.

However, one thing is clear: women that have been rejected, such as Betty in our story, have their emotions readily available due to early conditioning that predispose them to feel that they are not good enough. Usually, they can take a victim-mode behavior and, luckily, rely on a strong network of social support that allows them. Depending on what kind of advice they look for, they tend to process much better their emotions, such as our story. Just a few days after the disagreement between Betty and Mario, Betty started to look for a reliable source to talk about the issue. That's another marked trait of the gender; they usually look for someone to talk with, be listened to, and express their feelings to start processing the pain.

⊙   How do men deal with difficult times?

Men, on the other side, as they are wired differently biologically and emotionally, tend to deal with emotional issues as well usually by doing what they learn through history and evolution–isolating themselves, physically taking out the stress or sadly by being driven to take something to numb the pain, which can either be a stimulant drug, alcohol, or meaningless sex adventure to raise their ego. They just try to avoid the pain, trying not to deal with the situation.

Unless they have had this type of experience several times, and being able to see things from a more mature point of view, they will recur to speaking with someone. And even if they do it, they will tend to take more time than women, as they are also more prone to be ego attached and being conditioned to suck up their emotions and deal with the problems "as a man," swallowing everything. Moreover, the social network they rely on usually is less reliable in terms of maturity and smaller in terms of the number of people they can refer to.

II. What's happening inside many of us as women and men in terms of our biology?

Biologically. Women tend to feel more overwhelmed by hormones of stress; the levels of cortisol if they're not pregnant tend to go up faster than in men. However, when women are pregnant, a protective response of the body is to have already higher levels of cortisol than usual; this doesn't mean they can't take up more stress. This biological difference is justified by the protection that the fetus should have from this stress hormone (Feinberg 2013). High levels of cortisol may be damaging for the development of the fetus in terms of his/her immune response, mood disorders in adulthood, and (Suzuki 2014) it has also been documented that stress on early pregnancy may produce a lower cognitive development for the fetus (Davis and Sandman 2010). Being said that, we also can add that the cortisol levels triggered from a stress response produce a fight-or-flight response as adrenaline levels start increasing. However, if we remember our story, Betty's first reaction was not to run away. On the contrary, she wanted to stay and discuss the issue the day she said to Mario she was pregnant, even if, after all, she ended up running away that had much to do with Mario's panic response and the proposal to end the pregnancy.

⊙ In terms of biology, what happens with men?

Biologically, men tend to have an aggressive response when faced with conflict; they also have cortisol levels up when they are criticized, when they argue, or when they are threatened. In Mario's case, he was feeling threatened by the situation due to the fact that it happened unexpectedly and "interfered" with his plans. Cortisol levels in men also trigger the release of adrenaline, but they cope with it differently:

- *Men tend to react aggressively.* They either yell, hit something (or in the worst case, they hit their partner, which of course is not a justification for that behavior), or, another type of reaction which is what Mario did, just leave without any explanation or reason. This has to do with a biological component that men have of taking more time to lower cortisol and adrenaline levels until they find an outlet (yelling, hitting, or leaving). It usually has to be a physical way to release that amount of hormones.

- *Men isolate in the cave to process emotions.* An evolutionary component of their response to conflict is to isolate; however, they tend to take less time to forgive or understand the situation although they usually are not good with coping with the source of the conflict. Therefore, there's a high possibility that if they talk about the situation without processing the issue, they might explode again. This also has a lot to do with the way most men are educated; they're never presented with an opportunity to express their feelings or even recognize that they have them, as they are undervalued, criticized, and their masculinity questioned every time they feel or try to express an emotion (in most cases).

Gender may also condition the interpretation of a "regulated" cortisol response; previous work within the current sample showed that while depressed women had lower cortisol levels during discussions of conflict and delayed post-discussion recovery, depressed men had higher cortisol levels both before and after the discussion (Laurent 2013).

⊙ *Lack of attention is a stereotype of the male role.* This is the key component of many male problems related to how they handle the emotions. Since early childhood, men have a usually higher lack of attention as they are perceived to be more independent, strong, and able to cope with difficulties. This is also a very good feature of why Mario reacted in that way. If we remember his background of not being given the attention he needed, he also was compensated with material/economical possessions to justify or cover the lack of attention his parents gave him. It is not uncommon to hear that men statistically have more tendency toward suicide due to the lack of attention and social interaction and isolation that they have. Since they're growing up, they are thought to hide their feelings so they are not bullied. A famous phrase we have all heard is "Be strong, you're a man" or "Men don't cry." All those conditioning thoughts and expressions are being integrated in men's psyche, and when they grow, they are the fallback program that they have to rely on. Therefore, it is not unexpected that men have a very difficult time to speak of their emotions, and when they do, it is not easy to find someone they can trust or have good emotional guidance.

III. How do men and women process emotionally a difficult situation or discussion and how does the social environment affect each of the genders in terms of dealing with emotional and couple issues?

Women's emotional processing

On the *emotional and social side* of the reaction, women tend to look for support in other women; they are more prone to social interaction, and they want to verbalize what they are living. Making this distinction on the way we react to conflict doesn't mean all women or all men react in this way, but it's the majority of times that I want to represent with this outlook. Usually, women tend to avoid the person involved in the issue due to the fact that they sometimes think they're misunderstood.

⊙ They feel strong emotions. Due to the hormone pattern difference, women tend to feel more the aggression or discussions as they may have experienced them. This, of course, is also affected by pregnancy as hormone levels are completely disrupted and above normal due to the needs of the fetus.

⊙ <u>They take it personally</u>. This has nothing to do with biology; this feature has an evolutionary component, as most of women throughout history have been taught to be diminished, discredited, and also with low self-value. Therefore, many of the conflicts that involve rejection of something or withdrawal from their partners tend to be taken as personal.

⊙ <u>They hold on to the grudge or hurt for a long time</u>. As part of their security and safety, women tend to isolate sometimes more than men in terms of processing the pain and hurt. This is also explained by an evolutionary component and, of course, is higher when women are pregnant because they want to protect the unborn child.

Men's emotional processing

It is time to take the emotional processing of men in a deeper setting to differentiate the types of responses or reactions and to make it easier for their counterpart to understand some of those expressions.

Men, on their side, as we also have witnessed throughout history, have been conditioned since ancient times to deal with other kind of issues and leave behind the emotional component.

⊙ <u>Withdrawn pattern and isolation</u>. The demand-withdraw pattern also shows clear gender differences; women typically take on and show costs of the demanding role, whereas men more often take the withdrawing role and may actually be reinforced for such disengagement. It has been suggested that these gender-specific vulnerabilities derive from lingering power differentials–i.e., men enjoying more power in intimate relationships (Laurent 2013).

Taking into account these data in terms of how men process the emotional component, these can be clearly verified and just like in women has a strong evolutionary component that has been reinforced through endless decades. It has even been praised and forced sometimes that men have to deal with their emotional issues by themselves, alone and without even being able to ask for help.

Moreover, these kind of "processing," though it makes men less prone to ruminate on what happened, it certainly does not deal with the issue and instead just produces a swallowing-like behavior that allows to build up and slowly create an internal toxic environment, which has been proven by statistics that men tend to have higher rates of substance addiction, game addiction, or sadly, suicide rates. This also has a strong social component that will be discussed further.

Some gender role theories suggest that men are more likely to engage in suppression or avoidance, including turning to substances to avoid (Nolen-Hoeksema 2012).

- ☉ The reward loop. Men, more than women, tend to look for situations where they are being presented with a reward to what they are doing, giving, or sharing. These types of male behavior will have an effect in the way they deal with emotions as well.

One consequence of low effortful control may be that males are more likely to engage in impulsive, reward-seeking behaviors in response to negative emotions. Some studies suggest that the relationship between depressive affect and later alcohol use is stronger for men than women, suggesting that men may be more likely than women to seek the rewarding effects of alcohol in response to negative emotions. Indeed, studies of adults show that men consistently score higher on measures of "drinking to cope" compared to women (Nolen-Hoeksema 2012).

Consistently with the line of research and data, men have been "trained" and "programmed" to be task oriented. That being said, a rewarding expectation is triggered in them whenever they perform some task or behavior; therefore, when they are engaged in an emotional issue where they don't know how to react or what to do when failing, seeking for an outlet to their frustration and sadness guides them to any kind of rewarding option and usually is not one of the healthiest options.

Women's approach to social advice

Women, as mentioned above, have a more powerful group of social interaction and access to advice; however, they tend to take any kind of advice as reliable, and that can complicate the main problem. Therefore, as a woman, try to be very objective in what you say about your issue. The more accurate and truthful the story is, the more success in achieving your best solution it will be.

Whenever you solicit advice from another friend and you're sensing they are diminishing your partner or just attacking the male gender, try to shorten the story, change the subject, and look for a better option. If within your network of friends, you don't find anyone reliable, don't be ashamed to look for professional advice. Usually in serious resources of psychology magazines or journals, you can find some listed options to look for advice, which in general offer also affordable prices. Additionally, and if you are more of the self-taught kind of woman, look up the topic in serious resources and read a similar story or just type your question and see what comes out. Be careful to choose a good source, not just some people trying to flood the web with their emotions. This can help you find the answer you were looking for and allow yourself from your own inner journey to process what you really feel.

Men's approach to social advice

Men usually tend to close up more on the emotional side and pretend like nothing is happening, or in a worst-case scenario, they rely on addictions to make them forget what they're feeling, such as alcohol, gambling, or drugs.

Why do they react like that? This is an evolutionary component that as mentioned before, as children, they're encouraged to close up their emotional side and hold their feelings inside until many times it is too late and they start developing stronger emotions such as rage, illnesses, or severe depression. Opposite to what the greater public think, men suffer more from depression than women. The suicidal rate is also higher with the male gender due to this social stigma, labels, bullying, and gender prejudices that have been around for decades. So the outlook doesn't look good for men when they face an emotional issue, and this was not the exception for Mario in the story. Fortunately, he had someone in the family with whom he could open up.

To close, what kind of approach should men take when they encounter an emotional issue?

It is suggested that men should try to generate a strong though smaller group of friends that they could rely on for these kinds of problems, furthermore you could do the following:

- ☉ Find a close relative to talk about the issue. Ideally, your mother is the best option if you have the confidence to talk about your problems with her. (That is why it is also advised for parents to have a strong bond with their male sons.) If your mother is not an option, try to look for someone in your family whom you can trust. Why is it recommended as first option someone from your family? Simply because they usually know your parents and some background history of how they were raised; therefore, this background could be very helpful as many patterns tend to be developed and repeated from their parents' role model.

- ⊙ <u>Find a strong group of friends with whom they can talk about these kinds of issues.</u> It may not be so easy for a man to find that group, but he should have at least two to three friends with whom he can talk about emotional issues. Try to find people with stable relationships and, needless to say, mature male examples, so you don't have a worse advice than trying to find a solution by yourself.

- ⊙ <u>Start practicing some kind of mindful approach.</u> It can be meditation, yoga, or simply learning to calm your inner thoughts and finding peace of mind in silence. The walking meditations approach might be a good option as they combine physical relief as well as mental peace. Usually, men seek for a physical outlet for emotions, so any kind of exercise combined with some peaceful stress-relief technique might be your best option (Tagliabue et al. 2018).

V. What kind of agreements and strategies could be helpful to deal with those kinds of situations?

Take into account all the differences mentioned above when you are faced with a conflict in your relation because of the many biological, emotional, and social tendencies we were raised and inherent in our kind; and of course, they play a major role on how we react.

None of the strategies used by genres should be labeled or assigned to them. As we have been doing it throughout history, it is more about learning how to resolve conflicts in a much healthier way for both sides, caring more for the greater benefit, which is to maintain a positive and clean environment in the relationship, instead of looking for someone to blame.

Therefore, my suggestion for a healthier approach in terms of the possible solutions would be, as shown in the story, allowing some time to process feelings, trying to find someone to talk with, and if possible, with some real experience, determine criteria and good guidance to sort out the difficult situation. Finally, if along the way to resolving the conflict there are still feelings of pain exchanged, we should try our best to consciously avoid damaging the trust, deep feelings of the couple, or to diminish the value of the relationship.

If we have the knowledge of why and how we usually react, we will have more tools to face many of the conflicts that we may face in the future. Therefore, these actionable steps when facing a conflict in your relationship might come in handy sometime:

i. *Find someone reliable to talk with.* Usually when we have any sort of issue, decision, discussion, or self-doubt, we look for support in our family or social circle. This resourceful advice becomes very relevant to finding balance and self-reflection aided through discussion, and it will produce a much healthier approach and less bias toward your best decision.

ii. *How to maintain yourself unbiased from your social support?* This is a very solid pillar of the female gender, as they usually have a stronger network of support among them compared to the male gender. However, as they have easier access to this resource, it can also be sometimes biased and not objective in terms of relationship advice. As humans, we tend to tell our stories a little different from what really happened, which is the first biased point. Therefore, if you want objective advice from your friends, you should be very truthful in terms of how you expose the problem, issue, or decision you want advice on.

After being objective, you should look for the best possible example in terms of what you want to solve. It is not just about letting it out from your chest; it is about getting your best objective point of view and, if possible, from a person that you know has the experience over the topic and/or has more assertive decisions in her/his life.

iii. *Learn from yourself how to process emotions and allow a healthier outlook that promotes reconciliation.* Whatever is your best approach to dealing with emotions, something that is clear lies in the ground of being more detached from the emotional load rather than ruminating on blaming any of the involved parties.

Taking an attitude of self-reflection or mindfulness approach to dealing with emotions has now been a very helpful strategy used by many experts in psychology and psychiatry, as it has been shown to raise a powerful awareness and consciousness of the self-dialogue, the ability to find repetitive or ruminating thoughts.

Moreover, this approach allows your mind to objectively find a healing purpose to the emotional burden, reconcile your thoughts and emotions, create a healthier chemical profile in terms of your neurotransmitters and hormones. It also allows you to create compassion, empathy, as well as giving you a third-party perspective that will definitely aid you through the path of feeling better and aiming to resolve the conflict with your partner, which in the end is what we are looking for.

CHAPTER 3

Building a Healthy Ground

EVERY RELATIONSHIP HAS its ups and downs; however, the foundation of every family builds from there. All couples that begin or continue a healthy journey have better chances of creating a healthier family bond, a more promising future for their children, and a very important safety net that they will always be able to rely on. Betty and Mario's story is not the exception, and we're about to continue their amazing journey into one of the biggest adventures for them.

We left off our story after Betty and Mario's reconciliation, which, fortunately for both of them, happened without causing too much damage to the new member of the family in one of the most important stages of every human being–the process of conception inside his or her mother's womb, which many times is paid little attention to, even when it has a wide expanding variety of toxic effects and memories that a turbulent relationship might have in the baby's future.

After their reconciliation, they started to get along pretty well; however, as we mentioned before in each other's background, they share as with many couples a different upbringing, pattern issues, a set of programmed beliefs, etc., which will make more challenging and appealing the interaction that we will start to unravel.

Creating Opportunities

Betty's life was a little more stable after all this discussion and separation because she was a more focused woman, who knew what she wanted for her and the baby's future; she already knew the next steps in her life. She knew that first, she had to speak with her boss, Charlie. He is a very insecure man and obsessive/controlling of people's personal life, more when we are talking about women.

Why is Charlie so biased against women? Does this have to do with his family?

Let's find out a little bit of background about Charlie's past. He grew up in a family where his father was the dominating character, a completely patriarchal family. He belittled Charlie's mother every time she had an accomplishment related to her work. His father was a renowned scientific researcher as well as her mom. However, throughout most of Charlie's infancy and adolescence, his father was never present; and when he was there, he was just an image of fear that also made his mother develop a victim complex that Charlie could see very often. This kind of behavior made an imprint in Charlie's character, predisposing him to repeat that pattern due to the fact that several times he spoke with his mom and she just used her victim personality to avoid demanding respect from her husband (Charlie's father).

However, as mentioned and highlighted before, Betty was a very smart, intuitive woman; therefore, she did some research on Charlie's parents, which, as we mentioned, were famous researchers, whose some of their "private" life was available at interviews in newspapers and science magazines. With this information, she knew how to make things a little bit easier when the moment to face her boss would arrive, and she knew that she could use that background on her behalf.

When Betty started to discover this kind of environment in his boss's upbringing pattern, she understood why he treated women with disrespect and sometimes hate. Therefore, Betty knew how to approach her boss regarding the issue that she was pregnant. She developed a very clever and smooth strategy, as she already knew the reasons of her boss's behavior, which in addition to that now she could be more empathic and compassionate with him.

Her first steps to build her strategy were constructing a powerful and loyal reputation with him since some months before, she was "earning points" by being a very good, reliable, and responsible employee. In spite of the short time she had at her company, she never gave anyone the right or chance to make her feel uncomfortable or inefficient, as she always fulfilled everyone's demands and had amazing organizing skills, which made her a difficult prey for his misogynist boss. In addition to that, she was not a woman that played the victim role or complained excessively as many of the other women in the company did. That helped a lot with her image toward Charlie.

Betty knew that she had to win her boss's attention by doing something extra. Therefore, every time her boss seemed stressed by any other issue, she tried to be supportive and gave him what he needed—attention, validation, or someone that just listened to him. He was a very lonely man, as he created a tough image as his shield that didn't allow people to approach him or be able to sympathize with him.

Moving on to her encounter with Charlie, how did Betty prepare and handle it?

It was a Friday afternoon; everyone was gone from the office. The company just passed a financial audit, and they got a very good grade/review from the auditors. All the employees were very tired, as they had many weeks of stress and cumulative late shifts in addition to weekends sacrificed due to the amount of workload. Therefore, that day, everyone was gone as soon as the auditors gave the result of the audit except, of course, for one person—Betty.

She stayed late with her boss on purpose because she knew that it was the perfect moment to talk with him about her pregnancy and maybe some future plans that his boss could have for her as he mentioned something during the audit process.

Empowered Women

Betty knocked on Charlie's office and asked if she could talk with him. Charlie said, "Of course, Betty, what do you need?" Betty started by saying she was very grateful for all the opportunities to participate during the audit process, the freedom she had to guide some people on what they had to do in order to answer the auditors' questions with more evidence. She also told him that he was very generous and supportive during those new challenges. He replied, "It's the least I could do after all the effort I saw from your side even with your early experience and being a woman. You have proved to me that you deserve to remain in this company."

"Thanks, Charlie, I really appreciate your words and support. Well, I stayed late today as well because I wanted to talk with you about my future in this company."

"Hmm . . . Okay, could you clarify *future*?" Charlie replied.

"Don't worry, I won't demand anything from you or ask you for a raise. It's just that I have to tell you that I'm pregnant and the baby is going to be due on the first or second week of April. Therefore, I wanted to let you know with an ample time frame so that you could start planning who will be able to cover me during my maternity leave." Betty did a long pause and an anxious face, expecting Charlie's answer, which, by the way, was taking longer than expected.

After the awkward pause, Charlie confessed to Betty that he took time to answer because he was worried about the time that she was going to be absent and the help he was going to need during that time, as she had become a very strong role model for other assistants at her department.

Betty's face was relieved and surprised. She didn't expect those words or appreciation and less from him; therefore, that made her feel really happy, but she also compromised to do a better job until she was going to leave.

Charlie and Betty stayed a little longer just trying to have a storm of ideas that they could discuss later with more details, but they seemed pretty satisfied with each other's role and commitment to cooperate with the process. On the relationship side, Mario was aware of this audit. He also knew it was ending that week, so he expected to see Betty at his place earlier than before. However, the wait was taking too long, and he was a little bit worried by the late hour she was taking to arrive. When Betty arrived, they started discussing what happened at the office and her boss's response to the big news.

Betty was very happy about everything because she finally felt valued at her work, and all the late hours and sacrifices now had been worth it.

Mario's mood was angry and cold because that night was not, of course, the first one for Betty to arrive pretty late from work. Mario had already a lot of patience before and didn't want to mention anything because he knew how important was Betty's job and how hard it had been to climb or earn her respect. However, if we analyze Mario's position, we could understand his reaction. Mario was a man who was a little older than Betty (two years), without a career, just finally catching up with his academic background, and leaving behind a history of drugs, alcohol, depression, and a very toxic social circle where he wasted a lot of time trying to piss off his parents, but instead of making them disappointed, he just pushed them further away.

Therefore, it is not hard to imagine what kind of thoughts were crossing his mind with all of Betty's late arrivals, knowing that Betty's confidence in terms of her professional performance could be a magnet for other men, and the inevitable self-doubt that they could find her as attractive as he did for all those qualities, even with the fact that she was pregnant. All of these mental constructs, stories, and obviously self-created fear contributed to Mario's emotional response, creating a very different context for their discussion of such a simple story, which was the response of Betty's boss to her pregnancy.

Additionally, Betty was the one that had been making pretty much all the important decisions since they had begun their journey together. She was also supporting the two of them economically since she was the one with a degree, the one with a good job, and finally to add more "mental reasons" to Mario's suppositions, she was the one that lately had not been present when they were supposed to see each other, as well as arriving tired and not in a great mood. Thus, all of this list of factors was just building up in Mario's head, and they were just reinforcing his insecurity, lowering his self-esteem, and of course, judging Betty's behavior without even knowing what was going on in her mind.

Mario then took the lead in the conversation, and he said, "You know what, Betty, some days ago, I had been worrying about your 'dedication' to your work, but knowing your boss's background, the way he treated you in the past, and his behavior as a misogynist, it is hard for me to understand why you are so loyal to him and willing to stay late hours when you know he almost never recognizes what you do or your value in the company."

Betty, was a little disappointed and sad by Mario's reaction, but as it had been an amazing day, she just said, "You know what, Mario, give me some minutes to relax, get comfortable, and I'll explain everything to you."

Mario was angrier because she seemed to not care about his worrying state, but he decided to leave her alone while she got fresh and relaxed. After more or less thirty minutes, Betty was ready, and she approached Mario and asked him to talk, to be patient and open to what Betty was going to tell him.

Mario's face was even more worried and angry. Betty started talking, and she explained that she had been staying late hours due to the audit that the company was going to have. She explained that her strategy of making herself noticeable during those stressful moments and very important event for the company would show her boss once and for all how valuable she could be, even in the midst of chaos and stress for the company. Additionally, Betty explained that by staying late in those moments and showing her abilities to her boss, it was a very important step to gain his trust as he was not aware of them, and it could be a great opportunity to prepare the ground to tell him about the pregnancy in order to obtain a much better response from him.

She also explained to Mario that she had been doing some research about men with that kind of personality, and she knew exactly what to do in order to become a valuable asset for him and the company; all of her actions performed during the past weeks were perfectly justifiable. After doing that research, she knew what Charlie wanted from people regarding professional decisions and also how these kinds of men usually need someone loyal, reliable, one that can be a confidante for them. Thus, she had become almost an expert, and that auditing process was the perfect event for her boss to see her as a valuable asset, not just as an "assistant" but also as a supportive, reliable, and resourceful employee. Finally, all those factors could smoothen the path for her to tell him that she was going to be two or three months off after her pregnancy. She also tried to explain to Mario that during this audit, many people could be laid off; therefore, she was also worried that she could lose her job right after she came back from her maternity leave.

"Mario, please, you should understand that from the moment I became pregnant, I don't have to think just about myself, but I also need to think about our baby and you, in addition to trying to keep this job afloat while we settle and you're able to catch up with your degree and hopefully find a part-time job. I'm sorry if I didn't make a pause or took some time to explain my plan before, but I didn't know if it was going to work or not. Therefore, I preferred to not say anything about it because I don't like to promise or talk about things that in the future, I won't be able to deliver.

"We come from two different settings, and maybe that's why we decide our lives in a very different way sometimes. We shouldn't be doubting each other's actions because we are a couple and soon, we're going to raise a child together. Therefore, we need to be able to trust in each other. This doesn't mean, of course, that if any of us want some type of clarification to understand each other's behavior, we should always be able to ask for it."

Mario was speechless after listening to her and everything she had thought, all the preparation she did, and how she took care of everything. The only thing Mario could say was, "I'm really sorry for ever doubting your behavior or decisions. As you said earlier, we come from very different backgrounds, and that's exactly why sometimes I'm predisposed to think the worst-case scenario, but your amazing explanation and planning of everything just proves me wrong again. The way you investigated your boss, about his personality issues, and how you could make an impact with a perfect timing for the company is amazing all together. Once again, you show me with facts why you're the smartest and most valuable woman I have ever met. You really have a unique ability to sense and figure out people's characters, issues, or weak spots and use them in your favor in a very healthy way. Additionally, you showed me that your thoughts and the way you behave is not selfish at all. You're always thinking of us as a family and putting aside your own comfort to protect the baby as well as trying to please my own wishes sometimes.

"I have never received so much care or attention. That's why I probably react aggressively or insecurely about some things that you do, but now, I feel even more secure with you more than ever. Thanks a lot for explaining yourself so clearly to me and proving to me that I can trust you at all times, even when you don't even have to do it.

"The last thing I want to say is that what you just did with your boss in spite of the short time you were with the company is a real example of how women can overcome job issues in a very smart, polite, and healthy way. If you keep exploiting that ability to overcome these important issues, I'm certain that you can become an agent of change in your company and start becoming an asset for your boss and a true leader for women mistreated and frustrated by all the injustices at the workplace. I've always thought that actions are so much louder than words, and what you did just completely validates the saying and my thoughts."

Betty's face lit up after Mario's comment when she was explaining to Mario. She even felt more satisfied, appreciated, and grateful with him for showing his true feelings and recognizing all the effort she had to put through those moments of painful stress and demands from her company.

After that talk, Mario and Betty were apparently in good terms again.

However, the journey as a couple continues every day, and it's always composed of ups and downs.

Mario had the patience, and in this time, he could acquire more control to listen to Betty's explanation without letting his emotions drive him. He was even recognizing her, but what was happening in his mind after all this discussion? Was he still feeling bad because he was feeling diminished, not by Betty's actions, but by the fact that once again she had everything under control and again, he was not able to do much for the family either economically or in emotional terms? Therefore, as a man, he started to feel undervalued, not needed, and simply useless. Many of those feelings were exactly the ones that he constantly felt in his family when he was a child. Additionally, from his previous background and story, we know that he had suffered from addiction due to the fact that he wanted to escape precisely from those kind of unworthy feelings, and we also know that it is very hard to stop them, more when they have had so much reinforcement and there is still a lot of pain that had to be canalized in so many ways.

Toxic Environments

Thus, after their conversation, what happened to Mario? During the next few days Mario was having an episode of withdrawal, being isolated again; and instead of pursuing his plans and the necessary steps for him to begin his career and probably find a part-time job, he was tempted again with an urgent feeling and necessity to escape from those painful, unworthy thoughts as he used to do by consuming drugs. It had been a good while (more or less six months) since he tried any kind of drugs or alcohol, but the feeling and thoughts of unworthiness and not being able to perform according to all the society labels, as "a provider" and/or "responsible man" of the house, were daunting him from his previous experience. He already knew that the "easiest" way out was taking himself away from reality with the help of drugs. Therefore, he contacted one of his old friends Jonathan. This new friend was a guy that also had a family; he was not married anymore, but had two children of seven and eleven years. He was already a successful entrepreneur and owner of a pub in one of the most frequented commercial districts of Mexico City, Mazaryk.

He met Mario when they were both studying high school, and since then, he had been addicted to drugs and alcohol although not in a "highly destructive manner." Just during his teenager years, he crossed the line and had some destructive behaviors. Currently, he was more of an addict for "recreational purposes," combined with the "social" consumption of alcohol. Nonetheless, Jonathan had been around Mario whenever he was feeling the "urgency" to disconnect himself from reality or having a strong need to have "fun." Thereby, as you can imagine, this qualified as one of those moments. Mario talked briefly with Jonathan about why he needed some relief and escape. Being a recently divorced guy, Jonathan perfectly understood him;

hence, without too much questioning, Jonathan gave Mario a pack with five pills of ecstasy.

Mario took two pills. After an hour, more or less, he was already having the effects of the drug. In addition to that, he also took two shots of vodka to "increase the sensation." All of these events happened early in the morning; therefore, by noon, Mario was uncontrollably "excited/motivated" and willing to do anything to make himself "worthy." Consequently, he contacted one of his ex-girlfriends Kelly, a friend also from high school, a kind of hippie that enjoys living every adventure that life brings to her and also trying to escape her reality from her wealthy parents that never paid attention to her and always treated her as the black sheep. Hence, you can imagine that she and Mario used to be the "perfect couple" in terms of their childhood wounds and matching experiences, their lack of attention from parents, their unsatisfied needs as children, and of course, the isolation issues they both looked for in order to cope with the pain.

Kelly was really surprised by Mario's call, as they hadn't seen each other for at least five years. Nevertheless, she was also happy to hear from him. Kelly met with Mario at a nearby mall from her place. When she arrived, she immediately noticed that Mario was under the influence of drugs and alcohol; it was very easy for her to identify that level of excitement, the clumsy movements, and many other noticeable behaviors.

Still, Kelly was very happy to see him again although she felt disappointed at the same time, as she had been away from drugs for five years more or less. Coincidentally, it was the same time they hadn't seen each other. Mario was only looking for her because he was desperately needing someone with the same kind of experiences that could understand his addictive behavior, his desperation to be listened, and of course, someone with the same level of "unworthiness" that had a similar background. Why? Simply because he needed to feel understood without needing to use a "false" personality or being judged.

The first thing that Kelly asked Mario was, "Why are you taking drugs again? What kind of drug are you on right now?"

Mario just answered with a huge smile, "Ecstasy and two shots of vodka."

"Why, Mario?"

"Well, Kelly, it's a long story, but right now, I don't want you to judge me or feel sorry for me. I just hope that you have some time, and maybe you can help me understand somehow why I was lured again to this stupid drug."

Mario started to cry and laugh almost at the same time. He also started to tell Kelly everything about Betty, all her qualities, and he tried to summarize their relationship in order to arrive at the important issue, which triggered Mario's addiction and his need to look for someone with the same issues. Kelly was surprised, angry, disappointed, and happy at the same time. It was all too strange and apparently synchronistic because she remembered that just a few days ago, he was thinking about her journey through the addiction. Anyway, with all those emotions that she had inside, she didn't know where to begin or what to answer to Mario's request.

As best as she could, she said, "Well, Mario, let's begin by recognizing that you are acting as a complete idiot. I'm sorry if I'm being harsh, but by the story you told me with Betty, you are now a very lucky guy that has found a really valuable woman, who is giving you very valuable life lessons, practically rescuing you without knowing she was doing it. She is also finally showing you that after all you've been through, you are worthy, she loves you, and she was able to accept you with your addiction. I'm sure that when she met you, you were also being the same lousy employee at that sportswear store. If you were not able to perceive that and to appreciate it, let me just give you some news. You will lose her as well as the possibility of having once and for all the family that you secretly wanted. Having said that, and being a little more empathic with you, it is somehow understandable for me that you might fall for those stupid pills or any kind of drug again, as I myself was for a very long time attracted to their 'powerful effect' that they have over you, how they kind of take you away from your sad stories, and how quickly they provide an escape from your hurtful childhood issues.

"However, let me just tell you my story with drugs. From this past five years that we haven't seen each other, after we broke up, as you might remember, I was also addicted to ecstasy and sometimes to smoking pot. However, as of right now, you're feeling those kinds of effects from the drug and are able to completely 'forget' about your emotional pain. You will agree with me that once you start trying them, they produce a sensation of wanting to feel more and more, right?" Mario just nodded his head.

"Unfortunately, those fake feelings and sensations will start to increase the threshold of the experiences that you will want or crave. After we separated, I suffered a very severe depression and turned more addicted than ever, trying also intravenous heroin. In one of my lowest and darkest days, my mother humiliated me to my lowest point due to my inconsistency at school, my poor choices with men, and my stubbornness to continue being free and wild. Not long ago from that day, I also discovered that my father had an affair, which I discovered by accident. As you can remember, my relationship with him was also very deficient and toxic, but at least with him I was able to talk and could still sometimes remember we had some good times once in a while.

"However, that dark day, I also consumed two pills of ecstasy, one joint, and some shots of tequila. Therefore, as you might understand right now, I was feeling 'superpowerful,' extremely happy, and willing to do whatever may come in my way, meaning in those moments, talk with my father about his affair. Thus, I called him and asked him to meet me at a nice restaurant in Lomas of Chapultepec, and when he arrived, he took a deep look at me for a few minutes and perceived that I was high. As it was a fancy place, he couldn't make, say, or do any kind of scene or take me anywhere. Therefore, he had to listen to me and even answer every question I wanted to ask him regarding whatever the hell I wanted because he already knew that when I was under the effect of drugs, I could take everything to the extreme. Since I saw him noticing my state, I warned him to answer me politely and calmly to all the questions that I wanted to ask him, or otherwise I was going to burst into tears and make an awful dramatic scene in one of his favorite restaurants.

"Then after I told him that, my first question to him, as you might be guessing right now, was how long he had been having an affair. He answered that he had seven years with the other woman, and he was so much happier with her than with my mom. He also told me that I had a half brother from this woman, painfully for me. He spoke so good about his son with that woman. I could notice the happiness in his eyes and, of course, by the way he expressed about her and him, so in my mind I just couldn't stop thinking that with that other family, he was able to be the role model father that I would have loved to have. It was very clear that he treated completely differently my half brother from me. Therefore, as you can imagine, I was torn apart, and with the drug effect dripping off and now driving me to my lowest feelings, needless to say, I couldn't keep listening to him.

"So, I just left my seat, ran away to the exit, and started driving without any direction or destination, as you also know how these drugs make you do things that you have a hard time to remember, even after a little while. So this was one of those times. I quickly arrived at Cuernavaca, and I was just apparently looking for a 'high spot' where I could be completely isolated. I remember that there was this famous spot named Mirador, and it was the perfect place as it was kind of hidden in the woods. It was the perfect place to take my experience even to a higher level.

"Once I arrived at the place, I was desperate to feel powerful, worthy, and happy again, so I started looking for more drugs. 'Luckily' for me, I thought, I still had two vials of heroin left in the truck of my car for a 'special occasion,' and this certainly qualified for that label. So I got out of the car, opened the truck, and took out a syringe that I also had there. I looked for a quiet spot in the woods and began injecting what's inside the vials. As you can imagine, doing two vials of heroin, plus the alcohol and ecstasy still in my body, made me start to have a complete revolution inside of myself. Unfortunately, the words of my father, his happiness with the other family, the fact that he spoke so proudly of my half brother were spinning in my head that just made my feelings of unworthiness to become stronger, and instead of making them disappear, I started to feel incredibly sad, angry with myself, unworthy to an extent that my only clear thought at that moment was to throw myself over a cliff and end my failure of a life, end all the disappointment that I was to my mother and the invisible daughter that I was to my dad. By the way, a great place to perform my last action in this planet was not very far from where I was, so I began to walk toward the cliff. However, as I was pretty dizzy and clumsy with my movement, I tripped on a hole, hit myself with a stone in my head, and I passed out, just lying on the grass in a 'perfect' spot where no one would easily find me. Call it God, universe, or whatever you want, after a few hours, I was found by a couple lying on the ground. They were celebrating their anniversary in a nearby restaurant and where looking for a nice spot with a good view of Mexico City, so I just luckily happened to cross in their way, sort of saying. They found me unconscious, puked, and they immediately called an ambulance. As you can imagine, I survived that terrible last experience with drugs.

"More importantly, my point with this tragic story and your current state with drugs is to help you now in your journey because from that moment on, I began my own search for help. I talked with my father again at the hospital, apologized to him, kind of made amendments with him, and explained all of my deep feelings why I started to take drugs again. He was completely shocked, as he had never listened to the complete story of how I felt inside. Therefore, he made a compromise with me and enrolled me in a rehabilitation clinic in Guanajuato in the middle of nowhere. I was there for six months, and I could finally detoxify from everything as they have a very strict and complete program.

"Let me describe what I went through in that program so you can see a clearer picture of what you might wanna do some time from now, of course if you really want to leave any kind of addictions once and for all. And stop hurting yourself, now that it seems that your life can take another path and you are already a father, something that requires a lot of responsibility unless you want to repeat the circle with your child, Mario.

"The first stages of the program include a slow detoxification of your addictions to the substances, of course, and they include a healthier nurturing program, where you start finding natural substances that help you counteract the feeling of abstinence. It isn't easy at all—your body starts shivering, sweating, feeling anxious, and depressed at times, but it is all part of your dependent mind that is still craving for the drugs and is transitioning your internal chemical imbalance that you have. In addition to changing the food that you used to eat, they also complemented nutrition with exercise during those moments. I really realized that we don't know many of the benefits of exercise in terms of naturally releasing chemical substances that make you feel awful and how after a little while of doing it, you start releasing a self-made pharmacy that helps you feel better. All the positive substances that you release with it suddenly start replacing the drug effect. Some of them are dopamine, endorphins, and serotonin. All of this chemical cocktail eventually starts repairing your homeostasis and attaching to the receptors in your brain to allow you to overcome part of the anxiety and depression symptoms. You might easily relate to those feelings, as I remember that you used to swim to escape from your reality and feel better.

"Then they start incorporating meditation classes, where you learn how to breathe correctly, how to let your toxic or emotional thoughts pass, allow them to be with you, embrace them, and teach them a new path to move instead of becoming identified with them or rejecting them because they insist a lot in the concept that if you don't learn to cope with those kind of thoughts, then they internally become toxic energy that somehow looks for an outlet. These classes little by little start helping you to feel more whole, more connected. You start tapping your inner voice, which we all have within, but we never allow to be louder because we are trained to never listen to it. We usually are taught to be dependent on every outside stimuli and external rewards, but when we access that inner world of hearing your own voice, experiencing how your own heart can heal you, and all the possibilities that you generate placing yourself in that peaceful state. That's when your true self starts emerging, and that's the moment when you start understanding that before, you were simply lost, you were trying to be someone else, trying to fill someone else's expectations, trying to fill your huge emotional void that needed attention and a lot of love. Sadly, you want to fill it with external things, but in fact, you were drowning in your own self-awareness, your feelings, and most importantly your divine presence that always lies within you.

"You might think that I became so spiritual, and maybe even a fanatic, but actually, this kind of approach doesn't have anything to do with any sort of religion, cult, or esoteric way of living. It is, in fact, learning to live with your own divine principles that we all embody. It's an integral wellness path, more than simply a spiritual one.

"When we experience a true balanced nurturing process that comprises the major nutrients as well as the correct minerals, when we hydrate our body, when we admire it, understand what it does internally for us every day, we almost unconsciously access a gratitude field, from where it is easier to want to take care of it, as our most expensive and luxurious vehicle to access a physical experience in this world, and we get to enjoy more every day that we are simply alive!

"Exercise, as part of the program, now becomes a huge expression of gratitude as well to our bodies. We allow every cell inside of us to release the toxicity that we generate daily, clean our organs, strengthen our tissues, give flow, and channel our nutrients, fasten our metabolism, boost our immune system, regulate our millions of chemicals that affect our emotions and learning process, and finally oil all of our internal machinery, allowing it to recover, repair, and even start rejuvenating us.

"The spiritual path of meditation allows you to identify so many programmed thoughts, many erroneous beliefs that we carry that are not even from ourselves, that sometimes are not even from our parents, but unfortunately are just being passed on from generation to generation. They produce a lot of limiting beliefs, diminish your value, and make you feel that you're not enough. Hence, we tend to look outside either on drugs, stimulants, toxic relationships, gambling, or even on overworking, a relief, a feeling of peace, apparently obtaining instantaneous 'joy' because many of those substances or external aids provide just momentary feelings. However, as you know, they last very little, and the payoff after you constantly use them or recur to them is worse than the feelings you had at the beginning."

"Wow, Kelly," said Mario, "you have blown my mind with such a brief, but deep description on how powerful this program is! As simple as you make it sound, I now believe that is just what I need to finally leave my addiction issue. And what resonated a lot for me is the spiritual path, where you learn to master your thoughts, sort of saying, 'cause I believe that is the most difficult part of my journey. I think the reason I became an addict, as many of us look for an escape of our current or past reality, which is usually full of painful situations that we lived in the past, is we try to fill the void, as you mention it, that our families sometimes left or helped to create, in many cases not on purpose, but after all, the damage is already done.

"I'm very sorry you had to see me in this condition, but everything has moved so fast in my life that sometimes it is inevitable to listen to that voice that you were talking about, saying things like 'you don't deserve her,' 'you won't be able to succeed in this healthy life,' 'you won't be a good father,' 'you're not going to be a good husband,' 'she always takes care of everything, what are you doing to contribute?' etc.

"Many days I wake up, and those thoughts are just like my 'waking alarm'– they're inside of my mind, they haunt me all day, and just when I think I have been able to dominate them, Betty tells me another of her successes, another achievement that she just accomplished, and then I immediately feel less unworthy, and you know that path. Then suddenly, I start sabotaging myself until I achieve to provoke more new feelings of unworthiness that drive me directly to any kind of relief, which many times are the drugs. Unfortunately, I still have access to people that can provide me with them, so I keep falling again and again just when I started to think that I was tougher or I didn't need them anymore. I don't even know how, but I manage to get myself in the path to obtain them and use them.

"This might sound weird, taking into account our history, but I've never heard someone talk so clear, so blunt, and of course, that understands my path as real as you do. Would you be willing to be my sponsor through the path of my recovery?"

Kelly was shocked when she heard that. She paused, stayed still, started breathing faster, and then said, "Yes, Mario, I can be your sponsor, but given the fact that we had a story together and knowing that you have found an amazing woman with whom you're on your way to be a father, I will only do it if we explain to Betty together and you tell her everything that happened today with us—the feelings you just describe to me, everything that you feel when she accomplishes something, and of course that we have a past together, clarifying that we have been apart long enough to know for sure that there aren't any feelings behind that could threaten your relationship with her.

"I know it is tough what I'm asking, but it's the right thing to do if she approves that I can be your sponsor, and of course not just by myself but finding as well the support of my own sponsor from the clinic that helped me through my journey of recovery.

"Thanks, Kelly. Of course, I agree with all your conditions and sounds pretty fair to do it in that way, being completely honest with what I have felt and this new adventure that we'll embark on."

Thought Takeaways

Let's analyze some key points that can help us understand the building blocks of a healthy ground in a relationship:

I.   How can Betty's strategies help us in dealing with a difficult boss?

II. What did Betty take into account when speaking with her boss about her pregnancy?

III. How and why did Mario (or any man) feel ashamed, "humiliated," or simply not needed when a woman, Betty, is the provider with a successful career?

IV. What would be Mario's drug effects for him, the relationship, and his future as a father?

Let's begin unpacking these takeaways from the story.

I. How can Betty's strategies help us in dealing with a difficult boss?

Betty's strategies to deal with her boss were very powerful, proven techniques and handled in a way that almost any kind of boss would be surprised how a proactive employee can give a turnaround on a difficult personality.

First of all, Betty was, as mentioned in her background, a goal-oriented person that had to develop highly efficient organizing skills to get to where she is. In addition to that, she had always been the silent employee but carefully winning people over including her boss by paying attention to details, helping others with difficult tasks, becoming a source for solutions. Additionally, a very powerful strategy was researching about her boss's personality and background without seeming needy or eager to be liked by her boss. She also became a strong person to rely on and finally becoming the first line of support when an important event (internal audit) took place. All these attributes are the ones that any kind of boss no matter the kind of personality they could have would love from an employee.

Therefore, we can see that anticipation, organizing ourselves and helping others to do it, paying attention to details, giving solutions instead of complaints or gossips will most likely help you to succeed in your job no matter the area or the type of boss you can have.

Organizations should utilize mentoring relationships to facilitate informal and personal learning of both mentors and protégés. Perhaps training programs can help mentors and protégés explicitly discuss what they want to learn from the other. More broadly, organizations can attempt to foster mentoring by cultivating a climate that encourages informal developmental relationships and continuous learning. In particular, organizations should attempt to develop a climate of psychological safety, which allows employees to take risks and ask questions without fear of recrimination, resulting in increased individual learning (Turban 2016).

II. What did Betty take into account when speaking with her boss about her pregnancy?

Betty was very skillful in setting up the whole scenario to talk with her boss. She was very careful to follow a set of steps, some of which were already mentioned in the story, but we are going to put them here more clearly to be able to follow them:

- ⊙ She was careful to <u>analyze the personality of her boss</u>, to know his "biased behaviors" but not feel threatened, instead be more curious about his past and why he reacted like that, which we could call empathy.

- ⊙ She <u>paid a lot of attention</u> to what he noticed from other people, what type of achievements he celebrated from them, and more importantly, what was missing for him as he was an overdemanding boss; but she picked up those "extra" things as a leverage for her to try to do them without seeming just a pleasing employee.

- ⊙ Finally, she <u>waited for that "perfect moment"</u> to drop the news in addition to being previously a person that had already won the confidence of her boss and practically assuring that the feedback and response was going to be positive for her. Here, we can appreciate an attitude of service instead of just an attitude of extracting benefits from a job or demanding things without doing too much to earn them. Any kind of boss would be also glad to have employees that think ahead, that give more than they can ask without necessarily having to sacrifice too much.

III. How and why did Mario (or any man) feel ashamed, "humiliated," or simply not needed when a woman, Betty, is the provider with a successful career?

- ⊙ Men usually have a more competitive instinct, more in terms of career or provider roles, which have been conditioned for them since practically a prehistoric epoch. Therefore, usually, men that have as a partner a successful woman and they're not being a good provider or they have not been able to achieve bigger success than their wives tend to feel diminished every time their partner has a success.

⊙ Men's implicit self-esteem was lowered when their partner succeeded (relative to when their partner failed) in domains that were higher (academic) and lower (social) in relevance to their sense of self. There is some evidence that men automatically interpret a partner's success as their own (relative) failure (Ratliff 2013).

⊙ There are at least two other reasons why thinking about a partner's success might lead to decreased implicit self-esteem for men. One is that positive self-evaluation derives in part from fulfilling roles typically ascribed to one's gender. There are strong gender stereotypes where men are typically associated with strength, competence, and intelligence; a partner's success, especially if it is construed as an own failure, is not compatible with the stereotype and could negatively impact self-esteem. Men portray themselves as being more competent than they actually are, being reminded of a time that their partner was successful might pose a threat to their own view of themselves, thus lowering their implicit self-esteem (Ratliff 2013).

⊙ These kinds of comparisons or decreasing self-esteem can be overcome by improving the communication between partners and, in this particular case, trying to develop more empathy from the female side, in addition to highlighting the qualities and abilities that the man has in order to restore his confidence.

- Every time we are reminded of labels, roles, or society-imposed frames of success, men and women can fall into decreasing their self-esteem as we tend to equate our value to any external measurement or standard also imposed either by parents, society, or, in this case, both.

- However, it is important to remember that our worth is only given by the self-image that we have created; therefore, it is encouraged for both partners in a relationship to cultivate their inner worth, looking for more tools inside them, knowing their abilities and trusting their own value as adults.

IV. What would be Mario's drugs effects for him, the relationship and his future as a father?

We will briefly get into the world of ecstasy as a "recreational drug."

Ecstasy is a commonly used name for the chemical substance methylene-dioxymethamphetamine, which is abbreviated as MDMA. Ecstasy is comprised of chemical variations of amphetamine or methamphetamine (stimulants) and a hallucinogen, such as mescaline. In addition to MDMA or the related compounds MDEA and MDA, drugs sold on the street such as Ecstasy also contain other psychoactive or mind-altering drugs, like caffeine, ephedrine, selegiline, and ketamine (Morgan 2000). MDMA is produced in tablet or capsule form and is usually taken orally although there are documented cases of intravenous use. MDMA's acute effects last from three to eight hours, and its short-lasting effects include feelings of euphoria, enhanced mental and emotional clarity, sensations of lightness and floating, and other hallucinations. Users of MDMA also have suppressed appetite, thirst, or need to sleep (Gordon 2001).

In addition to the effects described above, when we combine any type of drug including the ones that are prescribed by a physician with alcohol, we will enhance and accelerate the effect of the drug in addition to increasing the side effects for our internal organs, such as liver, pancreas, and kidneys to process all the unwanted chemicals generated from their metabolism.

This a list of all the damage you can produce to your body and brain when mixing this kind of drug with alcohol, and I dare to say they are the same damages of mixing any kind of drug with alcohol repeatedly:

- ⊙ Serious dehydration is a potential risk. The use of ecstasy often results in hyperthermia (increased body temperature), and individuals begin to sweat profusely. Alcohol is a diuretic. This can lead to dehydration that can result in cardiovascular issues (high blood pressure, heart attack, and even stroke), delirium, aggressiveness, confusion, psychosis, kidney failure, and seizures.
- ⊙ Combining these substances results in a significant potential to develop liver damage.
- ⊙ People who abuse ecstasy often have problems with insomnia once they crash.

⊙ There is a significant potential to overdose on either drug. Most likely, individuals overdose on alcohol, but overdose of either drug can be potentially fatal or lead to long-term damage to areas of the brain that may produce significant cognitive issues, such as problems with memory, attention, problem-solving, and emotional regulation.

⊙ Individuals who combine alcohol and ecstasy often begin to experience issues with severe anxiety and paranoid thinking that can become quite pronounced.

⊙ Once the individual stops taking the drugs and they begin to leave the system as a result of normal metabolism, a massive depletion of neurotransmitters in the brain occurs. This can lead to significant issues with apathy, depression, and even suicidality.

⊙ Chronic use of either drug is associated with the potential for numerous neurological and cognitive issues as a result of damage to the brain.

⊙ When an individual combines different types of drugs, such as a central nervous system depressant and a dissociative hallucinogenic that has stimulant properties, the risk of overdose on either drug is increased. In most cases, overdosing on alcohol would be the most common occurrence as a result of mixing these two drugs, as individuals continue to drink more and more alcohol. However, it is possible for one to overdose on either drug as a result of the effects that occur when one takes both drugs.

⊙ When different drugs are combined, there is always the risk for unusual or unpredictable side effects from either drug or from the combination of the drugs.

⊙ The development of physical dependence on one or both drugs is markedly increased.

⊙ The development of a substance use disorder to one or both of the drugs is substantially increased.

(https://www.alcohol.org/mixing-with/ecstasy/)

As stated above in the side effects, the abuse of this drug can, in very simple and direct words, predispose Mario to more problems when controlling his emotional reactions, losing more capacity of his brain, which of course would have an impact on his academic and professional future. Above all, he will likely be having a lot of problems as a father in addition to setting a very poor example to his future child.

CHAPTER 4

The Snowball of Self-Sabotage

A S WE LEFT off, our story ended on the last chapter with Kelly (Mario's ex) and Mario's talk. They agreed that they were going to tell Betty about their plan, where Kelly was going to be his sponsor together, of course, with someone from the clinic.

However, in order for Mario's plan to work out, he realized he really needed more help to finally overcome his addiction; therefore, he found out more information about a three-month program in the clinic where Kelly was treated, which was located in the middle of the road toward Guanajuato. He also felt it was going to be easier on Betty if he commended the whole plan so she wouldn't misinterpret his intentions with Kelly or have any kind of jealousy thought about their relation. Mario agreed with Kelly that they were going to try to approach Betty in the most professional and respectful way. Thus, everything was set up between them. Next, Mario arranged an appointment with Betty after she came back from work at Mario's place.

When Betty received the call from Mario at work to set the appointment, she was already feeling something was not right, and with a keen agreement, she nodded her head and accepted Mario's invitation to dinner though at that moment Mario didn't even mention they were not going to be alone.

As the night approached and Mario was, of course, completely clean, he still was a little anxious, worried, and just feeling fearful that Betty would misinterpret something or simply just get angry and leave him again. Kelly was already with him, so she tried to calm him and convince him that everything would work out fine if he would just stop focusing on those imaginary thoughts that were not even happening at the moment, also trusting that if he started to mention everything he had already researched, then that could help prove to Betty that he really wanted to improve, to become a better partner, a better father. Probably that approach would minimize Betty's worry and any kind of threat that she might feel.

Your Actions Dictate Your Consequences

The night was settling, and Betty arrived at Mario's place. Mario and Kelly were eager to talk with her; Kelly was also curious about Betty for all the things Mario mentioned when they met. Mario opened the door, let Betty in, and as soon as Betty entered, she noticed there were three dishes and three sets of cutleries on the table. So, she asked, "Mario, why are there three spots on the table?"

Mario was a little nervous, and with a stuttering voice, he replied, "Well, Betty, we have three sets on the table because I want to introduce to you a very special person that I know from my past." Mario went to the living room and presented Kelly. "Betty, this is Kelly, a girlfriend from high school. Kelly, this is Betty, the future mother of our child."

Kelly replied, "Nice to meet you, Betty. It's a pleasure to have a face now for the woman that finally seems to have Mario seriously committed and a very different place from where he was and hopefully help him straighten out his life toward a much better future."

"Thank you, Kelly, nice to meet you too."

"Okay, ladies," said Mario, "let's get to the table so we can start eating as I am pretty hungry already, and we have plenty of things to talk." Betty's face was full of curiosity, and she had a touch of suspicious thoughts as Mario had never done anything similar to what was happening.

Mario started to serve the food, which also was unusual for Betty to see that kind of healthy food in Mario's place, but she didn't want to keep imagining things so she patiently waited for Mario's explanation for all this unexpected dinner. Mario began talking, and he started to talk about Kelly's past.

"Well, Betty, let's begin with a brief explanation of who is Kelly so you can be more familiarized with her and also understand what this is all about. Kelly, as I mentioned, is an old high school friend that for the sake of keeping everything honest, I wanted to tell that she was my girlfriend at that time. She is now a very successful free soul, who dedicates her life to the art and interior design of houses, as well as selling modern paintings. She loves to travel the world and enjoys life as it comes to her. However, and to link our stories, do you remember, Betty, that when we started dating, I told you that I tried some drugs in my past? And before you, I sometimes had a hard time using them and suffering their effects?"

Betty replied, "Yes, although you were not that specific. You just said you used to taste some of them."

"Well, Betty, never mind." Mario continued explaining about Kelly's past. "When Kelly and I used to date, we tried several drugs. Of course, the most common ones for us were pot and ecstasy, nevertheless, and to be completely honest and sincere with you, when people are addicts, they also have less fear to try almost any kind of drugs. Your life usually starts derailing from any kind of meaningful purpose, pretty much the only thing that matters is escaping the crude reality that you're tired and extremely resentful to endure, therefore you start trying these drugs more often than you would want or than anyone else would imagine. This happens because your body starts creating a very weak and low threshold to cope with reality, and each day you consume them, it all starts to grow as you expose yourself to more drugs or try a new one, or a more intense one, until your life starts to feel numbed. Well, that's exactly what happened to Kelly and me."

Betty's face was surprised, disappointed, and angry at the same time, so you can imagine the cocktail of negative chemicals that started flooding her body. She interrupted Mario and said, "Mario, why are you explaining to me all these drug effects, or why are you being so detailed about people's behavior under drugs?"

Mario replied, "Well, Betty, being as honest and specific as I can, I'm giving you this context because as you recalled before, and you already mentioned it, I wasn't completely honest with you when we first started dating about my story with drugs. Therefore, this time, I don't want anything to be left out, and I want you to be completely aware with the details of why I did it or why Kelly is here with us today. Please let me continue and listen to all the truth. I just kindly ask for your patience and understanding as these issues are not easy for you to understand them or much less become aware of them now."

Betty replied, "Okay, Mario, carry on."

"Well, as I was particularly mentioning some specific effects of the drugs, I wanted to be clear on that because as you might remember, recently just after we discussed your amazing solution with your boss and asking already for your pregnancy leave, right after we had that talk some days ago, I kept feeling really bad, diminished, humiliated, having a really low self-esteem, just like I used to feel when I was a child and my parents were never satisfied or pleased with my grades or behavior. Therefore, I couldn't resist my head, my painful feelings, and I called an old friend that gave me a small pack of five ecstasy pills, then in the bar where I met with this friend, I took two pills and some shots of vodka to numb my pain, sort of saying. Thus, in just a few hours, when the effect of the drugs started to kick in, I felt an extreme rush and a stupid sense of reckless power, of being able to do anything. I was afraid I would do something stupid, and I just could think of one person that could understand perfectly how I was feeling due to her journey with drugs, so I called Kelly, we met to talk, and then she started to tell me her story with addiction.

"To be completely fair with you, I'll try to explain it as lightly as possible to avoid more unwanted details for you. As soon as I met with Kelly, she noticed that I had taken some drugs, and she felt reminded of a similar event that she had experienced so she told me everything about it. She told me that one time, while under the influence of drugs, she did a very stupid act of looking for isolation in a spot in the outskirts of Mexico City and the road to Cuernavaca. You should know this place, as it's near where you live. Anyway, during that event in the woods of the restaurant Mirador, she was trying to kill herself, looking for a good spot to just jump off a cliff. However, she was very lucky and tripped into a hole, hitting herself with a stone on the head. While lying on the ground completely passed out, a couple that luckily was nearby found her. In that moment, she realized that she couldn't have any more risks or stupid impulsive behavior, so with the advice and help of her father, she decided to get enrolled into a program to be detoxified, completely heal, and clean herself once and for all.

"As you might start seeing the connection, Betty, when Kelly saw me that day, and right after I told her that I had taken those two pills and the shots of vodka, she and I agreed that maybe this detoxifying program that she kindly explained to me that day could also work for me, and finally I could be able to move on with my life, probably understanding more why these kind of diminishing thoughts and self-sabotage behavior is so strong and ingrained in me.

"I don't expect you to fully understand, Betty, and I'm completely aware that you might be feeling very disappointed right now or mad at me for not telling you all the truth of my dark story before, but as we started to move on in our relationship so quickly, and I started to feel something very profound and strong with you, I really felt that you are going to be part of my story and most likely the person I will end up with, so I couldn't really risk losing you if I told you the whole truth."

Betty was really confused with her feelings, so she just said, "Okay, Mario, don't worry, we'll talk later about our future. Right now, please go on."

"Well, Betty, I'm approaching the end of the story as you can imagine. The reason Kelly is here with us today is to tell you that I'm going to get enrolled in this program to detoxify myself because I really want a clean slate in my life. I really desire to be a different kind of man for you, for the baby, and most of all, for me. I am completely exhausted of this disease, of being addicted to some pills, of being dependent on their influence and effects that they have on me, and most of all of being just a slave of all these negative and addictive emotions that I have felt at least since I was eight or ten years old."

Kelly intervened, and she started to support Mario's explanation. "Betty, I can partially understand how you feel right now by my presence and, most of all, by the things that Mario is just telling you, so in the best interest of making this dinner and reunion a more friendly environment, let me just tell you that the journey of addicts is not easy at all. It's a very difficult reality that only the ones that have suffered the same or who dedicate their lives to help these kind of people are able to relate with their emotions, with their thoughts, or with the effects that these stupid drugs have on us and also the devastating effects they have on the families of addicts.

"Mario and I were very lucky to find a healing path before it was too late. Let me just tell you that during my journey in the clinic, I met some people that had completely destroyed their lives, their families, and of course, had damaged so much of their bodies that they are not able to recover many things of their lives. But even with those painful and grieving scenarios, they are still standing, and most of them are now in a completely healed path, rebuilding their lives even at their fifties or sixties. So, if we try to see Mario's case and now his decision to completely heal, we can be a little more understanding, compassionate, and able to empathize with him. It's all that we are asking from you, and we know that it is a heavy story, some hurtful truths, but in the end, this is a very lucky scenario than the one that could have happened if Mario didn't find his way out of the drugs."

Betty was completely stunned, a little scared, and deep down angry because in the end, Mario lied to her and had torn her trust although inside her she was feeling very sad for Mario and also helpless to completely relate to his story. Betty just said, "Okay, Kelly and Mario, I'm trying my best to understand all the plot, the past, and background of your stories. However, it is worth mentioning that I'm feeling betrayed, Mario, for your not being completely truthful with me, though as you explain to me more the world of addiction, it is easier for me to feel less betrayed and more empathic with you too. Thus, now can you both tell me exactly how this program will work and why you had to be here, Kelly. No offense, but this story seems too personal for Mario, therefore I was wondering why you were also here."

Kelly just said, "Yes, Betty, you're completely right, and I really appreciate your honesty about how you're feeling. Mario, please start moving on to the reason of me being here, please."

Mario replied, "Okay, Kelly, and thanks, Betty, for your honesty, as usual, and also for the huge effort you're doing to understand all this story that seems to be taken out of a mystery novel. Well, Betty, Kelly is here because as I mentioned earlier, I'm planning to be enrolled in the program very soon. As part of being in the program, I need to have a sponsor that will guide me, be with me, and practically be my standing pillar when I feel the need to relapse or when I start having the effects of abstinence from the drugs. Therefore, Kelly, together with another person, whom I still don't know, will be the sponsors during my journey in the program. However, we wanted to explain this to you together so you could meet Kelly, know her story, and of course, first give you an explanation on how all these things ended up this way. So, I would like, Betty, to ask for your opinion about Kelly being also part of my sponsor help after I enroll in the program. Are you comfortable with that?"

Betty's face now was a little upset and more disappointed. However, with all that, she said, "Okay, Mario, I'm fine with that. However, can you be a little more specific about the program, please?"

Mario knew Betty's tone, and he started to get worried about Betty's reaction after the dinner, but he still continued with the explanation. "Well, Betty, this kind of program is a complete detoxifying process that is not only focused on cleaning the drugs of your body, but it is also concerned about the root cause that generated the addiction. Therefore, it is a program comprised with four stages.

"The first stage of the program is detoxifying your body, so this means eating really different from what most of us consume and allowing your body to be cleansed of any traces of drugs or compounds that could still be provoking anxiety or depression in you. That being said, I will finally be able to lose some pounds and not be triggered by junk food as you know that I love and probably that was the first surprise when I served dinner.

"The second stage is the emotional detoxification, and this means that I will be guided by a psychology expert, specializing in the treatment of addictions without, of course, giving me any kind of medication. This process starts by going deep in your previous childhood issues, as they are the root of most of your addictive tendencies and self-sabotaging behaviors.

"The third stage has to do also with your body and about exercise, so in this stage, experts on biochemistry and metabolism explain how your body works internally, your multiple triggers that emotions or food have within you, and additionally a new approach that is trending in wellness centers named epigenetic processes. These are all the effects that drugs, emotions, sleep, lack of exercise, your social circle, and any stressful environment can cause in your genes. Thus, by understanding how your body works, you will be able to appreciate more of what it does for you every day, and also, you'll be more conscious to take care of it every time you have some kind of external trigger.

"Finally, the fourth stage is concerned about your spiritual health, and this is not at all related to any kind of religion. It is simply techniques on how to breathe properly, starting to learn how to meditate, understand how you can be in complete silence and stillness, becoming sort of an observer of your thoughts. Additionally, this stage is also concerned with aligning your inner body signals with your thoughts and feelings, being able to synchronize your heart and your brain by achieving a deep state of coherence without letting yourself be triggered by stress or sadness, and questioning more what is the meaning of your experiences, instead of trying to numb them with any kind of external distraction or drug. This, of course, doesn't mean I will become a monk or will live in isolation. It just means that I finally will be able to stop my inner toxic-thinking cycles."

Betty was a little relieved, though she was still confused and angry, mostly because it seemed that Mario wanted to set up the talk they were having with Kelly, so she couldn't say anything and she sort of felt compromised to agree with whatever Mario's plan was. Nevertheless, she replied, "Sounds good, Mario. I just have some questions."

"Of course, Betty, please let me know them."

Betty said, "Well, what is the success rate that they have with people that enter this program? How much time are you supposed to be isolated for? What's going to happen with us after you finish this program? How can I trust in you again with these kinds of issues if you are just telling me about a whole life of addictions, which I was completely left out? And I have one more request before you start answering, Mario. I would like to discuss the answer to these questions just you and me—no offense, Kelly, but they are too personal, and I would like to have this discussion with Mario alone."

Kelly's face was already ashamed and uncomfortable, so it was the best thing that Betty could have asked her. Thus, she replied, "It's completely fine,

Betty. Don't worry, I was just going to say kind of the same. That conversation seemed a lot more appropriate for you and Mario." Right after that, she just said goodbye to Mario and Betty and left.

Mario was a little afraid of Betty's tone, and when he said goodbye to Kelly, he just quickly whispered to her, "Please wish me luck." Kelly replied, "Don't worry, it'll work out."

Mario approached Betty to hold her hand, but Betty just stepped back. Mario then started to answer her questions. "Well, Betty, to answer your questions, which are completely reasonable and appropriate, let me start by saying that I really appreciate your understanding so far with all this situation. I can imagine by your tone and face that you didn't enjoy Kelly's presence. I'm sorry for bringing her, but I was really afraid what you could say after I told you all the truth about my past experiences with drugs."

Betty said, "Start answering the questions, Mario, please because we have some other stuff to talk about."

Breaking the Trust

Mario began answering Betty's first question. "Well, Betty, the success rate of the program for the research that I did and also Kelly's feedback is above 80 percent, so for me, it seems pretty high and reasonable, and for the cost of the program, don't worry, I have already thought on how I'm going to pay it.

"The isolation stage is only for the first month. The next two months, I can be visited as much as anyone wants to do it, and during the third month, depending on my progress, the trust that I have earned with my sponsors, and my results on some tests that they will apply, I would be able to be released for the weekend. Of course, I would be under supervision by my sponsors and the person that they assign me as my emergency contact. That, of course, is going to be you if you agree.

"For your next question of what is to happen with us when I get out of the program, I was thinking that if you want and if everything goes okay during that time, maybe you can put me on a trial for maybe another two to three months or more, and after that time, I would really like to start looking for an apartment for us and start living together, as I want to be with you during the last months of the pregnancy and, of course, for the birth of our child.

"And finally, for your final question, of how can you trust me again if I didn't mention anything about these issues before? All I can say, Betty, is that I'm deeply sorry. I'm completely aware that I screwed it up by not telling you, by betraying your confidence and also may be more by contacting an ex and bringing her to convince you about the program. Just let me quickly explain why I did it." Betty's face was angry, but at the same time she was a little empathic with him, mostly because she was really in love with him. Therefore, she just said, "Okay, Mario, please go on."

Mario said, "Well, Betty, if we are going to make a step forward for this relationship, then I better tell you also many of the stuff that I've suffered with my family and during my childhood. Let's start with my father. He is a very successful business man, and as you know, he owns many casinos here in Mexico City and two in USA right at the border of Tijuana. Ever since I can remember, he has been a very cold man, practically absent my whole life. I have had very few contacts with him, and in the few times we were together, he just mocked me, humiliated me because of my weight, my slow-learning skills, and also because I seemed to need more contact from him and he never had time.

"As you can imagine, the story or the relationship with my mother has been as well very painful. She has been a woman who withstood being around him practically for his money. She developed an addiction to alcohol since I was a child (probably around five to six years old), therefore she has been always relapsing and also being addicted to dating younger men from her gym. So you can pretty much picture the environment I grew up in, which I know is not an excuse, but for me it has been intolerable. I really have never felt what it is to be accepted, loved, or much less cared about. Thus, my only escape were three things—drugs, exercise, mostly swimming (though this one was really many times my last option), and lastly, women. Before I started dating you, I was a guy that just had fun with women, went out two to five times with them at the most, and then drop them. My mask or defense mechanism has always been the ability to talk, the way I move the conversation toward what I want, and of course, some of my charming personality."

Betty's face was really disgusted, confused, afraid; she was a real hot mess with everything she was listening. However, finally at the end, she was really knowing the man she was supposed to be with. Then she just said, "Well, Mario, it seems that you are a real 'piece of art.' It is a shame that I'm finding out all this now that I'm pregnant, now that you've decided finally to handle your addiction though if I can see some good in everything that I'm feeling and thinking, it is that at least our baby is not yet here to witness the mess of parents she/he has chosen."

Being Responsible to Start Healing

"The only rational, fair, and honest thing that I really can think of is that you go to your clinic and start the program. During that time, we'll be recovering separately from each other's past and emotions that we have been dragging. We'll think if we really want to commit to each other, and this time it has to be a formal commitment that we can both make. I'm not asking marriage, but it has to be a very serious and formal commitment. If in this time we figure out that we could be better off separated, then we'll do it. Right now, we're not bound by anything so it will be easier in terms of any administrative issues. You might be wondering why I'm saying this or you might think that I'm angry, but it's not like that.

"What I see is a man that is deeply hurt by his parents, by many things of his childhood. I'm sorry for all your past story and all the pain that you have been carrying. However, that's not an excuse to lie to the woman you said you wanted to be with your whole life. That's not a reason to even make me think that everything was okay, and after the fight we had when you found out I was pregnant, probably it would have been a better time to mention all this. But whatever, it has happened now, and I understand that sometimes we can't control the timing of things, but we certainly can control what we want to happen in the future, therefore that's exactly what I'm doing. I want to be sure that you and I can commit to each other. I want to make sure that you can really promise to yourself and be able to get out from any type of addictions, mostly, of course, for you and because I don't want our child to witness or to be around a father that will relapse, that will bring a very toxic example to her/his life.

"I also had a rough childhood. I myself suffered many emotional abuses from my father. I witnessed a mom that was and has always been a docile woman, who has denied herself the right to do what she wants, the right to enjoy many things, and all because of a dumb promise she made to God, all because of her old beliefs, and all because of us, her children, as she has been very clear with me every time I asked her why she keeps a marriage that is just a mask for the family and society. I don't want that future or any other toxic future, Mario, not for me and not for our child. Now I have to decide for someone else that is growing inside of me. And for that child that is coming, I will do everything in my power to heal myself and save him or her from that pain, but also I will be very clear that I want the same in a partner because I think that we are now in a perfect time to heal, to give our child a much nicer and healthier future than the one we had for ourselves.

"I think, and I'm sure you agree with me, that our deepest wounds come from our childhood. All the negative emotions or toxic experiences we had when we were children are the root cause of how we think now, why we suffer, and we sometimes keep repeating the same circles and stories. But I'm hopeful and positive that we can take this time, seeing how all of these events were unfolding, as an opportunity for both of us to clean ourselves, to know more what is bothering us from that stage, to let go of that pain, and to start again as new individuals. Let's do it for us, and let's do it for that baby that is coming because he or she deserves to have a better home and a better environment than the one that we both had.

"As you know, I'm not a woman that gets comfortable with a situation. I think I have proved that to you and to myself, and now it is a time for both of us to compromise with ourselves and with our possible future. I won't interfere with your recovery program, and instead I would prefer that we don't see each other for these next three months. But I propose to you that we meet again after you get out from the clinic. Let's see what happened with each other, and if we are able to heal, then I'm sure that we can pursue a healthier future together or we will decide at that moment what would be the best option for both and, of course, for the baby."

Mario's expression was speechless, sad, confused, guilty, but he was also aware that this time, he didn't have any other choice than to accept Betty's conditions as they also sound very reasonable after all he had been hiding from her. Thus, his answer was, "Okay, Betty, I agree with everything you just said. I'm deeply sorry and ashamed that we got this far as, of course, I would have never wanted to end like this, but I also agree that this time will be better to focus just in ourselves. From my side, I also fully commit to work really hard during the program, to really take advantage of this opportunity you're giving me to finally end my addictions as well as my painful childhood.

"My main motivation is now very clear–I really want to be a healthy father, I want to be a good example for my child, I want to give him or her a family like the one I never had, and more than that, I believe we also have the chance to break this toxic patterns and start a new future for the next generation that is coming with us."

Thought Takeaways

After witnessing a very hard and complicated outcome between Mario and Betty, I believe the powerful messages we can extract from the story are the following:

I. How can your childhood experiences mark your future relationships?

II. Why do we use masks to meet people, and how can these masks affect the couple's trust?

III. Is it fair to hide your worst qualities from the person you love even when you have achieved a certain level of confidence with him or her? Why do men or women keep hiding their real personalities?

IV. How can you really use a time off in a relationship instead of just wasting your time?

V. What is the effect of all these kinds of emotional arguments or separations between couples on the baby?

So, let's begin unwrapping these questions and extracting the most of them to have practical and applicable actions to your life.

I. How can your childhood experiences mark your future relationships?

Many of us experience some type of adverse experience in our childhood, and as a result, we developed masks, a type of personality that allow us to cope with that pain, or worse, an addiction that we thought could help us escape from that pain. The label of the mechanisms that we use is not as relevant as identifying what kind of painful experience are we allowing to make us suffer, what kind of message is still there lingering to appear at the least reminder or trigger, the kind of behavior that we are repeating even though we promise ourselves not to do it.

For the sake of identifying these types of experiences with a general label, we will name them adverse childhood experiences (ACEs).

Chronic exposure to ACEs, including abuse, neglect, and household dysfunction, can damage long-term physical and mental health. The effects of ACEs on neural circuitry are particularly salient during sensitive developmental periods and highlights the need for effective intervention during infancy and early childhood.

Parents with multiple ACEs are at risk for mental health and substance use problems, disrupted social networks, and limited educational attainment.

This is just exactly what has happened to Betty and Mario's relationship; they ended up taking things almost to an end due to the buildup of their problems and ACEs that they've suffered, and if we analyze more carefully each of them, we would be able to see that Mario had developed a personality of attracting women through lies or made-up stories to cope with the abandonment of her mother. He also treated them badly or was unable to fully commit to them for the same reason. All the anger, frustration, and pain that his mother caused him when he was a child and showing him that her addiction to alcohol was more important than the time he would have liked to spend with her provoked a wound in him that he transferred to other women, making them engage, sort of fall in love, with him and then disposing them. In the end, it was the exact same pattern; however, all those experiences that Mario created to "cope" in reality just repeated the pain over and over again, not allowing him to overcome the root issues. This was just to mention an example of the kind of behavior that we sometimes develop and we falsely believe is going to help us, but it just deepens our pain and generates more resentment.

On the other hand, Betty's painful experience of her dad being cold, humiliating her mother, and just being able to provide economically but showing emotional abuse every time he could, had an effect on Betty's personality to be strong, to be independent, but also to shut down her feelings and not allow herself to be vulnerable in addition to having troubled relationships with men that frequently needed to be rescued; and Mario is not the exception.

Whenever we cope with such profound emotional pain when we are children, we just tend to look for the easiest way out, the less painful, and we often develop some "clever or creative" way to hide it as we are not mature enough to find a better solution. However, doing that in a physiological way of speaking means hiding it, letting it accumulate, and therefore creating a higher threshold of endurance for the next time for a lower threshold for coping with everyday life.

This translates into having a personality that is more sensitive for certain issues or experiences in our real interaction with any person or event that reminds us of a certain semblance to what we experience when we were children.

Moreover, in our biological realm inside of us, there's a series of events that are triggered by the sympathetic nervous system (SNS), which is a section of our nervous system that is activated by this emotional or physical threats; and whenever it starts to respond to any stressful situation, it has three options to react—you fight, flight, or freeze. This is also accompanied by the production of more adrenaline and cortisol as we have mentioned previously; however, this buildup of substances in our body will trigger a cascade of negative responses in our body that include weight gain, obesity, high blood pressure/ hypertension, type 2 diabetes, frequent infections, hormonal imbalance, autoimmune disorders, etc. Of course, all of these diseases and events are generated through years of building up these negative chemical responses and being irresponsible about them.

As you can see, there are several problems that can be developed if you just keep building up emotional reactions and wounds and you don't make a commitment with yourself to heal them. You might think in the moment that you are okay, that nothing happens, that it is the person or event that provoke that response when in fact it is all within you, and the sooner you tackle those problems, the better it will be for you and for everyone else around you.

II. Why do we use masks to meet people, and how can these masks affect the couple's trust?

This is a really tricky path, as we certainly all have different personalities that we show depending on the interaction that we have. However, in terms of meeting a partner or getting involved with someone emotionally, the mechanism of developing a mask works to hide those traits that you usually are more afraid of. Therefore, generally speaking, people develop the opposite mask of what they really are. If you suffered from lack of attention or you were ignored or neglected of physical and emotional attention, you would be predisposed to look for some kind of personality that allow you to cope with those insecurities, as in the case of Mario, who showed to women how he was the charming, skillful, talkative guy that wisely enchanted them and who, once he was feeling confident and they were starting to develop feelings toward him and he could no longer accept that or feel he deserved it, rejected or neglected them or simply disappeared from their lives.

In Betty's case, we can see that due to the emotional abuse and the example that her mother gave to her for standing pain, humiliation, and diminishing acts from her father, she developed a strong, secure, and sometimes bold personality that was also complemented with a closed attitude toward getting involved or looking for a guy to fix and repair what she saw her mother could not overcome.

Therefore, she developed a mask of being strong, independent, and not open to being vulnerable; however, she was frequently attracted to men that needed to be fixed, and she felt rewarded by that kind of personality as she deeply needed to fix a childhood story from her past. Additionally, this type of men didn't repress her like her father used to do with her mom, nor did they abuse her emotionally. Sadly, what in the end was the case for her was that men got comfortable and didn't do much for themselves.

Talking about the relationship that Betty and Mario have, we clearly see that hiding in a mask either of overwhelming confidence as Mario or in a strong/independent one like Betty's was a disadvantage for them and for any other relationship, as they still pretend to be someone else and tried to cover the facts that they have wounds, unhealed stories, and a past that they needed to take care of. However, this type of conflict in couples is amazingly common as many people met in circumstances where they still have many things to be healed and recognized, but if they're handled properly and if you have the courage and the vulnerability to open up with your partner, they can be healed while you experience your relationship and the road will be more smooth if you are mature enough to accept that you and your partner have issues to heal and not to use those wounds or trigger buttons to your advantage or to hurt.

Then the best road to start a healthy relationship, in an ideal setting, will always be when you have healed many of your childhood wounds. When you have had the courage to go within and analyze yourself, list your qualities, list your opportunity areas and work in them, when you get to a point where you are healthy, you can love yourself without needing someone, you can accept yourself with all your scars, then you can attract also someone that matches that energy, that vibrational state, and probably he or she will be a healthier partner for you.

In the meantime, if you are in a relationship and you're having problems due to those wounds that you suffer in childhood, recognize them, take time to go deep within, heal them, and during your journey, your partner most likely will be inspired to do the same if you are really meant to be together and share each other's love.

Extreme personality styles have at its base biological differences in specific affective difficulties. Even these early deficits may be part of an early social history. They set in motion a contingent history of unfolding where early deficits affect later development in the manner of cascading constraints (McIlwain 2007, 2008). Being at extreme levels of some parameters early on has knock-on consequences for later development. Early deficits in emotional experience predispose the person to failing to develop other attributes crucial to empathy and morality. There is a dynamic, social aspect that is also part of this picture–scare giving. It entails having to hide from those upon whom one depends; the experience of abuse, threat, or attack from those who optimally would be one's protectors and guides, who would convey how to understand and soothe feelings. In such a case, avoidance in the form of a shamed retreat from feeling and from others may seem the only strategy. The outcomes of shame being added to the mix are many, depending on how one copes with it; but alienation, rageful attacks, and a fragmented self are among them.

We can clearly see some of these traits in our couple's story, and as referred by research, each person has a unique way or personality to develop in order to cope with all the emotional burden that has been suffered, mostly during childhood. Many times it doesn't have to be so severe as in other cases to cause damage; that's why many people that probably saw their childhood as normal or "not so bad" underestimate the emotional pain that might be underneath and is causing some repetitive toxic emotions and behaviors. All these justifies even more why we should be more concerned in knowing ourselves to the point where we are able to identify, recognize, and accept some of that pain and find it a proper outlet or channeling it in the right path.

III. Is it fair to hide your worst qualities from the person you love, even when you have achieved a certain level of confidence with her/him? Why do men or women keep hiding their real personality?

We all experience this type of dilemma, and I dare say we all hide our worst qualities mostly when meeting new people. It's completely normal because we have been trained that rejection is the worst thing that can happen to us, in addition to being programmed to not accept ourselves. However, hiding your true personality once you've passed the meeting stage and maybe also arriving at a stage where both are really compromised and they have experienced trust and more love for each other is not the healthiest way to continue a relationship.

In fact, the longer you wait to discuss or show your true character and personality, the more damage you will start causing to the relationship even if you want to deny that fact.

The chronic overactivation of neurochemical responses to threat in the nervous system, particularly in the earliest years of life, can result in lifelong states of either dissociation or hyperarousal (Karr-Morse and Wiley 1997, 168). Schore (2001) suggests that experiencing relation-induced trauma can result in "a blocking of the capacity to register affect and pain" (2001, 232). Connections between the amygdala and the orbito-frontal cortex atrophy in response to "scaregiving" (2001, 248). It is suggested that this means the fear/flight response can appear with diminished chance of cortical inhibition—a rupture between behavior and conscious control. Thus, there may be differential myelination of pathways if one lives in early terror or if one must hide out from the people upon whom one must also depend. Looking at degrees of attachment rather than the actual presence of trauma and "scaregiving," Ontai and Thompson (2002) found that more securely attached children show greater understanding of negative emotions, but this is only true at age five. At age three, attachment security has no influence on emotion understanding. At age three, the highest level of emotion understanding is in the context of pragmatic rather than elaborative maternal discourse about emotion and less secure attachment.

Insecure attachment may result in hypervigilance to emotion signals from an early age, but not necessarily greater understanding of them later on, without tuition in emotion recognition and coping with emotions. Hiding out may be linked with less emotional expressivity of oneself—a definite advantage for manipulative personalities. As supported by research, we can see that developing a coping personality and hiding your true self is a self-developed mechanism that allows children to withstand pain, rejection, and humiliation from their caregivers.

However, as stated above, keeping this pattern for a longer period in a relationship can and will make the other person think that everything is fine, that you are happy, that the relationship is flowing when in fact you don't really feel that and you're in fact disappointed, bored, or even resentful with your partner for not accepting when it all comes back to you, as you're not asking for what you want or you're not saying what you need.

On the other hand, as is the case of Betty and Mario's relationship, something toxic, something dark might be haunting you again, such as any type of addiction and covering up or not being honest with your partner will make her/him feel betrayed and will most likely break the confidence she/ he had in you.

IV. How can you really use a time off in a relationship, instead of just wasting your time?

Having time off in a relationship is often judged by society or sometimes has been labeled as if it were just an excuse or a way out to face problems. However, when a relationship has reached a point where things are just approaching a very toxic pattern or they just don't match with what you wanted, it is completely fine to take that break. Nonetheless, to make the break work, you really have to be compromised with putting yourself together, investing in knowing yourself, looking for help or enrolling into a recovery program depending on your needs. Of course, this will only be true if you really are committed with the relationship and if you truly love and accept the person you are with. If not, then there's always the possibility of making that break permanent, being honest with you and with your partner and end the relationship, which in the moment might be painful but, in the end, both people will be benefited. If there are children already, it would be much healthier for them than witnessing their parents fight, insult, humiliate, or discuss constantly.

In either case, the time off will be an opportunity to work on the issues that you already saw were not working; however, it has to be clear that you only can work with your issues, you can't keep blaming the other for your shortcomings or your wounds that obviously you have been hiding or you even buried deep inside so they don't hurt you, when in fact doing that just led to a more toxic inner environment.

Therefore, the best approach you can take for this process is first making a list of three to five deep wounds that you have from your childhood that most likely will be also the ones that were affecting your relationship. Then you can start owning the meaning of them.

For that, this model list of steps might become handy for you to start your healing process:

- Identify the message, wound, or toxic example that was left in you when you were children.

- See the lesson that is behind that painful situation; this would mean not to assign blame to anyone but to simply detect why it was done or passed to you and find out more about the story of your parents or the person from where that message or hurt came from.

⊙ Question yourself about why it was done to you; this step will detach the blame on the person that provoked the attitude.

⊙ Turn the feeling to you and see if you have developed that same attitude in any of your emotions or behavior with others.

⊙ Forgive and change the message of that thought or emotion into a positive one so that you release the negative power of the thought or experience and allow it to become a positive tool for you.

V. What is the effect of all these kinds of emotional arguments or separations between couples on the baby?

Repeated emotional stress that includes rejection, neglect of expression of emotions, constant examples of discussion, stressful situations that are prolonged for a longer period of time, emotional abuse, etc.., as mentioned above, are classified as ACE), all of which can cause several negative effects on the fetus and the development of children even to the extent of adulthood.

Early-life adversity in the form of abuse and neglect in infancy and childhood are a huge contributor to allostatic overload during the life course because of the biological embedding of those experiences in memories in the brain; these memories sensitize and also qualitatively change the ways in which the brain responds to experiences in daily life, particularly those that relate to reminders of early-life trauma. The responses include not only behaviors but also neuroendocrine, autonomic, immune, and metabolic responses. As a result, depression, substance abuse, and antisocial behavior are more likely to occur in those experiencing ACE, along with sexual precocity and higher risk for AIDS and an increased risk for cardiovascular disease and obesity as a result of greater allostatic overload.

Prefrontal cortical development is impaired by early-life adversity resulting in deficits in emotional self-regulation (McEwen 2017).

As discussed above, early-life experiences create an overload system at such a precarious stage where everything inside the baby is still forming and receptive to all the effects that can deviate the expression of some of the genes, causing a defective protein to form or simply creating the epigenetic labels that we discuss in chapter 1. All these toxic environment starts predisposing the child to develop lower-threshold reactions or increasing the amount of stress needed, predisposing them to feel attracted to higher doses of toxic chemicals that then in turn will bias them to develop an addiction more easily than others.

This is the major red alert that all future parents should be aware of; staying in a toxic relationship when you are already pregnant or allowing high amount of stress during those stages is highly toxic for the fetus and not only for him/her but also for the next generations that will inherit those epigenetic marks. Because as research supports this, most of epigenetic marks prevail for three to four generations, making each generation more prone to develop some types of diseases like the ones that are mentioned above.

All this information is very easy to verify if we just see the statistics of depression, anxiety, diabetes, obesity, cardiovascular diseases, cancer, autoimmune diseases that probably we're more prone to develop due to the epigenetic marks as well as to the excessively fast-paced and stressful environment that we have developed so far.

Consequently, we should start to be more aware of the kind of environment we want our children to grow into, start raising consciousness on emotional health, and being responsible for the pain and wounds that we have as adults in order to stop the cycle to be repeated generation after generation.

CHAPTER 5

The Healing Journey

WE LEFT OFF our story when Mario explains to Betty that he will he take the most out of that separation to turn himself into a new man. Betty on her side marks the path and clearly states that their relationship is a time off, to heal and not to interfere in each other's decision, allowing space to think what would be the best course of action to go on as a couple.

This sets the stage for a new paradigm, a new adventure in their lives, now in separate roles, not as a couple, and will reveal some of their darkest wounds and layers that have been dormant, nonetheless causing problems, addictions, and other struggles that we have witnessed in their story.

Let's start with Mario's journey. As we remember, he left for the rehabilitation clinic where he enrolled in a detoxification program. During the sessions he received, they explained to him that the sequence of disciplines was already researched and proven to be thoroughly targeted to eliminate, train, and face every kind of threat he could have when getting out from the clinic.

Owning Your Life

His most outstanding and worth mentioning experience was when he was faced to heal the toxic emotions that his parents had seeded in him, going through that experience with a technique that made him question himself about the type of behavior, rejection, or hurt that his parents had caused him. One of the most ingrained experiences that left him marked was the fact that his father constantly humiliated him by undermining his efforts to learn sports or any kind of activity he wanted to engage in. This pattern was also mirrored and repeated with his mother by making her feel dominated, worthless, and pretty much an object for his father's social events. He worked this kind of emotional abuse with his counselor, Mike, who began by advising him to place the experience in a new setting, where he could take out his judgment and pain, focusing his attention on the behavior that was being performed by his father. Then without knowing what happened to his father in the past, he was asked to see the experience as an observer, as a third party, and trying to question why his father was acting in that way. Mario started describing some of his father's behavior, in other circumstances, trying to identify some of his father's traits of character that could give him a more impartial answer about why his father was acting like that.

Mario started saying, "Well, Mike, my father was, since I could remember, a very strict man. I could definitely say he was a perfectionist with all the things he was doing. He didn't allow himself to make mistakes, also a cold man who was incapable of showing affection, though the only time he spoke something about his own father, he mentioned that he was a person who inflicted a lot of physical and emotional pain on him. Just by mentioning his name, his eyes would start to flood with tears, and then of course he would snap and yell at me about anything, changing the subject of the talk."

"Okay, Mario," said Mike, "now with those facts and knowledge of your father's character and reactions, what can you infer that he was withholding?"

"I don't know, Mike. It's hard for me to guess what was happening through my father's mind."

"Okay, Mario, I'm not asking to guess, I'm asking to do the effort off putting yourself in your father's shoes and feel what he felt every time you were near to achieving something, or every time he could see that you were going to succeed in a challenge."

Mario closed his eyes, and he started answering Mike, "I think that my father felt a lot of anger, rage, disappointment that I could achieve something, and I think deep down, he really wanted to recognize me, encourage me, or at least maintain a positive mind-set toward my experiences. However, I also think he was in a lot of pain and struggle due to the physical and emotional abuse he suffered in his childhood, as a consequence, being only able and programmed to attack me and undermine my efforts."

"Exactly, Mario," said Mike. "Your father as well was holding a lot of emotional and physical pain, so his 'only choice' with you at those moments was to humiliate you because he never allowed himself to forgive. He never even allowed himself to recognize that he had all that pain inside. He as well was 'programmed' and 'educated' to solve things with violence, whether it was verbal, physical, or emotional. Hence, your victories or achievements were a 'threat' for him as he was never allowed to feel those kinds of emotions. He was severely neglected of them; he was even beaten so many times when he dared to mention his feelings to his father. Therefore, the only escape he had was transforming all that pain into resentment. Now, Mario, are you able to see a pattern of behavior here with your life?"

Mario was shocked for a little while, and he just took a deep breath, his eyes starting to turn red and watery. He just couldn't hold the pain anymore, and he burst into tears. Yelling, he just stood up and looked for the punching bag that was in the exercise room (right beside where they were). Mike was not surprised at all, as he knew that those reactions were perfectly normal after going deep in the emotional pain; in fact, he allowed Mario to take all the anger, yelling, crying, and hitting the bag for about ten minutes, which was more or less the time that his negative energy lasted in getting out of his body.

After Mario finished his session and had released everything, he sat with Mike, and they started to talk. Mike asked Mario to speak about what he felt as he just released the physical stress about the event, but there was still missing the reflection/meaning stage of the process.

Mario said, "Well, Mike, I just realize that many things that I was doing with my life, my emotions, and women that I even did with Betty at the beginning of our relationship were exactly the same pattern that my grandfather and father did with me and my mother, so it was very painful to see that pattern reflected in me again. I felt frustrated, disappointed, and of course, as you could see, full of anger toward myself."

"That's okay, Mario. It's one of the purposes of the exercise, after all. However, right now, I'm more interested in knowing how you felt about your father. Do you still have all that anger and resentment toward him?"

"Not in the same degree, and not with the same biased point of view, Mike. Now I can see more clearly that many of my father's behavior were just emotions that were inside of him—pain, anger, disappointment, humiliation that he also received when he was a child. I now feel I can forgive him and release many of the things he did with me because I have a deeper understanding and empathy of his own story. However, I still have many questions, confusion, and contradictory feelings inside of me."

"Why, Mario?" asked Mike. "Because he was, after all, a successful man, a man with power and money, he didn't do anything about his pain, emotions, and resentment? I think you can now answer that one, Mario."

"Okay, Mike, can you help me here a little bit to get more insight?"

"Yes, of course. Close your eyes, Mario." Mike started playing a very soft nature song without any voice, just relaxing music, and then he started to give some instructions to Mario. "Well, Mario, breathe deeply, and every time you let the air out, imagine that your pain is leaving your body. Now imagine your best moment with anyone, a moment where you felt appreciated, loved, and grateful for being alive. Do you have it?" Mario replied yes.

"Okay, now hold on to it. Embrace it, live it again, feel the love, feel the appreciation, put your hand over your heart, and feel how it beats. Focus on being happy, grateful." The music kept playing, and Mike left Mario for some minutes to feel that sensation while he just spoke some words to give Mario some awareness to stay in that moment, to focus on his heartbeats and breathe deeply. After that, Mike asked Mario to imagine now that he was traveling back in time and to picture his father as a child, his grandfather beating and humiliating his dad about any stupid thing. Mario was still with his eyes closed; he had already picked up the image and was starting to cry. He was able to see the kind of pain that his father was suffering, the humiliation that he received when showing his feelings.

Mike said, "Okay, Mario, breathe . . . go back to your happy moment, put your hand over your heart and breathe." He left Mario for some minutes again and then asked Mario to open his eyes.

"Okay, Mario, do you have the answer now?"

"Yes," Mario replied. "My father was never able to see his pain because it was too much. The only thing he learned to do was withholding his emotions, feeling ashamed of them, and he was so scared after all to go there that he never allowed himself to go back and remember anything. Therefore, it was very hard for him also to ask for help or even recognize he needed that."

"Exactly, Mario. You see, it's a matter of going deep within you. It's all a matter of aligning yourself with your most powerful energy that is your heart. What we did in this exercise was just that—we first got you in a deep relaxation environment, where you felt safe, calm, appreciated, and then we started harnessing you to your heart's energy, to the synchrony of your beating, and we aligned your brain with those simple words of holding on to that moment, feeling your beats. Then I asked you to move to an observer position, where you also could see the pain that your father might have had, so once you were aligned for a vibration of love and coherence, it was less risky to move you to a painful situation, where you also could appreciate that not only were you in pain when you were a child, but also your father. By doing that, you generated a strong sense of compassion and empathy with him, which made it easier for you to see why he couldn't be aware of the damage he was doing to you, nor could he be responsible for his own pain by not allowing any recognition or self-awareness and, of course, never asking for help."

"Wow, Mike, I'm totally amazed by what I did, what you helped me achieve. I'm feeling very grateful, it feels as if I have taken a huge burden out of myself. I feel so empowered, energized, and totally aware of the steps that I would like to take in terms of my emotions toward my parents."

"Perfect, Mario, that sounds good to me. As you can see, your healing process will always start placing yourself in a place of connection with your heart, synchronizing your inner energy with the power of your thoughts, and allowing yourself to recognize the toxic emotions that you are still carrying."

External Slavery vs. Inner Freedom

"In the end, it is nobody's fault. It is just a matter of how aware we are of our own emotions, of our thoughts, and then placing ourselves as an observer of what happened, also being responsible enough to picture our parents in those painful spots and position that they also suffered. And finally, moving ourselves from the victim mode, from the place where we can't do or won't do any change other than looking for people to blame and excuses to remain in the same position.

"Moreover, as you experienced all those emotions that are building up, you are creating a burden that sometimes is so heavy that you want to find an exit, a way out, and most likely that exit door is confused with an easy opportunity (addiction) that 'takes away' your pain or moves you from your reality, when in fact, that opportunity (addiction) will eventually destroy you from within, will detach you even more from that pain momentarily. But after, it will sink you more and take you to a darker phase, where now you are really a victim of an 'external aid' and you no longer have power, trust, and confidence in you, so you think you are not able to get out from there and the easy way out is to consume more, and that cycle starts repeating over and over until if you're lucky, someone helps you. If not, as the statistics don't lie, you will soon want to finish your life because it has become a place where you are powerless, just looks painful and full of uncertainty, diminishing scenarios, dreadful events, or challenges."

"Exactly, now, I can really see it, Mike. Thanks a lot for these sessions, you've given me so much clarity on my life, on the path to follow; and of course, all these disciplines that create sort of a healing bubble, has helped me generate a different set of emotions, know and love my body, be conscious of what I eat, how to detoxify any toxicity with exercise, sleep, and reflection in my life, how to handle my emotions and feel empowered to do it, be able to feel more and also be more mindful to look for time to reflect, to be at peace, to connect with my inner self, with my heart. It has been an amazing journey, this last twelve weeks. I'm also very grateful for being here and be surrounded with people that has the same mind-set and purpose to heal—that certainly helps a lot. "Finally, I just have some fear about going back to the real world. Am I going to be able to handle it?"

"Yes, Mario," said Mike, "you will. This bubble, as you accurately call it, is not about creating any kind of dependency in you. It is more about, as you also mention it, empowering you, teaching you how to do it by yourself. That is why we also allow you to have time for yourself and practice, understanding what is happening inside of you with each of the disciplines, pillars, or components of your inner health. When you get released from the program, which is in the next few weeks, you will be able to get back to the lessons that were taught to you, to the tools, and you will still have some support from your sponsor to help you whenever you feel that you're falling again or when you have a tough day.

"However, the next two weeks, which are the last part of the program, will be about simulating stressful situations and scenarios, where you will be the one applying the tools, where you will be able to overcome those last fears that you have and where we are going to close the gap between the bubble and reality. It is worth mentioning that these weeks will be challenging, and you will have to recall, train, and work on yourself almost alone, sort of saying."

"I know, Mike. I will be ready because I have a purpose now. I have a much stronger reason to go on, in addition, of course, to the most important event in my life, which will be the birth of my first child. I also want to amend every possible mistake I did at the beginning or before coming here with Betty. I'm now more aware of the problems that I might face, gaining again her trust and taking my life back again."

"That's good, Mario. You'd better use all your resources and extract all your learning experiences and knowledge during these last two weeks, so you can sustain and overcome the transformation that I have witnessed in you. I have seen a very deep transformation, I've witnessed all the effort you have placed in this program, and I feel confident that you will be ready for the real world. Just always remember that everything we have done for you here is an aid in showing you the path, but you have walked it by yourself, and you have shown to yourself that everything is inside you. So just recognize that all the tools are within, and anything external can change what you are made of. It might throw it out of balance, you might trip, probably fall and get hurt, but you can always get back on your feet and stand up stronger, wiser, and always with more experience for the next challenge."

"Thanks, Mike, I'll do my best, and I'm confident now as well that I will succeed."

On the other hand, Betty's path toward recovery was not so taken care of. Though she was emotionally stronger than Mario, she was having a very hard time too in being alone, to face what she might have done wrong, and even though they were apart, Mario wrote her two or three letters where he tried to give her a glimpse of his experience, of the things that he was living with in the clinic.

Those letters from Mario made Betty reflect on her past, on her open wounds as a child, and also realize she had some emotional baggage as well to work on. So she decided to design something similar to what Mario was living in the clinic, and she started working on her eating habits, caring more for her body, reading more about how the things she used to eat and the hectic life she was living was impacting her internal organs as well as the baby's health. As we mentioned at the beginning of the story, she had also started to do exercises even though she was pregnant; she set for herself for some walking and swimming at least four times per week for about forty to fifty minutes.

She started writing about her deepest emotional wounds and trying to replicate a similar exercise to the one Mario talked about. While doing that exercise, one of the most profound and heavier emotional issues she was carrying was the fact that her mother had always been so controlling, submissive to her father's will, and almost every time, she chose the victim standpoint to excuse herself from any responsibility of how her life had turned out to be.

Those examples, those dialogues, those comments and endless complaints of her mother had made Betty a woman that was strong in character, but felt almost no love for herself. Her self-esteem was pretty low, even though she was many times trying to mask it with the image of a successful career-driven woman.

Living with Resentment or Forgiveness

But Betty felt it was too much emotional pain to handle it by herself, and she was afraid that she was going to fail doing that exercise alone; thus, she remembered that Karen had helped her before. She knew already part of the story, and she was very helpful the last time. Therefore, she approached Karen, contacted her, and they set up a long emotional release session. Betty explained some of the steps that Mike did with Mario, and they tried to replicate the exercise with Betty and the pain she had with her mother's attitude.

During the session, Karen asked Betty to try to get some extra information about her grandmother and how she treated her mom. Therefore, Betty tried to randomly talk with her mother by questioning her about her past, to sense the ground of her childhood, and obtained enough information to work it out in the exercise.

During the questioning, it turned out that Betty's mom suffered severe emotional pain from her mother too. Betty's grandmother was a very cold woman, an alcoholic; therefore, every time she had some extra drinks in her body, she humiliated Betty's mom. She even hit her so strong that Betty's mom many times lost consciousness. A younger brother of Betty's mom tried several times to stop that kind of abuse, but he was too small to stop it; therefore, the abuse continued for several years until Betty's grandmother killed herself by an overdose of alcohol and intoxicated herself with the fumes of the stove that she left open and kept inhaling until she just died. Betty's mom was just a teenager of fifteen years, the younger brother six years old; therefore, Betty's mom was raised by an uncle that took the responsibility of raising them, but just over the surface, as he also used to drink, not so frequently as Betty's grandmother, but was still an addict.

With that in mind, she had enough information to work with Karen, so Betty set up another session with her to handle that emotional pain and burden. Moreover, Betty was also facing some stressful confusion in terms of how things were going to evolve for her and Mario. She had many doubts about going back with him, as he had betrayed her confidence with the addiction issues. She was also stressed that her family could find out more about those addiction issues of Mario and judge him or make their relationship more stressful. It is worth mentioning that Betty's mom and some of her aunts were already trying to decide how the first months of her child should be, where would be the best place to raise the child, what kind of care he or she would need, etc.

That made Betty angrier because she was fed up with the excessive control and meddling with her life since a long time ago. It is also important to mention that many of Betty's past relationships were also affected by her family's meddling with her life and the narrow religious judgment that they had. All of these situations had Betty's mood and performance at work very undermined, which was something that her boss, Charlie, was already starting to notice. However, he was waiting for a good time to speak with her about it.

In the meantime, Betty decided to first work out the issue with her emotional burden and the information that she already gathered from her mom, so she set up another meeting with Karen to handle that.

When Betty and Karen met, the session developed not in the way that Karen expected it to be because right when Karen asked Betty to relax, to start listening to the music and finding a very happy moment where Betty could feel grateful, appreciated, loved, she was having a hard time to find that moment. Thus, Karen was afraid to take Betty to the next level, which would be to start seeing her mother as an observer and trying to picture her as a child. So Karen stopped the session and started to question Betty more about why she was stuck and she couldn't find a happy moment or a moment where she could feel appreciated and cared.

Betty started to cry, and she told Karen that she was frustrated, confused, that she had too many problems that were fuzzing her mind and stopping her from going back and picking a happy memory. She started to tell Karen that she was really afraid about what was going to happen with Mario and her, that she also felt out of place at work, that she knew these past weeks she had been having a bad mood and sometimes a bad attitude with her coworkers and even with her boss. Finally, she just said, "It's too much, Karen—my emotional wounds waked up by Mario's letters, my family that doesn't seem to understand that I'm an adult already, and I need to decide my life and my baby's future probably by myself, and on top of that, my poor performance at work."

Karen tried to calm Betty, and she said, "It's okay, Betty, I completely understand you and empathize with you. I know what it is to be pregnant and having, in my case, just some stress, so I can imagine what you're feeling with all the things that seem to be falling apart. But hey, as I'm seeing it from outside, I can just tell you that this process is completely normal. It would have happened eventually, hence the most important thing right now is that you start solving each messy loose end step by step. This baby that's coming is giving you that energy, trying to help you from within with her or his positive energy, to clean your emotions because she or he already can feel them inside. If you don't want to harm her/him more, please listen to your heart, listen to your intuition and your whole body because the answer is right there."

"Okay, Karen, you're right. I'll focus on now on today that we're dealing with my emotional childhood and the pain I've been accumulating over several years. It's not healthy for my child to carry all that burden, and of course, I don't want her or him to repeat any cycles in her or his life."

"Exactly, Betty. Let's clean that negative energy out of you, and let's go one by one. You're not alone in this. If you have been in touch with me and have trusted that I can help you, I'll do my best to accomplish that. Just remember that this is not a one-time thing. From here on, you gotta be more aware of these kinds of emotions and allow yourself to recognize them and just let them go."

"Yes, Karen, let's try again to relax and fix that resentment that many times I feel toward my mom."

"Okay, Betty." Karen started to set up the environment. They were in a silent room in her house, where there was very dim light, so she started to play some relaxing music, speaking some words about being focused on the breath, allowing Betty to concentrate on her breathing, and also giving her time to smooth her heartbeats. Then she started asking Betty to put her hand on her chest and the other one on her belly so that she could feel the baby's heartbeat at the same time. After that, she asked Betty to allow herself to bring back a happy memory. Betty started to breathe a little bit faster, but now she was able to find her happy memory and stay there, Karen could notice that because of her breathing that was more synchronized, as well as noticing a smile on her face and some small tears. In addition to that, they were both surprised, though they didn't lose the concentration on Betty's belly, that the baby was kicking and moving, probably because he or she felt the energy coming and just enjoyed that.

All those signals were enough for Karen to start asking Betty to go back in time and try to imagine her mother as a little child with her grandmother. Betty started to do the exercise, and she pictured her grandmother yelling at her mom. She was trying to stop the yelling by crying and telling her mom to run, when suddenly the grandmother hit her mom and started telling her that she was not a good daughter, that she always complained about everything, that she was guilty of her father's death, and that she regretted having her. During the argument, she was really scared because her mom was drunk and during those moments, she could do anything to her and to her little brother; therefore, Betty's mom ran out of the house, picking up her little brother and they went to look for one of their aunts. During that vivid image of Betty's mom, she saw why her mom always acted shy, submissive, and usually prefer to be the victim of everything, and Betty literally knew that her mom's attitude was always to be seen as the victim. Betty started to cry, the baby started to kick again, but of course, everything now seemed as a stress reaction. Therefore, Karen asked Betty to relax, to breathe more deeply, and to go back to the happy moment. She even hugged her and tried to comfort her pain. After some minutes, with the relaxing music continuing, the deep breathing started to have an effect on Betty's stress, so Karen asked Betty to open her eyes.

Betty was surprised a little bit; she was still in shock due to the images and the scene she witnessed with the exercise. Karen asked Betty to keep breathing, and instead of asking things about her mom's scene, she asked her first to visualize a very happy memory.

Betty explained to Karen that it was her graduation from college because that day was the first moment where she really felt she could accomplish something worthy, and that it was pretty much on her own all the effort and struggles she had to surpass. She also emphasized that was the only day that her mother seemed really proud of her in addition to also seeing her father happy. They were not discussing, neither of them was sad or bitter as they used to be, and pretty much they remained happy for the whole night. So that made her feel really at peace, appreciated, and ironically it was the one time both of her parents really showed their emotions without worrying about what anyone might think. They were joyous, and they even danced for a good while during the party.

Karen was consciously listening to Betty's memory, and she was also happy and relieved that Betty's face changed from scared, shocked, and confused to happy, appreciated, and grateful. Now was the moment to start asking the difficult questions.

"Okay, Betty," said Karen, "it seems to me that now you're calmer and at peace, I can start asking some questions. Are you ready?"

Betty replied, "Yes, I am."

"Okay, first of all, how did you feel when you started to picture your mom and you witnessed the abuse she suffered during her childhood?"

"It was really shocking, Karen, because when I started to see those images, I really felt the terror, the stress, and the strong pain that my mother could have felt, more due to the fact that my grandmother was drunk and she repeatedly hit her. I also felt that I had been very unfair with my mom's attitude to judge her, criticize how she is, and to blame her for many of my low self-esteem issues that I had during my teenage years, when in fact she never really did anything to me. She was just so self-immersed in her pain, so her attitude was just plain. Of course, many times she seemed cold, but more than that, now I can see that she was still depressed due to the huge emotional burden she had been carrying even up to now. I also could feel a lot of compassion for her, for the struggles and difficult childhood she had to endure and survive, for all the years she couldn't even enjoy her childhood, but instead having to take care of her brother as he was younger. I don't even know now what to do, should I apologize to her for being so judgmental and sometimes unfair?"

Karen said, "Well, Betty, don't overthink so much what to do. Whatever you have done in the past, I'm sure that your mother doesn't even registered that so much with all the pain she's been enduring. However, in my humble opinion, I think that inviting her to dinner and giving her a letter with all the things you've reflected, highlighting all the good things she did for you and your father, and closing with an apology would be more than enough for her.

"Okay, Betty, let's move on to the next question. Can you understand now why your mother wasn't able to demonstrate love to you or sometimes recognize the accomplishments in the way you probably would have wanted?"

"Yes, now it looks clearer to me, and I will tell you what is my best assumption and then you tell me what you think please."

"Of course," replied Karen.

"Well, now is a very good moment to understand this because just a few days ago, I felt really bad for all the issues that I have to handle, and they are much less significant, realizing what my mom went through. I think my mother developed a very strong and thick shield toward allowing her to feel worthy, happy, to feel she deserved something more than a husband that practically consider her as an asset to clean the house, feed him, and play the role of a submissive wife. Moreover, she also did a very good job not giving my father any reasons to get angry, to even think of leaving him, and of course she was always very responsible with my well-being in terms of all my basic needs. It seems reasonable to me that she didn't even have a clue about what I needed in terms of emotional support, as she never experienced that. Even though I sometimes clearly asked for that, probably the only thing she could hear when I blame her was her own mother humiliating her for not being enough, for causing her father's death."

Betty started to cry. Karen approached her and hugged her. "It's okay, Betty, we often overlook that our parents also had many issues as children, and usually we're not even interested in their stories as we get dominated by our ego and immediately start blaming them for how they treat us, but they also had tough stories, though now you will understand that when we are parents and more as mothers, we often tend to build up emotions, and the last thing we want to do is worry our children with our lives or pain.

"However, if you let me continue . . ."

"Of course, Karen, go on."

"When we do that, when we reject or neglect our feelings by swallowing them or by developing a personality that protects us, we often tend to create a snowball that starts growing inside of us, and that is the main trigger to many other conditions such as the victim mode, anger, frustration, anxiety, sleep disorders, weight issues, and many more. Nowadays that we have so much tools and information, we should be more concerned for ourselves because only by healing our past wounds we would be able to feel worthy, to feel confident, and to vibrate in another frequency, where we will attract a whole different kind of people.

"As women, we should never take the road of the past conditioning or justify ourselves that is the society that has trained us. Today, all of those are just lame excuses to avoid our responsibility, and they are also an excuse to typically blame men when they don't really have too much to do with that. It is always a shared responsibility. When there's an abuser of someone, most of the time there also exists a person that let the abuse happen, and that didn't do anything or just looked for excuses or more people to blame."

"Thanks, Karen," said Betty. "Now I completely understand many things that I did with Mario too, blaming him of the way he sometimes told me to take care more of my image or how I was eating, and also about my obsession to be extremely responsible with my job, but forgetting that I also had a partner that wanted to be with me. It is amazing how all our past wounds, our parents' wounds, and probably all the messages before them are passed on without even noticing or without us being able to see them in our everyday lives. There's just so much noise outside, so much obligations, roles to fulfill, but doing this work now before my baby is born is just the perfect timing.

Now I have a much more conscious awareness of many things. I can be more vigilant of my thoughts or attitudes without obsessing, but allowing myself to heal because I guess this is just the beginning, right, Karen?"

"Exactly, Betty, this is just the tip of the iceberg that we're now melting, but don't worry, the path won't be as rough as this first encounter. Every time you decide to invest in yourself and go within to peel the toxic layers, it becomes easier, and the sensation of not carrying so much weight on your back, sort of saying, gives you the drive to carry on with this path.

"It will be become a lifestyle, a different reality for you to live, for Mario and for the baby, which after all is what everyone of us want. We all want to live a more fulfilled life in all aspects of our being, not just thrive in one of them. However, we have been domesticated to believe there's just one life, one set of steps and that's it. I can even dare to compare it to what they do with racehorses when they cover their side view so they can just focus on the road they have in front of them, on the goal. However, all the side view is what complements life, what gives the flavor, and many times is what sets you free from that program you were installed as a child."

"Wow, Karen, I feel so blessed to have a friend like you who doesn't judge me, who has invested in her own healing, knowing herself, and who doesn't blame the external circumstances to justify a poor behavior. I feel so empowered, so light, and joyful to continue the journey with Mario. Ironically, this exercise has released the stress, the fear, and tension that I had toward other areas of my life."

"Thank for your kind words, Betty. For me, it is so gratifying seeing you much better, seeing the smile on your face again and not seeing the sad woman you were becoming. I'm sorry if I'm being too straight, but you really appear to be a completely different person.

"I can bet you that Mario is also another man for the things that you told me about his letters. Even though you didn't reply to him, he should know more than ever that he wants you back, and now you know and you're sure that you want to be with him as well. I deeply believe that every relationship we have has a unique purpose of approaching us to be the best version that we are supposed to be, and when two persons find each other, even with a dark past, even with some conflicts, even with unhealed wounds, but they decide to face them and allow themselves time to be apart but compromised with each other's healing, they start aligning again and they kind of fusion their energies into one single beam of light, which in this case is the baby you both created and share!

"That light, that energy you needed to work on you is now inside. The baby you are about to have is already making wonders inside you, and it is also impacting Mario. Even if it is not physically inside him, the energy that is being emanated from that new human being is so strong, so pure, so mystical, divine, and magical that it's able to heal you and Mario with peace and also giving you both part of his or her wisdom to find your own light.

"In the end, we are all the same energy, we are all raising or lowering our vibrations with the thoughts, with the emotions, the actions and behaviors that we choose to have in our lives. We have been so stubborn and selfish to see it, and that is exactly the reason why the world and so many people are living in darkness and egoistic paths, which will only lead to separation, despair, and will just replicate the pain and the negative energy around them.

"So, Betty, from now on, please just promise to yourself, to Mario, and to your baby that you will be aware, responsible, and will allow your ego to step aside whenever it has to do it, and express the love and the light that you have inside and that it will always be more powerful if you share it. It will pulse and allow Mario's light and your baby's light to shine stronger and merge into a family unit."

Betty had her eyes full of tears; she was even trembling for all the words, wisdom, and energy that Karen was displaying with that explanation. The only thing she could say, after all, was, "Karen, I don't have enough to pay you for all this help, but I will be forever grateful to you. My best gift and way of paying you will be to emulate your steps and to create that enlightened beam of light called family now. I really love the description, and it would be so powerful that everyone could see families as a merged beam of light instead of a boiling cooking pot of pain that one day can and will explode and hurt everyone inside."

Karen just finished saying, "Now, Betty, it is our job and endeavor to dedicate our lives to change that concept, and the most powerful way to change it is through the example of us being that beam of light. There's no distinction of nationality, ethnicity, gender, sexual preference, or any other invented boundary. All people are included and will be impacted if we display our energy, and we are able to impregnate them if they want!"

Thought Takeaways

What are the key messages here after witnessing the path of recovery for Betty and Mario, and how does the light and energy of the baby helping them get together again, stronger and more aware of their past wounds?

I.   Is it really your parents' fault the way your life is unfolding?

II. Why do we place so much attention on the external things, and why is it so hard to go within?

III. What are the consequences of living a life of blame and resentment?

IV. Is a baby a healing energy for the parents?

V.   How do you let the ego blame your partner and concentrate on becoming stronger?

Let's begin to unravel all the information about these important takeaways and help you formulate practical steps toward your own life and recovery:

I. Is it really your parents' fault the way your life is unfolding?

This issue of blame is the root cause of not wanting to see the things as they are. As we all know, every time someone calls you guilty of something, they try to detach from their own responsibility. Every kind of relationship, whether it is with your parents, siblings, cousins, teachers, friends has an impact on you when you are a child. Therefore, assigning all the weight on two persons shouldn't be fair, and there comes a time when it is even ridiculous to look for someone to blame. Therefore, the first step toward owning how your life is unfolding goes back to you.

However, yes, there is a strong influence and bias on how our parents raised us, most of all due to the dynamic of communication, behavior, and attitudes that we witnessed as children.

During the time in the womb up to seven or ten years of age (there's still discussion about the length of time), most of the evidence indicates that the way we display our own emotions as parents impacts our child's behavior, and as mentioned in the takeaway message on the first chapter, there is each time stronger supported evidence that the emotions of the mother during pregnancy are key to impact many of the autonomic nervous system functions, such as respiratory sinus arrhythmia (RSA), emotion regulation, the development of the receptors for oxytocin and glucocorticoids, which include many of the adrenal cortex hormones, such as cortisol and other immune and metabolic hormones that act together to regulate many of the main pathways inside our body. They are imprinted in your immune system's maintenance, memory development, stress-response predisposition, metabolic functions, body fluid homeostasis, to mention a few; if you analyze this critically, it is almost every internal major systems of communication. So, it is of paramount importance that we pay more attention to the gestational period, as many people forget, and it is many times where mothers are most exposed to stressful stimuli, marital discussions, work-related problems, and a very poor diet that also impacts strongly the epigenetic development of the fetus.

From the environment end, the critical component is the species-specific maternal behavior that is adapted online to the infant's cues and changing state. Animal research has shown that well-adapted parenting specifically impacts systems that subserve the management of stress, organization of arousal, and adaptation to the social group (Feldman 2015)

For instance, maternal postpartum depression limits the mother's capacity to provide reciprocal parenting, and the reduction in reciprocity disrupts the emergence of infant ER, leading to higher negative emotionality and ineffective regulation in children of depressed mothers. Similarly, premature birth alters the infant-context exchange because of the infant's immature brain at birth, which results in low physiological regulation, high negative emotionality (Feldman, 2007b), and low regulation; and these in turn disrupt the mother's capacity to read the infant's signals and establish a reciprocal dialogue. Both conditions, each from a different end, alter the bidirectional field, and each has been shown to predict greater psychopathology and compromised social-emotional growth (Feldman 2015).

Baseline RSA at birth has been shown to predict regulation of negative emotions at three months, attention regulation in the second year, and lower behavior problems at six years. State regulation measured by the Neonatal Behavior Assessment Scale NBAS indexes the neonate's ability to maintain an organized state and display a range of adaptive states, from sleep to alertness, in the face of incoming visual, auditory, tactile, and multimodal stimuli (Feldman 2015).

Many of the interactions that we develop with our parents when we are children reflect mainly attuned to the attention, patience, response to children's needs, and interaction with them. During their birth to at least three years of age, children will be guided by the behavior of the parent and the response that is given to their demands, as they move their brains, neural connections, and different waves of neural activity. They can be more self-regulatory and start developing their own ego image, their self-attitudes, and claim their independence in certain tasks; however, what has been proven over and over is that when children lack attention, there's a repression of their emotion or there's no signs of affection from them, they start developing an internal "protection" boundary that predispose them to become more aroused to external stimuli, to have more difficulties to regulate their stressful factors, and to cope with relationship interactions.

How do infants shape their own growth? The data suggest that infants may influence development via three avenues. First, infants' regulatory abilities at birth trigger the development of regulatory abilities at later stages. Thus, infants who are born with more regulated dispositions will acquire mature forms of regulation with less effort and will move with greater ease from one regulatory task to the next, facing growing environmental challenges with better tools. Second, such infants elicit more reciprocal and well-fitted parental investments that, in turn, provide essential nutrients for further growth, leading to even finer regulatory outcomes. Third, infants' inborn dispositions may establish a psychobiological birth milieu that can directly impact long-term functioning, possibly through the construction of a more mature and resilient system. These results underscore the importance of studying infant effects on their own growth (Feldman 2015).

Every one of us is a unique mystery of possibilities. All the facts discussed above are a strong evidence of how our parents can "influence and predispose" our behavior, development of certain types of receptors, neural connections, triggers of dysregulation that we'll make sometimes more difficult to cope with our lives.

Nevertheless, in any kind of research, unless of course it is too continuous and excessive, there's something that proves or demonstrates that such changes, such predispositions, are permanent or are impossible to repair and reconstruct.

As mentioned also before, we are energy systems, we are constantly expanding or contracting, therefore as adults, we have to own our responsibility to repair any possible damage that our parents or any other external influence may have caused us. As noted during our story as well, we made it clear that our parents' story is also tainted, also damaged, and that they did the best effort they could with the small degree of awareness that most likely they had for the period of time they lived.

Now, the ball is in our hands, and the ability to change future generations is our duty as individuals, as couples, as families.

If we keep clinging to the fact that there's someone to blame, the only effect that we're going to have is what we're witnessing time after time–more egoistic behaviors, more separation, the destruction of the nucleus of the family; and of course, the reflection of all those negative behaviors is the reason why so many people's lives are faced with stress, addictions, selfishness, etc.

II. Why do we place so much attention on the external things and it is so hard to go within?

Having answered some of the consequences that you might have as a parent, being able to establish that responsibility for your life as the solution, we get to the point of why it is so hard to pay attention to the internal effects than to the outer external consequences.

It is simpler than you expected, probably, but we also like to overcomplicate things. We pay so much attention to the outer effects, first because we are used to that, because it is what we saw everyone else did, because most of us need to fall, get hurt, and get back on our feet before we are ready to look within. Nowadays, it is even more difficult if you want to see it like that, because we have a massive amount of external stimuli, as well as the same amount of information, but now many times we don't know what to do with it, and that behavior reinforces the attention on the outside.

However, as we all have lived and experienced in our lives, the more we place the attention on something, the bigger it gets. So, it is not unreal or inexplicable why we keep attached to the same issues. It is because we're obsessed with blaming, with external responsible people or events, and the more you think is something external that drives your life, the less power you have to see that there's another universe within you, a universe that will only be explored unfortunately when you get tired of failing to find the perfect external solution to your problems or, if you're lucky, when you have an encounter with someone that has done that inner work and inspire you to follow that trail. Whichever be the case, it will only happen when you're ready to do the work, to release the blame, to stop looking for external justification or validation, and when you realize that the inner work is everyone's final purpose in this material/physical world.

We all were created to live our best version of the inner self. Some people get to realize that during the course of their lives, others just react, reflect, and navigate a turbulent life that most likely doesn't end the way they would have wanted it to be and that is also nobody's fault; it is just the accumulation of negative energy, of toxic cycles that, of course, had a very sad ending.

However, no one is cursed or destined to have a sad, torturous life full of blame, resentment, and selfishness. It is an individual decision, an individual compromise that you should elicit from that inner universe that is full of endless possibilities. The only requisite that might be required is your gratitude to be able to appreciate it, see it, and enjoy all the love, the coherence, the peace, the energy, and the healing power that is behind it.

Even with all the early programming of your childhood, there's still a big chance for you to overcome it because no one can own your mind-set unless you allow them to do that. So the more you step away from the distractions, from the society's triggers, from other's people reinforcement, the easier it will be for you, and this of course doesn't mean that you become isolated from everything or everyone, but only means to start having your own criteria of what kind of activities, food, people, environment expands your energy and which kind of them contracts or drains your energy. This task is trial and error and individually experienced, but the good news is that the perception and feeling of it is almost immediate.

We all have experienced certain times in our lives when we talk with someone, watch something, read something, eat something, and immediately after sense the feeling of sadness, anger, desperation, or anxiety. All those signals from your body are the ones that you should start paying more attention to, and just by doing that, you by yourself will start knowing what type of decisions, encounters, and environments you decide to let in your life.

III. What are the consequences of living a life of blame and resentment?

Well, now this answer seems to have more foundation, living examples, and proof than the other one, simply because it is what most of us have lived at least during our first twenty years of our lives. Many of us are in constant interaction with the consequences of living with blame and resentment.

However, many of us deflect or deny that we live with blame or even worse with resentment, validating it with its first symptom, denial, and the most common answer is saying two phrases: "I'm fine" or "I don't want to talk about it." But once I enlist some of the most tragic consequences of living with blame and resentment, I believe you'll no longer use those two phrases.

Blame is a "mixed" feeling sort of saying because it is always accompanied by some of its best buddies—anger, frustration, and resentment. And just to clarify this, we are usually blamed for not achieving many things in our lives due to the poor care given by our parents, and we also mix it with a feeling of blame toward them, which make it even worse and more prone to be derived in anxiety and depression symptoms.

The frequent and persistent experience of anger, depression, and anxiety has been linked to numerous negative health consequences, ranging from occurrence of cardiovascular disease to the progression of cancer as well as the onset of behavioral and substance use disorders. Although the exact mechanisms through which the experience of these emotional states cause cellular or organ dysfunction remains to be elucidated, considerable evidence has implicated various components of the physiological response to environmental stress, including the autonomic nervous system, the hypothalamic-pituitary-adrenal (HPA) system, and the inflammatory response mediated by the immune system (Larkin 2015).

When we persist on building up all the known chemical substances released when we are stressed–discussed at the end of chapter 1, such as cortisol, adrenaline, and noradrenaline–these substances will in turn cause a disruption of many of our metabolic hormones and immune-response helpers that will leave our body weakened to cope with our everyday events as well as predisposing us to catch any opportunistic disease or developing some of the chronic diseases, such as diabetes, obesity, hypertension, autoimmune disorders, or even some types of cancer.

Because resentment, rumination, and worry represent cognitive phenomena, it is likely that engaging in them chronically, as an unforgiving person does, influences cortical functioning (Larkin 2015).

Using a sample of healthy adults who imagined a hurtful event with either instructions to forgive the offender or not, researchers reported cortical differences between forgiveness and unforgiveness using functional magnetic resonance imaging (fMRI). In this regard, this study involved exposure to an actual hurtful event rather than fictional scenarios used in the studies described above. Findings revealed that forgiveness was associated with activation of brain regions involved in emotion regulation and moral judgment, including the medial prefrontal cortex MPFC, amygdala, anterior cingulate, and striatum (Larkin 2015).

What these data means in a more colloquial way to explain it is that when we want to maintain a toxic state of blame either to ourselves or to someone else, some key areas of our brain that influence our behavior, our mood, our peace of mind are altered and triggered as if we were on a real threat. However, we all know and have experienced the feeling of blame and can relate to this kind of imaginary scenarios or self-created stories where the objective reality is lost and we're being dominated just by anger, resentment, and fear, which create an internal chaos in our mind that impairs more the area of the brain in charge of bringing clarity to you, hence the addiction to continue ruminating the problem, looking for people to blame, or even recreating the scenario but now with more elements so that you appear as the victim.

However, when we give a 180-degree turn to the objective fact, to what really happened, and we abide to a more objective version allowing a sense of empathy with the person(s) that "provoked" the pain, then we are more prone to arriving at a state of forgiveness, which in turn releases the key areas of the brain (prefrontal cortex, amygdala, anterior cingulate, and striatum) that will allow us to detach from the emotion and find peace, clarity, and a better sense of empathy with the other people's situation that might have caused the painful event, giving as a consequence the feeling of relief and facilitating the path to be able to break the ruminating blame cycle.

IV. How is a healing energy loop fostered by parents and boosted by the baby?

Everyone that has experienced the birth of a child has certainly experienced the deep bond that is created, stronger felt by the mom and also by the father. How can this extremely powerful bond be fed, mostly during the womb? Is it affected by the energy of the surrounding? Is it then a circle of energy that is created between mother, child, and father?

There are still so many things to be researched within this realm of our lives, but what's now very clear is the effect that toxic emotions have on the baby, some of them discussed in chapter 1; however, we focus on the other side of the source of the energy, now coming from the baby. That's where I believe we have many of the answers on why children have a very powerful and positive effect on us even in the womb.

My theory based on the heart and brain coherence allows that we are really being influenced by the most powerful force and synchrony of energy, which is that one of the baby, as he or she is pure, has no bias, full of love, as I believe that the soul's energy chooses us to heal some or many of our deepest wounds if we are conscious enough and ready to see the answers. The coherence of their hearts when they are in the womb also emanate a field that can reach and will reach the father whenever there are some types of struggles, discussion, sadness, or any kind of stressful event.

Many of us as parents have experienced that kind of love for our children even when we are apart from them. When we have pure love for our child, we experience also a sensation of wanting to be better, of wanting to do a good job as parents, of giving them the best of us that in turn activates positive feelings within us that if we are aware of them, we could use them as fuel to heal ourselves, to cure those old wounds that we suffer in the past, so we can give our baby the best and not the same childhood that we experienced.

Researchers have refined good-enough mothering to include her resilience—moment-to-moment adjustments that help her stay in synch with the infant's volatile body and mood states. Instrumental to this synchrony and bonding is mutual mirroring of gazing, vocalization, and touch. In caring for her baby, every facet of the mother is also stimulated. Their relationship activates new behavioral and neural pathways in each. Developmental growth in baby is matched with changes in the mirror neurons of the mother. Using the fMRI, researchers demonstrated matching cellular changes in child and parent's brain (Kafka 2008).

Research has shown that our emotional state, as measured by heart rhythm coherence patterns, affects how our brain matures. Our emotional state affects others in close proximity via the heart's electrical field. Stressful, incoherent emotional states in a primary caregiver impair development and learning in children while positive emotional states enhance coherent maturation and learning (Pribram 1998).

So, the pathway of early learning would be from the parent's or caregiver's heart electrical field to the baby's heart electrical field then to the brain. This is especially important in the first years of life. Touching, singing, talking to, or reading to young children won't be effective if the parent or caregiver is anxious, angry, or stressed. If the mother is trying hard to be nice and read to her child while she is anxious, the HRV patterns pick that up and go direct to the baby. The heart and nervous system detect the real signal (Pribram 1998).

There's plenty of evidence that every emotion or state of mind that we as parents experience is transmitted to the baby. Of course, this is deeper in the case of the mother due to obvious circumstances—the baby is completely embedded in her. However, father emotions are also perceived by the baby when they are closer to a magnetic field where heart waves can be perceived, which is, as science has stated, at least 8 to 10 feet (2.4 to 3.0 meters) of distance.

Because feelings and emotions are energies that emit powerful magnetic fields, the stronger the elevated feelings, the stronger the magnetic field. In fact, the heart produces the strongest magnetic field in the body—five thousand times greater in strength than the field produced by the brain. Place your finger on your wrist and feel your pulse. That pulse is a wave of energy called the blood pressure wave, and it travels through your entire body, influencing everything, including brain function. Not only does the heart's magnetic pulse reverberate through every cell of the body, but it also produces a field around your body that can be measured up to 8 to 10 feet away using a sensitive detector called a magnetometer (Dispenza 2017; Childre 2000).

Soon, it will be demonstrated that heat coherence from the baby can and is also a powerful healing energy that in many cases influences parents to work out their issues; it is that "strange/beautiful" sense of connection that we have as parents and that guide us to become aware of our own wounds, holes, and triggers that we still need to work on.

V. How do you let the ego blame your partner and concentrate on becoming stronger?

As discussed very deeply in question 3 of this chapter, blaming and creating resentment toward any person can lead you to self-sabotage yourself, predispose you to develop anxiety, frustration, and probably depression as you are just placing the responsibility of your life, thoughts, and emotions on someone else.

Moreover, usually when you want to see other people's fault, lacks, or actions, it is because you're letting your ego dominate and narrow your perception on what is really happening, meaning this outlook on your life will start provoking a lot of conflict in your relationship because you will be more concerned on your partner's actions and behavior than on what you're doing to sometimes sabotage your interaction and the way the relationship might unfold.

As a means of conceptualizing personality constructs central to motivation, emotion, and behavior, Jack Block (1980, 2002) proposed "ego-resiliency" as the dynamic capacity to regulate one's level of cognitive, emotional, and behavioral control in response to situational challenges and affordances. Across several different research methodologies, researchers have found that individuals higher in ego-resiliency are better able to recover from negative emotional experiences and flexibly adapt to the fluctuating demands of stressful experiences (Caldwell 2012).

Repeated experiences with sensitive and responsive attachment figures increase a person's general sense of safety and security and encourage the use of security-based strategies of affect regulation. These strategies are aimed at alleviating distress and maintaining comfortable, supportive intimate relationships, and they generally contribute positively to personal adjustment. They include optimistic beliefs about distress management, beliefs about others' trustworthiness and goodwill and a sense of self-efficacy about dealing with threats (Caldwell 2012).

Based on the research evidence, it appears clear why Betty and Mario's relationship had been biased to the latest challenges, reaching a point where both needed to separate and take time off each other. If we analyze their childhood stories as explained at the end of this chapter, we can see that both of them had challenging situations with each other's parents that clearly marked them to develop a poor sense of safety and security that could allow them to overcome the now-exposed challenges in their relationship.

Many couples struggle with this kind of issues, as we have discussed previously because many have emotional holes and deficiencies when they were children. Moreover, this kind of repetitive pattern is fostered when people don't want to work in their own self-knowledge, which is most of the case; therefore, there are many examples of this kind of twisted or chaotic relationships where there's a lot more damage, which ironically triggers the same root cause–feeling unsafe, unworthy, and unrecognized.

The only way out to overcome this kind of behaviors is allowing yourself and your partner to take a serious approach to heal all those childhood memories, lack of love, and work on your self-awareness of the thoughts you know that are controlling most of your emotions and sabotaging your path toward a healthy relationship.

I firmly believe that almost every relationship can be repaired if there hasn't been a profound damage to the integrity of the other person as well as committing both to pursue a better future even when there are no children in the picture.

In fact, healing as individuals, facing the wounds, and committing to a recovery is the core of breaking the toxic patterns that we will be facing time after time when we deny, reject, or get comfortable with a toxic life and, of course, toxic relationships.

CHAPTER 6

A New Member Brings Peace and Wisdom

A S WE MOVE on in our story of Mario and Betty, we hopefully start realizing how important it is to heal all the inner wounds, all the past scars, ideally before starting your own family. As you can see in the story, it is never too late, and your children will always be thankful if you decide to do it on time, giving them an opportunity to witness more awakened parents that promote the concept of emotionally healthy families. We left our story with the strong lessons that Mario and Betty received from friends or the coach in Mario's journey to recovery.

The day they were to be together again came. Mario was nervous, excited, and fearful because he really didn't know if he was going to be able to win

Betty back. During his recovery at the clinic facing all his struggles, pain, and self-reflection, he realized that he really screwed up the trust that Betty had for him by hiding his addiction problem. On top of that, he involved her ex Kelly in the recovery process. However, he had also learned not to predispose himself to any result or create fake scenarios because those two elements played an important role in creating more anxiety and desperation for him, which was a dangerous ground that could eventually lead him back to consume any type of substance to numb the pain or discomfort caused by those emotions. Therefore, Mario started using the tools learned in meditation and maintaining a journal to exteriorize his inner concerns and cope with those anxious situations.

Betty on her side had a clearer mind. She was feeling hopeful and ready to accept Mario again in her life; however, she was also realistic, firm, and knew that she had to be strong to set boundaries with Mario's addiction issues as she didn't want to risk her daughter's well-being due to a relapse that Mario could have.

Going Deep in Your Relationship

Their encounter was set to happen at a restaurant where they had celebrated the last reconciliation after the news of Betty's pregnancy. The place was very special for them, the night was warm, and everything seemed to fit so that they could achieve again a reconciliation and this time it was going to be for a good while!

Mario arrived first at the restaurant. He was a little bit anxious and worried, and he wanted to be there before Betty arrived. Betty had already started to care more about herself and her external outlook, as she also understood through Mario's letters and stories of the program that how you eat impacts your health, the baby's health, and your emotions. Both looked different, both had a glow that had to do, of course, with all the inner work they had performed during the past six months. When Betty arrived at the restaurant, she looked amazing, full of confidence and joy, excited, a little nervous, but willing to fix things and become a family with Mario.

When Mario saw Betty approaching the table, he immediately had a huge smile, and his eyes seemed sparkling with joy. He was really impressed with how Betty looked, as he never imagined that she had lost some weight too and had groomed herself like he had never seen her before, something that he would have wanted, but now she did it for herself. That was more meaningful for Mario, in addition to now having a completely different inner work that allowed him to see things with a much clearer mind.

He pulled the chair for Betty to sit. Betty also looked surprised at all the weight Mario had lost. He looked like a new man—slim, secure, also very handsome, and most of all, he had a different light in his eyes. He seemed, as many would say, enlightened; but of course, everything was the result of also six months of hard recovery, struggles, pain, and responsibility to know himself, dedicating his time to put everything together. That confident and healed outlook made Betty feel so much secure that they had many possibilities for them to have a future again, to continue the journey, and to become a healthy family, such as the one Betty had already pictured in her mind since she talked with her friend Karen.

Mario told Betty that she looked amazing, that he was really proud of the change he saw in her outlook, and he also expressed his gratitude to give him another chance to prove that he had recovered and had become a different man. He asked Betty to begin talking and just waited patiently for her opinion.

"Well, Mario, before I begin talking, I would like to recognize that you also look very different. I'm amazed of how much weight you have lost, how different you look, and that gives me confidence although I would, of course, like to hear more about your recovery and your plans. But from what I can see, it really seems that you're different now. I'd like to begin by telling you that I'm really sorry for many of the things that maybe also triggered your past emotional wounds. I would also like to thank you for all the letters you wrote me and all the details in your recovery process. All that information worked for me as well. In my case, I also took advantage of our time apart. If I have to be completely honest with you, it took some couple of months to realize that I had to also detoxify myself from my past emotional wounds, most of all from my childhood as well. Actually, I used one of the techniques that you described with Mike, your emotional coach. I asked for support from Karen, again, as she already knew some of our past story and I completely trust her in these kinds of emotional issues. She was amazingly helpful, and we ended up digging very deep into my mother's past and why her behavior triggered me so much, what kind of things I was also replicating in my life due to the programmed behavior we are many times exposed as children. During that inner journey, I realized that I was also being emotionally pulled from you, I was also shutting down myself from feeling more love, and ironically, I was also placing myself as a victim of the circumstances, exactly as my mother did it with my father.

"Now, after having gone through some deep meditations, some heart coherence techniques such as the ones you described, and a lot of journaling that has been pouring out from me, I'm really aware that we were both trapped in our childhood wounds. We were replicating our parents' behavior, and we were really recreating pretty much the same circumstances we wanted to run away from. For me, it has been amazing all of this encounter with a new person, a renewed inner self, a woman that now feels light, motivated, and full of energy to heal my path as an individual, as a mother, and of course, as your partner."

When she said "as a partner," Mario's eyes were completely full of tears, as she was already opening up the door for them to continue their journey as a couple.

"I want you to know, Mario, that for me, now there's a new outlook that I see for us, there's a new path, but also there are some conditions I would like to express and leave very clear because I'm also aware that I don't ever want to repeat any past pattern. I don't ever want to recreate the life I saw with my parents, and I would really love to have a very different story for me, with you, and our baby.

"Thus, I want our life, if we both agree here, to continue this path together full of honesty. I don't ever want any hidden information to come up. Of course, I don't want and I'm not going to tolerate any relapse from you in any type of addiction. I would also like to know in advance of any ex you would like to be in touch with, would like to know why are you interested in maybe seeing them or very rarely gather with them and have an update of their lives. I'm being very honest here too. I don't believe in prohibiting anything, that's why I said know in advance. I would also like that we could be very open with our feelings and be completely honest and direct with any kind of behavior that doesn't fit with our new way of being, try to have an agreement as soon as possible without feeling that we don't trust each other.

"Ideally, I was thinking that we can set up a biweekly or weekly heart-to-heart talk about how we feel, the things that you like or don't like about me, the things we can improve as a couple? Of course, very soon, we will have to add one more topic, which is the education of our daughter and her well-being. I now believe that the more communication we can have, the easier it will be to handle the problems or disagreements that we might have. In addition to that, I want us to create a different kind of relationship where we are the priority, where we don't ever lose time for ourselves, and just keep doing fun activities as a couple. I'm now more aware than ever that we're very close to starting a new stage in our lives. We both know many people that have experienced a challenge with their first baby and have let their relationship become monotonous, sometimes—as harsh as it sounds—boring or repetitive. Let's not be another couple that adds to that list, please."

Mario's face was full of happiness. He had a huge smile; still, some tears were dropping from his eyes because he didn't expect at all that Betty was going to be as open and willing to continue as she just expressed it, so now it was his turn to say what he wanted, his new outlook for the relationship, and of course, his new commitments.

Thus, Mario started saying, "Thank you very much, Betty, you've been amazing with me since the moment we met each other. I really felt that day that I had met a very special woman. I even thought and now I think that more, you were a gift from heaven. Many times, I didn't even think I deserved you due to my toxic childhood examples, poor care that I received, and also the strong conditioning that my parents left on me. However, this detoxifying time that I received in the clinic, which by the way was very complete and integral, made me realize that I had to start thinking differently, that I could reset my old patterns and program, I could be able to install a new software, which of course is going to be healthy, emotionally confident.

"Now I become committed to you not only by words, but also with my full commitment that from this day on, I will be a better man, I will be aware of my toxic patterns and stop them before I act in a stupid way and screw up. I, of course, will be a much better partner than the one I have ever been with you, and finally I commit to being a very congruent and coherent example to our baby and give him or her all the love he or she deserves, to break as well the pattern you and I share coming from toxic families.

"I have learned as well during my detox that the more communication you have with your partner, the better the relationship will be. Therefore, I'm completely committed to the scheduled meetings that we are going to have to check on ourselves, sharing how everything is going, and discussing any possible misunderstandings or issues that we might have. I loved the idea when you mentioned it, makes me feel even more appreciated that you said it first. Also, I'm completely on board with the dynamics of having a fun day or afternoon as a couple, where we get to do different things, being able to maintain the passion and love for ourselves.

"I also wouldn't like to be a number with the majority of marriages that just 'survive' the years, but who are just two strangers living in the same house, or worse, just fighting and pretending just like what we experienced from our parents.

"I want to be a very caring, conscious man with you, Betty, always reminding you how beautiful you are, how lucky I am to be with you, accepting each other's flaws and qualities. Today, more than any other day, you have been the ray of light that I needed to be transformed.

"I want you to know that I admire a lot your discipline, persistence, and resilience that you have had with your life. You have showed time after time that you really possess and express congruency with your values, your words, and your actions to achieve the things that you want. Proof of that is what you did recently with your boss, the way you earned his trust and your place in your company, all those attitude and behavior have allowed me to be very confident that you will keep your word and you will have my back if I also do my share.

"Finally, and this might catch you by surprise, I can't think of any better moment to become engaged with you." Mario got down on one knee and put out a small box with a gorgeous ring. He said, "Betty, since the moment I met you, I unexpectedly felt that you were my destiny, and today I'm the happiest man on earth and the most confident to tell you that I want to spend the rest of my life with you. Will you marry me?"

Since the moment that Mario got down on his knee, Betty was already happily crying, filled with joy, hope, and peace. All the energy that they managed to raise caused an amazing and surprising effect in the baby. Betty's belly, by the way, was pretty big by then, and she felt a huge kick that struck Betty with pain, but also with joy because she just knew that it was the baby feeling all that loving energy flowing through her veins and her heart producing coherent waves. We'll get deeper into that, but all the energy that Betty and Mario were emanating was able to repair any possible predisposition or damage that they could have produced before with their discussions or disagreements.

Now it was the time for their love, the time for their healing journey together, the time to start a new stage where more challenges were about to arise.

Betty, of course, without any hesitation and with a huge smile, her face flooded with tears and her voice trembling, said, "Yes! Of course, Mario, I accept to be your wife from now on and for as long as we last."

They were both amazingly happy, reconciled, joined, and having a new member that was expected to be born by the end of the following week.

They had a very peaceful dinner, chatting with more details their journey, sharing also some past memories from them. That night was marked as the beginning of a new relationship and with the birth of a new beam of light as Karen and Betty had agreed to become.

Your Reset Point

However, during that night, Betty and Mario also discussed the fact that they needed to quickly start looking for a place to live, something that Mario had also planned during his stay at the clinic. He had an account with a decent amount of money that his father opened for him to be spent for his college education. However, during his stay at the clinic, he managed to convince his mom to use that money to start his journey with Betty. She, of course, was not as happy as he would have liked; but after she talked with Mike, the emotional coach, she was more confident and was aware of how Mario felt not only his deepest wounds, but also the fact that since the moment he met Betty, she had never seen Mario so committed to any other girl. Therefore, as a mom, that made her feel confident he was making the best choice.

Thus, Mario also told Betty that he had already paid two months of deposit and the first month of rent for an apartment in a decent neighborhood near Betty's job. Betty was really surprised at how Mario in just one night proved to her so many things, giving her a lot of confidence that they were going in the same direction and walking a more enlightened path.

Now, it was Betty's turn to talk with her parents, about this engagement, and the plans they had together as a couple and the baby. For that, Betty thought it was going to be more formal and easier to organize a dinner at her parents' place; therefore, she arranged everything so they could gather the following weekend, as the birth date was approaching very fast.

As we know, Betty's parents have a very religious approach toward the formalization of a relationship, and they had previously thought that the baby and Betty were going to be at their house, at least for the quarantine period– that is, the period as believed by tradition wherein pregnant women have to remain indoors and with certain traditional homemade remedies. Therefore, those factors were going to be a matter of discussion over dinner.

Mario was a little nervous as the time for dinner with Betty's parents approached. This kind of social encounters were very different from the ones he had without, of course, having suffered that kind of pressure from anyone in his family. He didn't really know if he was going to be able to control himself and not answer in a rude or disrespectful manner.

Nevertheless, he still had the support of Mike from the clinic and his sponsor Joe. Thus, he contacted first Mike some hours before dinner to see if they could talk, but Mike was overseas and couldn't help him, but he gladly referred Mario to Joe. Mario contacted then Joe, and they discussed some strategies that Mario could do before dinner to overcome his anxiety and to control any kind of anger impulse he might have during dinner.

Joe told Mario to perform a meditation where he tried to visualize every step of the conversation with Betty's parents, trying to add as much detail as possible so that his brain could be more exposed to the real experience prior to the dinner. In addition to that, Joe recommended Mario to journal three to five possible scenarios of what could go wrong and how he could handle them with Betty's support to also develop a united front between Betty and Mario, giving their parents at least the assurance that they have talked all the arrangements before, as well as showing them that they are really committed to avoid any overwhelm placed by Betty's family. This, in fact, was a very good start for Betty's independence, marking her way through a new stage with Mario and the baby.

Finally, the time for dinner had come. Betty was also kind of nervous knowing, first, her parents' narrow criteria toward her independence from them; second, the sudden twist of events in Betty's life as they didn't know much about Mario's detoxification process; and finally, the family traditions or patterns that they had been programmed to believe were the right way things should be done.

Mario finally rang the bell to enter Betty's house. Betty's mom opened the door and received Mario with a warm gesture, something that, of course, Mario didn't expect. As Mario entered the living room, he was approached by Betty so that she could take him to the dining room and introduce him to her father. Betty's dad was a man of few words, not with a friendly face and a frowning outlook. Betty introduced Mario to her dad, and Mario raised his chest and gave Betty's father a strong handshake, showing confidence and respect toward her dad. Betty's father greeted Mario, and his first words were, "What a surprise, Mario. We thought Betty had invented a character as we haven't seen you here before at all."

Mario just nervously laughed and said, "I'm sorry, sir, but my life has been a little bit complicated during these past few months, that's why I hadn't been properly introduced to you. I guess Betty already explained you that me and my parents were out of the country for some weeks."

"Yes, Mario, Betty already explained something about you. However, now is a good chance to know you better."

Mario's face was more worried now, as he knew he might be questioned about some values, principles, and maybe some private matters about his life, which of course he didn't really want to get into details or arguments with Betty's dad. However, he was very skillful, and as he noticed that Betty's mom had a different reaction, he just thought he might get out from some explanations through being charismatic with her.

Everything was ready for dinner, and Betty was helping her mom prepare and serve all the food they were going to have. Therefore, Mario was left alone for some minutes with Betty's dad at the table, who started asking some basic questions to Mario. "Mario, please tell me, what do you do? How many brothers or sisters do you have? Where do you work, or are you still studying? What are your intentions and plans with my daughter?"

Mario started to have sweaty hands, and he started to feel a little bit anxious. Betty's dad was drinking tequila, and he offered Mario some, which made everything worse as he, of course, was not supposed to have any drop of alcohol. Thus, Mario excused himself and went to the bathroom. He started to feel dizzy, nauseous, and just couldn't hold himself and vomited.

Betty could hear something in the bathroom, and she quickly got there, knocking on the door and asking, "Are you okay, Mario?" He just answered quickly, "Yes, Betty, don't worry, I feel better." Betty was still worried so she waited outside until Mario finished.

When he got out of the bathroom, Betty asked Mario what happened. He told her that her father had started questioning him about his life and the intentions he had with her. So, Mario asked Betty, "Did you mention something about my addiction, Betty?"

She quickly answered, "Of course not, I kept everything very simple with them because I know them, and I know I could get you in trouble and myself as well. So, don't worry, the only things they know about you is that you work in a sports goods store and you are studying to become a systems engineer at the Autonomous Metropolitan University during these last few months. I just didn't mention anything about you, but my father just asked me quickly how were you and why you have never been to the house, to which I just answered that you were on a long trip with your parents and that was it."

"Okay, Betty, I think we should have talked about all this before, but whatever is fine that you're giving me the update so that I can know what to mention. I was just thinking that in order for them to stop asking questions about why I don't accept any kind of alcohol, I could say that I caught a very aggressive bacteria during my trip and I am not allowed to take any alcohol as I'm taking strong antibiotics."

"That's perfect, Mario, yes, just say that, and I'll also try to deviate conversation if they start asking more. Please calm down. I know they seem a little bit snoopy, but it's completely normal for me. Just try to be empathic, they love me and they have just always been overprotective as I'm their only daughter."

"Yes, Betty, don't worry, I'll try to keep myself calm. It was just too much for me after not having almost any kind of interaction with anyone for the past six months and much less of this kind of social questioning. Sincerely I've never arrived so far with any woman as to meet her parents, so please try also to understand my anxiety or worry."

Betty held Mario's hands as in a gesture of confidence, and she hugged him, telling him in the ear, "I will support you, and don't worry, we'll get out of this dinner just fine. It's a necessary step we need to take in order for us to have freedom and start our own new family."

Mario felt a lot better with those words and the hug, so they just returned to the table. Betty had to keep helping a little bit more, but Mario was no longer anxious as he already knew what to answer.

Betty's dad asked him, "Are you okay, Mario?"

He just said, "Yes, sir, I'm sorry I had just been feeling a little weird, and my stomach hasn't been so good since we return from the trip."

"Okay, well, Mario, don't think that you will escape my questions just because you have a stomachache. Could you please answer what I asked before?"

"Of course, sir. Well, I work at a sports goods store in Polanco for six years now. I don't have any brother or sisters, and I'm currently studying to become a systems engineer at the Autonomous Metropolitan University, and the last question about my plans with your daughter, I think that we should wait a little bit so that everyone is at the table and I tell everyone else too."

"Okay, Mario, I'll be patient and wait for my wife and daughter to be here too. Meanwhile, would you like something to drink, Mario?"

"No, sir, thanks for your kind attention, but right now, I can't drink any alcohol as I got sick with a terrible bacteria during my trip with my parents."

"Okay, Mario, may I ask where did you go?"

"Yes, sir, we went to Seoul, South Korea, where my father owns many companies and he had to make a business trip there to fix some issues, but my mother and I thought it would be a good idea to join him and know that city that we have heard a lot of good things about."

"That sounds interesting, and how is the city? The people? And the food?"

"Well, sir, the people are very educated and friendly, the city very clean, though people have very different customs and traditions to eat, which for me were not so easy to pick up, but I certainly enjoyed trying new things, food, and adapting myself to the customs of a new country."

"Could you just share one of them, Mario?"

"Yes, of course, sir. Seoul is a very technological city with a lot of first world services pretty much like some countries of Europe or cities in the USA or Canada. However, something for me was very 'strange,' if I could use that word, and at the same time hygienic was that Koreans don't enter their houses or some restaurants with shoes. They leave them in the entrance, they eat a lot of things raw, or they just use the same fat of the meat to cook the dishes. For me, it was funny and surprising that they also like spicy food. They use a sort of toothpaste that is made of a very spicy pepper, but it is very tasty, similar to what we here in Mexico know as tree chili pepper. They add it to soups, salads, or to almost any type of main dish, just like we do here in Mexico with any kind of hot pepper."

"Wow, I wouldn't think that any other country would eat as much chili pepper as us, but now I know they do sometimes."

"Yes, sir, actually, India and some other Asian countries do use those spices in their food."

Betty's dad had been detracted from the topic of Mario's plans with her daughter; however, that didn't last for too long as Betty and her mother were finally finished and have started putting all the food on the table, so that was all the prelude Mario and Betty were going to have, as Betty's dad was very persistent and now her mother was interested to hear their future plans.

Now, it was Betty's mom to ask Mario what were his plans with Betty, and of course, she also looked at Betty, sort of giving her the hint that she wanted to hear also her opinion and part on it.

Therefore, Mario stopped eating for a little moment and stood in his place and said, "Well, as now both of you have been very clear that you want to hear our plans, let me begin by saying that I'm really grateful with you, even though this is the first time I officially met with both of you because you have an amazing daughter. She has been since the moment I met her, the light of my life, the compass of my destination, and of course, now that we're expecting a child very soon and we have spent, in my opinion, enough time together, we would like to get married. So, Sir and Madam González, I would like to ask your permission to marry your daughter."

As soon as he said those words, Betty's mom became very emotional. She started to show some tears in her eyes while Betty's dad was a little bit in shock. As for him, they had not met for a long time, and he thought that Mario was very irresponsible for not showing up before as Betty was already pregnant so he just needed more than those words to convince him and start being more empathic with Mario's feeling. Therefore, Mario stood up, not knowing exactly what else to say; then Betty intervened and she said, "Well, Dad, don't be so harsh to Mario. He never showed up here because he knew you and Mom are very strict and sometimes controlling, even if you don't like that word, but he has the best intentions for me and the baby."

"Okay, Betty, so let him talk and explain."

Mario took the word again and started saying, "Well, sir, as Betty just told you, I have a very different set of traditions and values in my family, and speaking just for me, I really have never been good to interact with any kind of parents. In fact, you're the first parents I have ever met in my life. Don't get me wrong, sir, but I have never met any woman that really interested me so formally and deeply as your daughter. For all the things that Betty told me about you and your values, I was very intimidated, so I didn't want to mess anything up. Let me just share something very personal with you and your wife. My parents are not the best example of traditions, values, or a healthy marriage. I have had several disagreements with them because they are completely the opposite to you or practically any other Mexican marriage. They also have left me to decide and do with my life almost anything that I wanted. However, and as I mentioned before, your daughter really set a very huge example of values, clarity, discipline, drive, and confidence that made me realize that she is a gift of heaven for me, maybe because I suffered enough reaction from my parents or maybe because I needed someone like her to take my life more seriously and start maturing and behaving as an adult and not as teenager anymore.

"Moreover, during these past few months, I have been in an emotional retreat as well, where I also realized that we as a couple are very fortunate to have found each other during the time that we did because otherwise, things would have never been able to happen the way they did for both of us. Now more than ever, I can assure that I will be a very responsible, caring, thoughtful, as well as a good provider for your daughter, so please rest assured that your daughter is now in good hands and she will always be supported, respected, and of course, loved by me. In fact, proof of that is that I already have an apartment for us to live in and start our new family."

Betty's eyes were full of tears, as she never expected Mario to say the things he said with such confidence and also being able to open up himself with his privacy, all that left her father with nothing much to say.

"That's very good, Mario. I, as a father and soon as you will be one, just want to ask you to be very careful of how you treat my daughter, very careful what kind of example you want to give to your child, because I myself maybe haven't done my best job with her, but what I made sure she had was a very strong image of hard work, constant endurance toward life challenges, and hopefully I have set in her a high standard toward the man she deserves. So please, be up to the task, Mario, and I thank you for your honesty, openness, and for being straight with your words."

Betty's mom was still emotional after Mario's words and his husband's reaction, which she never expected to be like. The only words she could also say were, "Thank you, Mario. Even if you have never been in the house before and have had very few opportunities to let ourselves know you, with those words, the trust in your eyes, and the way you open up to us with your own childhood and the story of your parents, I am satisfied and hopeful that you will abide by your word and treat my daughter well. One last request from me would be to not ever let yourself think that just because she accepted, we have accepted your proposal and that new future that you are offering her, you have no longer the duty to tell her how much you love her, how much you appreciate all the things she will do for you, or even the silence and time you will share in common because we, as women, need a lot more than what you think our partners need by caring, loving, and reminding ourselves that we're doing fine, that you love us and that you appreciate what we do.

"As my husband said, maybe I also haven't been the best example to my daughter in terms of how she should be treated or acknowledged, but with your story, you touch some of those wounds that I really wish my girl would never repeat."

"Thank you, ma'am, I certainly won't take your daughter for granted or her efforts to be a good wife and a good mom. I know for sure that I will be more surprised for the rest of my life for the things she will be able to accomplish."

Betty was just ecstatic with Mario's attitude. If she had any doubt that he could put up with a new role, new endeavors, her doubts and questions were very quickly dissipated, as Mario proved that he was ready to be a different man from the one he once was.

After all those emotions, sharing, and display of commitment, they didn't have too much to do but to continue with their dinner and enjoy the night, so that's what they did. Mario and Betty were extremely happy. Mario's soul and shoulders rested like never before, and he really felt good and happy just like when he proposed to Betty.

A New Fresh Start

The next days passed with Betty dedicating some time to put her things together; Mario, of course, helped her with the packing and moving of things. They didn't have too much time to plan things because the next Friday, the baby was due and they had to be at the hospital very early in the morning. While doing the packing and moving her things from her room, Betty's mom approached her and said, "Betty, are you sure you don't want to stay here for a few weeks with Mario and the baby? I know that you want to prove your point and demonstrate you can do things alone, but having a child is not easy, and Mario is also in the same situation."

Betty answered her mom, "No thanks, Mom. I know it won't be easy and I know Mario is also new to these things, but my first tough proof that I can do things right is this one, Mom. I really want for us to be a new family, and of course, that doesn't imply you won't be involved, but if Mario looked a house for us, if he said all those things to you and my dad, if he already proposed to me, it wouldn't be fair to him to take all those efforts and authority down just because I want to be more comfortable in my house and with you. We really want to do things different, Mom, and part of that starts with the birth of my child and all the challenges ahead for us. I now know that we'll overcome them, and I know we'll be a different kind of family, which by the way just in case you were worried, you will be able to visit us and be with your granddaughter or we'll come sometimes here, but just as guests."

"Okay, Betty, I understand and I admire your strong character, which I didn't know so much up until now. That also leaves me confident that Mario is doing a good job by giving you more confidence and support, and it makes complete sense that you want to be reciprocal with him. I wish I have had the nerve to be the same with your dad although our journey was an entirely different story for the things you now know, but I think I would have loved to be as strong and confident as you're being now."

"Don't worry, Mom, it's never late to start. If you really want to heal from your past, if you still want to change the years ahead with Dad, just think about it, commit to yourself, and I'll be there to help you in the journey."

"Thanks, Betty, I will think about it."

Betty and Mario were really tired from all the moving and packing, but they were ready, just in time to get in the hospital and receive their new member of the family.

Finally, the day arrived, Friday, October 5. They were early in the hospital, and both were nervous. Betty's parents were there some minutes after them, and Mario's mom was going to arrive later. Mario was a bit nervous and anxious; he was at all times with Betty. The doctor approached them so they were assigned a patient room, and they could wait there for the checkup of the nurse, waiting for the proper indications so that Betty could get into labor. Mario stayed there for a couple of hours, but around noon, he told Betty that he needed to get out a little bit and do some exercise as he was feeling very anxious and nervous. Anyway, Betty was going to enter the operation room and Mario wouldn't be allowed to get in, as it was a public hospital and their policies don't allow the father to enter the operation room as part of its safety procedures.

While all those events were developing in the hospital, Mario left for his gym and went swimming. While he was at the pool, just trying to get rid of the nervous and anxious thoughts, he was thinking in his head first about the gender of the baby as they didn't want the ob-gyn to tell them beforehand, then about the health of the baby considering they have had some discussion during the first trimester of the pregnancy, and then right in the middle they were still having some issues with his addiction problems and Betty's stressful situation at her job. All those flashes started to come along during his swimming time. However, during the swimming session, there was a time where he felt something strange inside.

Suddenly, some images started to appear in his mind about the gender of the baby and a huge bright light. He stopped for a moment and felt an intense love in his chest, which just made him cry and feel really grateful for everything in spite of all the struggles, emotional wear out, and the everyday situations that were combined during Betty's pregnancy while he was having those emotional moments. He now was seeing images of enlightenment; and he remembered all the key moments that happened during his recovery, how he was able to handle all the emotional abuse and rejection, how all the anger was left behind, the encounter of their reconciliation at the dinner, meeting Betty's parents and being able to talk to them the way he did it. All these succession of images and positive flashes gave him a lot of gratitude for everything, a lot of love for his life, for Betty, for the baby, and a really strong feeling of resilience and strength that allowed him to visualize his future;

to feel confident that he was going to be able to be a good father; to leave behind all the sorrow, pain, and addictions; and to be now a role model for his daughter (that was what the gender that first came to his mind while he was visualizing), for his future wife. All of these experiences, brain flow of images, heart coherence, and opening of emotions in order to arrive to that experience of visualization, which was enhanced due to the exercise session and the amount of neurotransmitters liberated Mario without him knowing what happened, just experiencing a moment of physical and mental flow.

Meanwhile, Betty was already recovering in her room, and the baby was kept a little while in a sort of nursery care area where all the babies were kept and fathers and moms could see them through a big glass. They had schedules for the children to be visited and seen and also allow the mothers to have some interaction. This kind of isolation is where they protect the babies two days more or less from the environment and allow a softer adaptation to everything. Nurses and physicians monitored all the babies in case some health issues happen.

After some hours after the birth, Mario arrived at the hospital. He met with Betty's parents downstairs, and he also saw his mother, who gave him a huge hug like she had never done before. She was very emotional and started crying on his shoulder and whispered in his ear, "I love you, Mario, I'm sorry for all the pain that I have caused. I'm really proud of you and this new stage in your life." Mario also was very emotional since the swimming session, so he started to cry too. They kept hugging for some minutes, which was a small healing experience for both of them, most of all because Mario's mom was pretty cold and distant. Mario then went upstairs to Betty's room to check how she was and, of course, have some news about the baby. Betty was still a little numb by all the anesthesia and medications she received, but she looked pretty good and happy to see Mario.

The first words she said to him were, "She's so beautiful, Mario. It's amazing the love and energy that I felt when they let me hold her." Mario was shocked as when he was swimming, he had pictured a clear image of the baby being a girl without, of course, knowing that. Mario immediately shared the experience he had with Betty. They hugged for a good while, and they were both crying in happiness and gratitude. Mario was still feeling a powerful gratitude inside him, as if his heart was going to come out. Betty even felt it, and she was feeling also very protected and safe. After some minutes of the hugging/crying experience, Betty told Mario that he could call the nurse and ask her to take him to the nursery care facility so he could see her daughter. All babies had a number and letter code that was attached to the mother's wrist and labeled in the cradle where the baby was kept at the nursery. The nurse took Mario to see his daughter. Mario was anxious, but this time it was a healthy anxiety of seeing her, knowing how she looked. She was held by the nurse who approached the glass so he could see her closer. Mario placed his hand on the glass, and his baby moved her hand. He couldn't resist the emotion, and he just let some tears drop. Inside his mind, he was just thinking, *My beautiful daughter, I will always love you so much, take care of you, and I will become the father you deserve. Deep down in me, I know you have chosen me and your mom to be your parents, therefore we will honor that decision you made from above, and I promise you that you will have a very unique and loving family.*

They just allowed some minutes for the fathers to see the babies, and as Mario's time was almost up, the nurse put the baby back in the cradle. She stepped out and took Mario to Betty's room.

Betty was trying to fall sleep for a while, but when she felt that Mario entered, she woke up and asked Mario what he felt and thought about the baby. Mario was really overwhelmed; he told Betty that he loved her so much, that he was incredibly grateful to her staying with him, for giving him the chance to be a father, and for trusting him again after all that happened. Betty smiled and answered, "I love you, Mario, and despite all the struggles we had at the beginning or after, today, I just can't think of a better man for her. Our discussions, arguments, or pain that we suffered at the beginning, now they just represent blocks of steps we had to climb to be able to stand here stronger— as a couple, as two parents that, of course, had some or many flaws, but luckily, we discovered them on time to be more aware now with our daughter."

Mario nodded his head with approval. He approached Betty and told her, "Exactly, I also think about all the struggles. In particular when I was swimming, I also witnessed my life in flashes of meaningful moments good and bad, and I realized that if I didn't have some parents like the ones I had, if I didn't have my addiction to escape from those childhood wounds, certainly I wouldn't have had the opportunity to access and be in the clinic. With that kind of recovery program that I received, I never would have written those experiences I shared with you, and you also wouldn't have had some kind of awareness of your own wounds too. We are exactly where we belong, where we would have to be, and now we are a more awakened family than the one we could imagine, we now are more committed to giving our beautiful baby the best in us, and we have a long way to enjoy our journey as a family."

Betty was also very grateful, emotional, and completely satisfied with life. Mario told Betty that he was going to leave her to rest some more time, and he was going to go downstairs to talk with their parents, to share how the baby looked and how she was. Betty agreed and continued her efforts to fall sleep.

Mario gathered with their parents and told them, "She's just amazing, she's beautiful, she's the biggest of the babies in the nursery. To me, she looks just like Betty, thank God, but I think she has my eyes. They are both in perfect condition, Betty a little tired, of course, so I left her falling sleep."

Their parents were extremely happy; they seemed very proud of them, and after all, Betty's parents had accepted Mario's character of being more independent and away from family. Mario introduced her mom to Betty's parents; with all the anxiety and emotions, he just forgot to do it since he arrived.

They all went to eat something and talked about life and, of course, about their children. During the meal, Mario mentioned that Betty was going to be released the next day; she had been recovering pretty well, and her doctor told him the news.

Mario was excited to start their life completely anew; he felt as if he had a completely clean slate with a whole new outlook for life, a renewed drive to accomplish many things, and to be the man he once dreamed he could be. Another adventure is awaiting for Mario and Betty, in a new place, with a new member, and a whole new set of challenges.

Thought Takeaways

What are the key messages that we can take from our story, Betty and Mario's healing journey reconciliation, renewing their hopes as a couple, establishing new goals for them as a project to become a healthy family, engaging their families with them, sharing the wisdom and peace that their new baby was giving them, and most of all, extracting a huge breath of fresh air with a very different landscape for their lives, both committed to really heal and become a different kind of family from the one they had?

I.   How can a reconciliation help couples to engage in a deeper relationship?

II. How does humility of your own wounds create empathy?

III. Can your baby's birth give you a new fresh start?

IV. Is it possible to create a new healed family?

V. How can you construct a resilient model for your new family?

Let's dive in.

———————————————————————————————

I. How a reconciliation helps couples to engage in a deeper relationship?

As we witnessed in our story, conflicts, separation, and struggles between the actors of any relationship often seem very similar, often are repeated, and many times start with a small event or spark that ignites the pain and the wounds that most of us are not aware until we see the mirror of our partner, until we come into account that the circumstances are similar, that the image flashes of something we already lived repeats. I would dare to say that more than 95 percent of the population suffered some type of neglectful, hurtful, and sometimes even traumatic experience during childhood either by their caregivers, any other member of the family, friends at school, teachers, etc. The odds are pretty high as we all move in environments that are cultivated under the roots of unawareness, ignorance, shame, guilt, selfishness, pride, narcissism, and egoistic behaviors that are self-perpetuated over and over, generation after generation. We are just witnessing some of these results all over the world; in many types of societies, with all kind of ethnicities, nationalities, languages, they are all bound by the same toxic behaviors.

However, in the best purpose and intention to solve once and for all many of these types of behaviors, we all have to become aware, enticed, and interested to know why they keep repeating; and ironically, they seem very similar across the globe.

The central difficulty with ordinary forms of systemic analysis, including conflict resolution systems design, is that they do not begin by prioritizing the emotional and affective significance of conflict within the relationship, nor are they grounded in heartfelt communication and are therefore not able to work well with the intimate, relational aspects of marital, couple, and family conflicts. These are deeply sensitive, highly complex emotional relationships that require an approach to conflict resolution systems design that is profoundly informed by the heart (Cloke 2015).

At the beginning of every marriage, there is attraction. Later, this often becomes "the story of how we met"–stories of serendipity, romance, and burgeoning love. But stories are not always factually accurate–rather they sacrifice factual for emotional accuracy. Moreover, there are ways that even romantic stories can distance people from each other, diminish their problem-solving capacity, and reduce their capacity for authenticity (Cloke 2015).

The rise of all those difficulties and struggles leads to a breakup point, where both parties of the relationship arrive at a decision point where there are just two options: end the relationship or have a space to breathe and align again.

However, what makes a successful reconciliation more prone to last and hopefully to sustain over time? Even of course, with the possibility of having more discussions or arguments that will be eventually initiated by again some small disagreements that touch some past wound?

As we saw in our story of Betty and Mario's reconciliation, there were some key behaviors that made them, at least for the time being, able to be in a better place, able to have a much enlightened outlook of the future, and also able to overcome some of the challenges that probably seemed more threatening than they really were.

First of all, as we discussed in chapter 5, the commitment of both of them to heal and to own their past wounds was a very solid beginning that allowed them to have a better insight of why they reacted in some unconscious manner toward each other, that healing path of going deep to the meaning of the experience that marked them and allowed them to be able to raise an awareness, to become empathic with their parents' history and also their wounds, to realize that they were not treated badly on purpose but because there was an underlying program in their parents' brain and behaviors.

Second, both of them communicated all of their wounds to someone—in Mario's case, he was supported by a coach; in Betty's case, it was a well-prepared (could also be called a professional) friend that also had experience in helping people and being deeply committed to learn techniques to help couples. Moreover, as we saw in Mario's healing journey, he even shared some letters of his recovery sessions with Betty, with a lot of details that allowed Betty to replicate one of the techniques used by the coach, in addition to giving her a whole different perspective of Mario's childhood issues that allowed her to understand him better.

Third, they both had a new purpose to improve their own self, but also, they established new boundaries and expectations that were now clearer and had a benefit for both of them as a family, orienting their efforts to stop the self-replication patterns that they "inherited" from their parents. They had a lot more information clues and reasons that allowed them in the end to develop a much peaceful awareness path toward detecting their own faults or opportunity areas.

II. How does humility of your own wounds create empathy?

Being humble in a relationship is more important than anybody would think so, and to clarify, being humble doesn't mean you don't have boundaries or you are submissive. It just means to be able to recognize your own wounds, triggers, mistakes as well as being able to relate to your partner's pain, wounds, mistakes without being harsh or rude about them.

This ability is something that has been diluting over time with overemphasis on defending your voice, saying what you feel, and defending your rights. However, if you're not able to be humble in your relationship, you certainly will be overstepping the voice, the rights, and the wounds of your partner; and that will ironically make you an abusive person.

During the journey of our story, we could appreciate how Mario experienced some feeling of humility when he was understanding his own pain, his own program and patterns of the wounds caused by his parents. During those moments of reflection, he could also relate to some moments or events of his relationship with Betty where he could now clearly see that he was abusive or had overstepped Betty's boundaries without noticing.

Betty's experience was similar when she started to read Mario's letters, as she found out all the pain, rejection, and of course, emotional abuse he suffered. She felt empathy for him and could understand better why sometimes during their relationship he reacted aggressive, angry, or just simply looked for comfort in drugs.

Tangney (2005) proposed five factors that make up humility: realistic appraisal of one's own limitations, openness to new ideas, viewing one's abilities and accomplishments from a broad perspective, other-focus, and valuing all things. Davis and others (2011) consolidated the definition of relational humility to three aspects: an accurate view of the self, a modest portrayal of oneself to others, and an interpersonal stance that is other-oriented rather than self-focused (Ripley 2016).

Based on research evidence, we can relate many of the characteristics of humility to a relationship environment; and if we applied some of these principles, we would be able to overcome our arguments or discussion in our relationships in an easier way, without being biased, to amplify the effect or the real reason of them.

And probably here many people would say, it's easier said than done; of course, everything is easier when you say it than when you do it. However, in order to succeed practicing humility in relationships, you have to be able to let your ego out of the equation. As discussed in chapter 5 takeaways, placing your ego in your relationships will often lead to overreacting to any argument, any emotion, and of course, that will trigger your partner as well as ending everything in one big fight that usually just drains the energy and conduces to resentment and anger in both sides.

However, if you are able for some moments to stop and be open to the point of view of your partner, if you expand your vision to what the other person is telling you, if you objectively analyze a request or an event, you most of the times will end up realizing that what the other person wanted was to help you and what the other person was telling you was his or her perspective and that it had nothing to do with what you were already creating in your mind due to your old beliefs and programs.

The more you're able to own your holes, wounds, and opportunity areas as an individual, the more empathic and understanding you will be. Or in other words, the more you get committed to knowing your reactions, triggers, and emotions, the more freedom and empathy you will create with your partner's wounds and story.

Perceived humility is positively associated with relationship satisfaction among intimate partners. Estephan (2007) found that viewing one's spouse as having a humble self-focus correlated with marital satisfaction while perceiving too much self-focus was found to be characteristic in distressed couples–marital satisfaction was related to the individual's healthy self-focus (Ripley 2016).

Among intimate partners, perceived humility of the partner is associated with a willingness to forgive the partner's transgressions within the relationship and decreased avoidance and revenge (Davis et al. 2011). These findings, coupled with previous research on the virtues associated with humility, suggest that humility contributes to social bonds reciprocally between individuals within their relationship (Ripley 2016).

Many times relationships can turn into a game of counting each other's faults, transgressions, or discussions; and keeping that kind of score just shows that you're letting your ego act out as "it is being offended" and you can't let that happen, therefore you start developing a sense of revenge, a feeling that you will be more vigilant of the other behavior or you will be obsessively looking for the other person to make a mistake so you can point out that you're the "good of the movie" letting the mistake pass or forgiving "without complaining" when in fact you were just being obsessed about what the other was going to miss or fail in order to get back from the last time he/she hurt you, said anything to you, or he/she just made a mistake.

Those kind of "ball games" of keeping score of the mistakes, discussions, or things that happen in a relationship will only lead to a buildup environment of stress that will eventually explode on both sides, hurting both parties involved.

That's why humility of being more concentrated on your own life and understanding objectively the circumstances that can be presented sometimes in everyday situations will automatically create confidence and a sense of empathy in your partner, allowing more space to be rational and conscious to look for a solution and not looking for someone to blame. Practicing this kind of humble approach in your relationship not only will create freedom for you, but it will also help you to be more accountable for your own mistakes, triggers, and wounds.

III. Can your baby's birth give you a new fresh start?

The opinions and real effects of the birth of a child in any couple relationship can have multiple effects. However, these effects have nothing to do with the baby per se; it has a lot to do with the stability that the couple had before the child, the attachment patterns that they had with their own caregivers, and the ability to couple the new responsibilities and schedules with their previous dynamics.

All couples that are faced with the challenge of having a new member of the family will have an increase in stress due to the demands of the child, mostly during the first year, while a new dynamic setting is being established as well as the lack of time to engage in couple activities that were common before, such as very simple things like going to the movies, having dinner, or just peacefully watching TV, or reading a book. However, many of these challenges will fail to become a stressful situation if couples have enough maturity, previously they didn't have a hectic social life, or simply they are just committed to maintaining priorities in their new dynamic, meaning they should be able to keep the other person in the loop. Mostly this happens with mothers that for obvious reasons are more focused on the needs of the child, but sometimes forgetting they have a partner to pay attention to, without of course feeling an obligation or overwhelm with all the new activities that will be piling up in their lives.

The transition to parenthood is a stressful time (Rossi 1968) in which couples must renegotiate their roles as partners and new parents. As a result of this stress, the attachment system activates (Rholes et al. 2001), and parents begin to display attachment-related behaviors that likely impact their own and their partner's relationship commitment. The activation of the attachment system induces comfort-seeking feelings and behaviors. Avoidant individuals seek comfort in solitude and withdraw from their relationship during times of stress (Feeney and Noller 1990). Thus, they may experience (a) decreases in their confidence due to their reliance on themselves for comfort and their diminished need for partner support, leading to the devaluing of the relationship's future; (b) decreases in their dedication, due to their preoccupation with comforting themselves rather than fostering their relationship; and (c) increases in their felt constraint, due to a conflict between their desire to withdraw from the relationship and their new parenting responsibilities. Avoidant mothers may be more susceptible to increases in felt constraint because women shoulder a greater share of the child care and housework burden after the child's birth (Ferriby 2015).

We all have seen how the ones with children have experienced this kind of stress levels raised during the transition to parenthood, and as mentioned before, the result of how you handle those new stress levels or your success in coupling those new demands from the child, from the economic point of view or from the availability of time, will be directly related to your attachment pattern. If you are a person that has a pattern of avoidance whenever you are faced with a stressful situation, you will tend to literally run or cover up your isolation pattern with the fact that you have many responsibilities that have nothing to do with parenting. This is more likely a male behavior, where they find an easy way out by justifying the workload with not being present during the child demands or sometimes even completely making up a new promotion, new traveling schedule, or any other kind of work-related demands in order to avoid the responsibilities of parenthood. However, this can also be present in women that used to have a very busy work schedule, and this will have a much more profound effect in the attachment pattern that the child can develop in the future, as the child needs more the mother figure mostly due to the breastfeeding schedules, demands, and the bond that is formed between the mother and the child. Moreover, there's a strong hormonal link between mother and child in this aspect that we will later discuss more deeply, which is the effect of oxytocin in the neural and emotional development of the child.

What would then be the best approach to fuel the relationship when a child is born? And take it as a new start instead of just letting the new responsibilities, schedules, and child demands to completely disrupt the relationship bond.

Both schedules will be disrupted, both partners are being affected, and here is where the humble approach can allow you to shift those new stress levels into fuel to become a better partner and a better parent for your child if you aim to see this new parenthood reality as an opportunity to grow, as an opportunity to demonstrate to your partner that you will be with her even with all the stressful situations that she will be facing also as a new mom, and on purpose I'm referring here to the mothers because it is pretty obvious that the burden of demands will at least double for them in terms of the breastfeeding and attention demands that the baby will have. However, you can be a different father figure, helping with changing diapers, helping with bathing your child, helping with any other domestic chores that you can, and push yourself to organize your schedule in order to at least lower the stress from some of the angles where you can impact. That kind of approach, without expecting recognition (but of course, women, it is highly appreciated if you give it), will allow your partner to feel safe, to lower her stress levels, and that will in fact help your child to develop a less anxious or demanding behavior from you and be more at peace because at least for the first three years of development and for a good period of time, the hormones and emotional state of the mother will deeply impact the emotional state of the baby not only for her first years but also for many of her adult life.

Thus, it is a win-win situation—if you both step up as a different model of parenthood, you both will have an easier time during this transition, and along the way during the first years, that will be decisive in forming neural connections, emotional patterns of attachment, and confidence in your own child. Moreover, if you really behave as team players in this parenthood challenge, you will both benefit from it, and you will succeed in lowering the stress levels in your family environment.

IV. Is it possible to create a new healed family?

Oftentimes we feel trapped in a movie that seems to be an "updated" version of many behaviors, scenarios, and even dialogues that we already witnessed as children because we have a strong reinforcement of many emotions, attitudes, and of course toxic examples that we are so afraid to repeat that we end up doing many of the mistakes that we once promised we were never going to repeat. Nevertheless, there's another possibility, another option, and certainly there are many other choices that we could start to consciously produce in our lives; it is just a matter of deciding to do it.

If we feed the recently discussed paradigm of taking the birth of our child as commitment to do a better job than the one we received, we will certainly find motivation in doing so, just by the amazing surprises, the wondrous surprises that our child will give us; and just being open and receptive to all the love and energy that she or he will generate in us will be enough to start giving you the first ingredients to create a new healed beginning, to really start modeling a new family setting just like the one we would have wanted.

And be careful here in not trying to force or to use your child as the "experiment" to cure your emotional wounds or fulfilling the dreams you "never" could have achieved because that road will only take you and your child to live a frustrating model that will eventually end in another version of the previous movie you were trying to avoid.

As we experience our environment and learn new skills, neurons connect in a web, or network, forming intricate ensembles-neural circuitry, as it were, that underlie our perceptions, memories, behaviors, and habits (Childre 2000).

It is a matter of taking the attention from those old patterns in order to be able to dissolve them, engage in rewriting them, start creating new healthy choices, and always maintaining your consciousness to be able to catch yourself when the old pattern wants to arise.

Building a nurturing environment where you also have people around you that will enable you to be aware of the thoughts, attitudes, behaviors that you want to follow and detect the toxic ones can be also a very helpful solution to support the new model that you want to give your child.

If we take our story as the example, Betty and Mario have the perfect people to create that environment; Betty has her friend Karen, and Mario can rely on Liam to cultivate that mind-set of a new model.

The social environment that we decide to surround ourselves with will be the perfect "mixing pot" where we are going to generate healthier or, again, toxic behaviors. Therefore, you also have to be very conscious of what kind of people you want to be surrounded with and what kind of friendships then for your child you want to cultivate. Our social environments account for more than 50 percent of the behaviors, attitudes, and of course, thoughts that we are allowing to enter in our family environment.

Therefore, it is very important to be aware of the type of emotions that you want your children to be surrounded with. Whenever you have some challenges outside of your house, either in your job, family, or any other friends and you don't have a better emotional state, what can be a good option for you is that you start practicing some type of meditation or inner reflection right before the interaction with your children so that you don't transmit those emotions to them or you become an easy prey to be triggered by some minor incident.

Keeping and sustaining a healthy environment inside your family is a big challenge, most of all due to the amazing amount now of information and toxic media that all the other people that is around you will be filling you as the day goes by; that's why including a spiritual practice that allows you to cope with those kind of emotions is the easiest way to purify your emotions.

The difference between the past experiences, the way your parents treated you, and the opportunity that nowadays you have is, ironically, the access to information that will help you to awaken to a new state of consciousness, where you are more able to control your impulses and diminish the reaction that you might have or, even better, you could start working toward completely avoiding to be in a reactive state.

Moreover, creating that new paradigm of a healed family is complemented by allowing yourself to form a team with your partner as mentioned in the humility approach, discussed in question number 2 of this chapter. The more you're able to share your household chores, the demands of your job, and the interaction with your family in the best possible way to give each of the partners a good balance and agreement, the easier it will be to achieve that healed family and the easier your life will be as well.

V. How can you construct a resilient model for your new family?

Most couples, even when they have a perfectly planned pregnancy, during the transition to parenthood and without sometimes noticing have a tendency to increase the stress in their lives; this is due to all the factors discussed above that will impact the couple's dynamic and schedules. However, if you are able to manage some of those factors and create an environment where the stress and social environment is contained and even diminished, where of course the political family is included, then you will be able to cope with a smoother transition during your parenthood.

The different social background, attachment patterns, and even some "trivial" customs can disrupt the education and behavioral image that parents want to give the child; therefore, it is of paramount importance that the more you can have a very clear communication with your in-laws and the more you proactively discuss all the possible scenarios where they might meddle and establish your own rules as a couple and as a new family, the stronger your inner education and behavioral system for your child will be and the outlook of your relationship will become.

New parents are often unaware of these potential problems and can be surprised by the postnatal difficulties that emerge in their relationships. After the birth of a child, parents are also at increased risk for depression, stress, and declines in psychological well-being, in part because of the additional demands on time, adjustment to new identities and roles, and lack of sleep that can accompany having a child. When parents are unhappy in their relationship with each other, it often impedes their ability to parent effectively (Gambrel 2014).

According to interpersonal neurobiology, children's development is affected by whether or not they receive attunement from their caregivers. Attunement is a process whereby people connect deeply with others' emotional states, see their perspectives, and then respond sensitively and effectively to their needs. If early relationships are characterized by interpersonal attunement, then the neural pathways in the brain develop into a complex web of integration across regions and spheres, leading to increased capacities for empathy, self-awareness, coping with stress, and processing information. Research supports this in that the hippocampus–the part of the brain associated with managing stress and emotion regulation–is larger in children with supportive mothers even when controlling for social and economic factors (Gambrel 2014).

Attunement is equally important for adult relationships. The health and longevity of couple relationships are influenced by the mutual attunement abilities of partners to each other. Psychoeducation that focuses on promoting four aspects essential to attunement: presence (being aware in the present moment), clear perception (the ability to take another's perspective), emotional resonance (feeling another's feelings), and effective action (responding in a way that another can receive as sensitive and caring) (Gambrel 2014).

As mentioned by research and also emphasized above, you and your partner should be able to understand each other's emotions; the more sense of emotional resonance you have with your partner and you abide to the humility model highlighted above, the easier it will be for you to support each other for the common front that you have to create for your child. If as a couple you reflect support, emotional understanding, congruency between what you say and do, the first years of your child's development will be less threatened by confusing models. Children during the first years are completely based on mirroring the behavior that parents have, whether they notice or not, and it is not a matter of competing for who can do the best job or who is more successful in some areas than the other. In this ground is more about complementing each other's lack or abilities to better function as team, as a strong model for your child.

If you are almost completely aligned with your partner and your child sees that example, then that will give her/him a much solid security, personality, and confidence outlook to be reflected on.

The same will happen when you are faced with discussions, arguments, or any kind of set boundaries that you previously discussed with your partner; and the fact that in any social or family gathering that can be disrupted, if you give in to the social pressure and you modify your behavior just for the fact of "social image" or avoiding conflict with anyone outside from you and your couple that is also perceived by your child as a mixed signal of behavior, then that, of course, repeatedly will cause confusion or, worse, give an image to your child that in social situations, rules don't apply or they can be bended to others' will. Sounds harsh or strict, but the more consistency that you have, the more respect that you give to your partner in front of anyone, the easier the mirror it will be for your child to follow. Additionally, congruency and coherence between you and your partner is the strongest bond you can form because that will also impact your partner's confidence to feel supported no matter where or with whom you are.

Many "small incidents" or discussions can be deviated to a more threatening situation, when you don't consider that contradicting or diminishing the image of your partner in front of other people is a major factor of distress, as those incidents can't be resolved during the social situation. The stress generated in a social interaction with family or friends will be accumulated and internalized, creating a toxic emotion that will be building up until it finds an outlet, which, in general, will be a much stronger discussion or argument than it really is. Therefore, try to abide by what you previously agreed with your partner, be consistent with the type of behavior you want your child to be guided upon, and above all, create that connection with your partner that allows you to feel supported, to feel that the first line of decisions is taken by you and your partner, and any kind of recommendation or suggestion needs to be discussed with each other before taking any kind of action.

Moreover, be aware and careful in addressing any situation that might be left pending or you don't feel comfortable with, faking an agreement just to be polite with others, which in the long term will lead you to generate resentment and grudge toward your partner when, in fact, the one that is denying the ability to express the disagreement or dissatisfaction is yourself.

CHAPTER 7

The Clearest and Toughest Mirror: Your Child

WE LEFT OFF with our story right before Betty was discharged from the hospital, Mario's excitement for a new life, and a whole new beginning for them as a family.

Focusing on Parenting without Forgetting Your Partner

Mario went to pick Betty up from the hospital. He already had everything prepared at home, as he had everything fixed in the new apartment for the baby to come. He had already bought a bassinet and a crib for the child's room, and he also fixed some painting that the apartment needed and put Betty's things out of the boxes and shut them up in a closet because with all the rush when the baby was going to be born, there was no time to do all those things.

However, during the time Betty was in the hospital, he hurried up and finished everything so that Betty and now the baby could have a nice welcoming home.

When Betty arrived at the apartment, she was really surprised at how Mario had put everything together, as well as making time to welcome them. Her face was so happy that she shed some tears of joy. Mario thought she wasn't feeling good, but Betty clarified that. "Wow, Mario, you really made some effort with the apartment! It was just a few days ago that we left everything in boxes and it was a little dirty, but now it looks like a brand-new home. Thank you for being so thoughtful for me and the baby."

Mario just said, "It's the least I could do, Betty, as you have given me my place with your family and decided to come to our house instead of accepting the help, they were going to give you. Before everything happened, I was really nervous about becoming a dad, most of all because of these moments that we're about to share. But now that we're together, I realize that I have more positive emotions and expectations that everything will turn out to be just fine, that I didn't even have the time to be nervous at all. Haha, isn't that ironic?"

Betty just smiled, and she told Mario that she needed to feed the baby because some time has passed since her last meal. Right after finishing her sentence, the baby started to cry, so they just laughed about the timing and how she already knew what she needed without too much effort.

While Betty was feeding the baby, they started to discuss about possible names for her. They hadn't done that before because they didn't want to create too much anxiety into knowing the gender, so they left everything for the time that she would be born. Even the traditional baby shower that was organized prior to the birth, they agreed with Betty's family and friends that they were going to do it after the birth.

Mario had some names in mind, as he was the one who presumed the baby was going to be a girl, so he started telling Betty the possibilities, which were three: Solange, Megan, or Vilma. Betty stayed silent for some minutes. She was looking at the baby and at her eyes, and she repeated the names to her in a soft voice while she was feeding. When the name Vilma was pronounced, she smiled and kept feeding so that was the chosen name then. Betty just said "Vilma."

Mario agreed, as he liked that name more; that's why he left it at the end. They both hugged for a while and repeated the name to the baby. After Vilma stopped feeding, they were both curious with the meaning of the name, so they looked up the meaning and found that it was "determined protector, born intelligent and powerful, you'll do well in life, and agile." Thus, those were enough reasons to start liking the name even more. Additionally, Betty and Mario's last names were long, therefore she would be better off with a short name. Betty's last name was González; Mario's, Lizarraga.

Right after they agreed on the name and Vilma had fed, Betty started to close her eyes and Mario was also a bit tired from all the excitement of the first day at home, so they decided to fall asleep while they could as they both knew that Vilma had some three to four hours of sleep before the next meal. The nurses and medical interns had already warned Betty about the strong character of Vilma when she wasn't fed almost when she asked for it.

Betty and Mario's journey was going just fine, trying to get along with the schedules, Vilma's demands, and regular house chores that mostly Betty knew how to deal with. However, Mario was having a bit of a hard time, as he was used to being attended and mostly everything was taken care of in his parents' house and they had the money to pay for house help and maids. Therefore, he was getting pretty tired with the house chores. In addition to that, Betty's mom and one of his father's sisters that was very excited about Vilma wanted to help and to meet her, starting to push a little bit to help Betty by inviting her to go to her parents' house for a weekend and just have some help. That invitation, plus Mario's mood due to the chores, started to create tension between them, which Vilma at her very young age was already feeling and complaining about. How could she notice that? Easy. She started to develop some rash on her skin because she felt that there was some tension between her parents, and of course, in addition to that, she was in a crankier mood when she was hungry.

Political Family Interference

Betty accepted the invitation to go to her parents' house for the weekend. Mario was there too, but he was not comfortable at all, mainly because Betty's aunt was prying into how they were taking care of the baby. She was giving a lot of natural remedies for Vilma's rash, asking a lot of suggestions on how to tuck her in, how to bathe her, etc. Mario was just listening, but he was not at all happy with all the prying behavior of the aunt.

Betty could perceive Mario's mood and how he was getting upset about so much "attention and overprotection." To make everything more complicated, Betty's dad and her mom were already suggesting different names for the baby as they didn't really like Vilma and they hadn't officially registered her yet.

Therefore, Betty approached Mario, and they went to the bedroom to talk. Mario was angry because that's what he wanted to avoid by living with them even if it were just for a short period for time. Betty understood Mario's mood, though she just told him that it was a weekend and she was not going to give in again and accept future invitations if the snoopy aunt is present because she didn't like how they were meddling in their decisions as parents. Those advices and the way of prying by her aunt reminded Betty how this aunt, in her "naïve" but snoopy way of acting and being, had caused a lot of problems between her dad and mom.

"She used to talk bad of my mom, turn my dad against my mom, and also advising me in excess on what to do, how to behave, so that's why I was not surprised of what she did, but I didn't think that my dad would invite her knowing that I never had a good relationship with her."

Mario was glad that Betty understood and also didn't like that degree of control again; he didn't suffer that experience himself of having a meddling political family, but he knew about the toxic environments that could be created by family as his mother suffered a lot from that, and actually as a result of that kind of environment she had developed her addiction for alcohol that she could never give up; it was just controlled for some periods of time. When Mario was a child, he suffered a lot of indifference, sometimes blame, and of course, emotional deprivation from her mom.

As both Betty and Mario suffered from those environments directly or indirectly, as soon as they saw what was happening with the snoopy aunt, they decided to leave first thing in the morning from the house of Betty's parents.

Meanwhile, as all children, Vilma was perceiving the surroundings, observing her parents, but she was also starting to show some signs of her strong character by deciding what people she was comfortable with and who she didn't feel as comfortable as she would.

There's an old saying that only drunks and children say the truth, but there's ancient scientific facts that children have heightened senses such as the olfactory and perception of vibes. As young as Vilma was, just one month old, she already perceived and sensed very differently from other babies, which made Mario and Betty a little worried of how she would express her feelings about a person or even how she reacted when listening to the name they were going to give her.

Therefore, they tried to look up or ask their trusted friends if they have ever heard about that, or if they knew any baby that reflected those strong insights of people. Mario turned to Liam, who was the only one he trusted and had helped him to figure out what he wanted with Betty, and Betty on her side relied on Karen to discuss the same concerns and perceptions that they both had.

Let's start with Mario's experience when he talked with Liam. First of all, he was tremendously happy about all the news and in fact they were going to see each other in the –baby shower that Betty had planned, but Mario was a little concerned of Vilma's reactions and couldn't hold on for that party. Thus, Liam started by saying, "Well, Mario, you just keep amazing me on how you have turned your life completely from what I know from you, your past, and you truly surprised me with the news of the engagement, the baby, and everything. Now you're from the club of fathers, ahah." Mario laughed, and of course, he thanked Liam for his words.

"I know, Liam, I never thought also I could turn my life just like it has been the past few months. Actually, I had another relapse, but it's not even worth mentioning again. What is worth mentioning is that I'm recovered, and it has been two amazing months since I left the rehabilitation clinic where I had an amazing wellness program, which completely changed my lifestyle. That's why I also lost a good amount of weight and gain a lot of confidence and knowledge of why I did many of the stupid decisions, such as drugs or engaging in fleeting relationships. that's why Betty and I finally are on the right track."

"I'm really glad for you, Mario. You really deserve that, as I was a far witness of all the toxic environment you grew up with. So, what do I owe the honor this time of your visit?"

Childhood Awareness and Smoothing Couple's Interaction

"Well, Liam, Betty and I have been having some concerns about our baby, Vilma. Even at her young age, one month, she has presented some 'strange' behavior, sort of saying. There's nothing wrong with her, it's just that she's extremely aware of her environment and she has an amazing capacity to perceive the mood of others near her."

"Wow, that sounds interesting as you said strange. Tell me more please."

"Well, just last week, we were in my in-laws' house, trying first to interact a little bit with Betty's family as well as accepting an invitation from her parents because they were a little worried for all the burden of new chores and duties for becoming new parents. However, every family has its perks, ironically saying, and Betty's family had an aunt that is very prying into other people's lives and way of doing things. However, during that weekend, we noticed that Vilma was very reluctant to be approached or left alone with Betty's aunt. She also did that with Betty's father, just before we came to their house. Vilma had been fine and almost completely healthy, just a small rash on her tummy and buttocks, but we asked her pediatrician, and he told us that she was just having a normal reaction to clothes and the soap. So, we followed his instructions, and she was just fine.

"However, when Vilma was around the aunt from Betty's father side, we could notice that her rash was getting worse even though nothing else was changing because we were using the same soap to bathe her. Another incident was her facial expression around them and the fact that a month ago when we were deciding her name, Betty did this exercise with her by mentioning names, sort of like whispering to her and when she said Vilma, she drew a big smile in her face, and that's why we chose that name."

"Wow, Mario, I've never heard such stories of babies at such a young age. However, now that you mention it, I remember a friend from childhood that had a sister, and I always find her strange and a little bit isolated from the others. She liked to read science books and science fiction since she was very young, around seven years old, and she had a very acute sense of perception similar to what you mention with Vilma. She used to freak out with people that for us kind of seemed normal, but who after some time acted different and, in the end, turned out to be very mean and aggressive children.

"Thus, what my friend and I did for a good while was take her to important events where we could use her 'sixth sense' and her accurate perception with people. Additionally, she was very smart, but she had some issues to relate with people. She felt really misunderstood and rejected."

"Oh my god, Liam, I guess we'll have to wait and be very careful with Vilma and the social interactions that we have, but I think she might turn out to be like the girl you're describing."

"Right now, there's still nothing to do as you say, Mario, but keep an eye on her behavior and also try to see if she's faster and smarter in developing some behavior."

On the other side, Betty visited Karen, and she also explained the same incidents to her about Vilma. Karen was very surprised as well, and in her case, she didn't know any person that had a child with those abilities. But fortunately, she had read something about those kinds of heightened-perception skills, as she had experienced some similar things with her daughter, just not that strong and neither on that early stage.

Therefore, she mentioned something to Betty about children that are born with those special abilities. They used to name them "indigo" children, so she started chatting about what she read although the information was too general. She told Betty that these children have higher perception skills that allowed them to perceive with stronger, keen senses their surroundings—the tone of voice, the smell of people, and even as esoteric as it may sound, the vibrational mood of people, which pretty much by now covered what Betty experienced with Vilma. Karen had a good energy to calm down Betty, and she also was a reliable source; therefore, that left Betty at peace and able to start discussing about the baby shower, which, of course, involved Karen.

Mario and Betty came back with a deeper understanding from each of their friend's point of view, and they discussed the information to decide if they were going to do something or if they will just allow more time for Vilma to grow and, of course, still keep an eye on those behaviors from her.

Everything was getting easier to get along although Betty was having some issues regarding Mario's behavior in terms of the mess he left in the house, not helping to pick up his things, and when taking care of Vilma, leaving a complete mess of the house. She was tired and in addition to that was starting to get a little worried for the expenses, Mario's contribution, or his future decisions. She only had one more month to come back to her job and time flew really fast, so she spoke with Mario and asked him to start applying what they said at the reconciliation dinner about having time of at least every two weeks to discuss important matters that they were worried about or that they might fix to have a better communication and less arguments, more now with Vilma and of course with all the changes that both had in such a short span of time. As a result of that little chat, the first talking meeting was scheduled for the following week.

Although to Betty's eyes Mario didn't seem to be doing anything, he was already thinking of asking his father for money, but handling it as a kind of loan, to buy a car and start working as an Uber driver while he is also engaged with his school and continue with his plans. He was also noticing that Betty was not in the best mood, so he also was looking forward to talk about all the possible issues that they might have and fix them before they started to grow and become more complicated.

Vilma was also adapting to the dynamic with her parents; she didn't show any "strange" behaviors lately, but she was indeed a superperceptive baby. Betty was more aware of that as the emotions from the mother at this stage are easier to be shared, to have an impact in the child, and to build a bridge of connection that is exclusive of them. That doesn't mean that fathers don't possess those abilities; it's just more powerful for women due also to the breastfeeding span, where they are still exchanging a lot of nutrients and hormones from the mother.

Well, finally the first talking meeting arrived for them, and they were a little nervous on how to handle it as they had never done something like that, but Betty's obsessive compulsive behavior to make things right, traceable, and impactful saved them although it made it a little bit too intense for Mario's character.

Betty started to talk. She had a notebook where she wrote the bullet points she wanted to discuss and also keep track of the important things, dates, and be able to have a follow up on what they agreed. Therefore, she explained that to Mario. "Okay, Mario, as this is our first meeting, I wanted to propose to you that I will be writing my discussing points in this notebook, tracing important things of the answers as well as important dates, and maybe we can post a calendar in the fridge so we are both aware of our next meeting and maybe two to three important things to be reminded of. What do you think?"

Mario didn't know if he was feeling afraid of her intense tracking device or if he was glad to finally have some structure, so he just answered, "That's fine for me, Betty. I just wouldn't like these meetings to become stressful, but I agree that we need something to be able to follow up on them."

Betty said, "I don't expect them to be stressful, Mario, but I do expect to have commitment to them for both, as I firmly believe these kinds of tools will help us have more communication and be able to handle issues in an easier way. Actually, Mario, I learned this from your letters of the process you followed at your rehabilitation clinic, so if they do that there to improve such challenging issues for addiction, that should be a good approach to help couples have more stability and guidance, so don't worry, it will be just like taking your sessions at the clinic. Well, Mario, let's begin because Vilma's wake-up time is about to come and I will be with her, I don't want to talk about these things near her."

"Okay, Betty, shoot!"

"Okay, Mario, first of all, I would like to say that these past months that we have had, of course, a lot of contact, which is different from what we used to have even before you went off to the clinic, I have observed a pattern in you that I don't think I will be comfortable with, and it is the mess that you have with your things and cleaning of the house. It seems that you were very used to people helping you, and of course, that made it difficult for you to realize that here, we don't have that kind of help, so I would really appreciate if you're more careful with your clothes or with Vilma's things when you are in charge of her. I'm really grateful that you are doing an effort to help with her, to change diapers as well as bathing her sometimes. However, please help pick up the mess. You might not understand why this bothers me so much, but let me explain why I'm very tired, first for the short spans of time that I have to sleep, second because of the energy that Vilma takes from me in terms of breastfeeding, which by the way is a painful process, and third because I also have to clean the house including the things you leave all over. So for this first point, what's your opinion?"

Mario was kind of mixed up. First, he was a little bit angry to be honest; then with the more detailed explanation, he could empathize more with Betty so he said, "You're right, Betty. Another bad habit that I picked up from my house is that I always had help for any house chores, so it's difficult for me to adapt to this new environment, but I'll do it in the best way I can because I really would like to see a happier face in you. Don't get me wrong, now I understand why you have been so moody or sometimes angry."

"Thanks, Mario, I know it must be hard for you to pick up your own mess, but that's the way most people live. In that aspect, you were very fortunate that your father had so much money to have a person help in your house all the time. Before I move on to my next point, how can I tell you in the best possible way that you're doing it again? Just give a simple signal that you can pick up."

Mario said, "Hmm, let me think, maybe you can put on my side of the bed some of the clothes that I'm leaving around so I can get that I'm doing it again."

"That's fine for me, I will just leave on the floor on your side of the bed so you pick them up and put them where they belong. Okay, my next point is our expenses. I know that I thought I was going to be able to pay everything with my salary and told you that you were going to be able to dedicate to your school, but seeing the reality these past months, it might not be enough, so could you think of something that you could do to help with some money, maybe just the food and services of the house while you finish your degree?"

"Yes, Betty, actually I already thought about that, and I asked my father for a loan, sort of, to buy a car and start working as an Uber driver while I take some subjects at school as well. That's the easiest way to earn money and keep the school in addition to be able to pick up Vilma from the nursery when she goes there because I suppose she will be there in probably the next month, right?"

"That's fine, Mario, I really appreciate you worrying about the money issue before I told you. About Vilma's care, I guess it would be best to send her to a nursery even though I know it will be hard for me to do it, but I prefer that than your mom or mine to take care of her, I sometimes believe that children from school have at least less family patterns permeated to them although there's always the risk that in the school, they'll have a hard time, but we don't really have too much choices. So yes, she will go to a nursery soon.

"My third point and last one is about us. I really believe and I saw with some of my older friends at work that when they had a child, they completely forgot about their husband, which, for most of them, brought them a lot of issues, fights, and discussions. You and me grew up in a 'hostile' environment in terms of the bond that our parents had, and neither of us want to repeat the history. So I was thinking—and this is something I will propose to Karen, of course, and maybe you also can speak with Liam, which I guess are the two people we trust the most and both of them have helped us—if they can take care of Vilma on a Friday afternoon and part of the night or Saturday.

"During those hours, we could have some time for ourselves to keep being a couple, have fun, and not fall in the monotony of most of couples, which I think leads to a disaster little by little because each person starts becoming self-involved in his/her dynamic, either with work duties or child-related issues, until the two people involved are just strangers living in the same house and sharing parenthood, but they are no longer a couple. It was so sad, listening to some of my friends, who are women and men, complain about those monotonous days that they had, asking them about their weekend and seeing that the only words they would produce were, 'Ugh, pretty much the same as others.' I don't want that future for us, Mario. I want to be a different kind of couple, where we really have time for us, even if it's one afternoon per week and maybe after, we're able to find a nanny who could help us with Vilma, and have some short trip for us to relax, to maintain the concept of couple, and to be able to share more than talks of diapers, food supplies, or household chores."

Mario was very surprised that Betty touched on that topic and was concerned about that because he had the idea that they were going to fall into those standard couples, who just talked about children, house, and education issues and stopped being lovers, partners, and sharing their passions and future endeavors.

Therefore, Mario's words were just, "Thank you, Betty, I really appreciate and value your concerns for being a couple and having time for us and not just for parenthood. Don't get me wrong, but due to the background that you had and the patterns that you saw, I thought it was going to be more difficult to break that idea for you, which of course now you're proving me wrong! So, count me in, I will be completely involved in making those plans happen. I would certainly talk with Liam in our next baby shower event and start finding out if he can support us in the future."

"Thanks, Mario, I would really appreciate that so we can have at least two choices to rely on and, of course, from people we completely trust."

"Well, now is your turn to start telling me what you have felt or any important points that you would like to discuss."

"Thanks, Betty, I just have two things. First, I would like you to support me as I know you will do in terms of having more strict schedules for our responsibilities with Vilma or with house chores because as you know, I will continue pursuing my degree and combine that with the Uber business, but

I'm guessing that I will need to be very strict in the time that I dedicate for studying, reading, or school stuff."

"Of course, Mario, if you want. I think it is a great idea, maybe the activities that we share, such as Vilma's care or house chores, we can build a schedule/calendar so we are clear of the things that we agree on and respect those times off each other where we can dedicate time to read, study, or whatever we want."

"Sounds great, Betty, let's do that! My next point, which I believe now you will be on board, is that you and I start doing something for our nutrition, exercise, and probably we can add meditation to our activities to take care of each other. Since I was in the clinic experiencing those different activities, I felt really good. All those tools allowed me to quit my addictions, to have a very clear mind, to start looking after my body, and to worship all the things it does for me, having energy and a good mood to interact with people, which for me has always been an issue, as my childhood experiences together with the drugs threw me or let's say made a detour in my life several times to have either no friends or very toxic friends. I believe that if we replicate the environment that I experienced in the clinic, we'll be just fine. Of course, we will have our fights or discussions, but I'm thinking they will be much less in number and intensity. Plus, I don't ever want to fall again into any kind of addiction because I really want to do a good job as a husband and as a father for Vilma."

"I'm really surprised with your last suggestion, Mario, and of all the things you wanted to say, you didn't complain at all for my obsessive behaviors or my intensity to be neat and structured! That has been an issue many times for me, as my friends always saw me as the nerdy, strange woman that in addition of also not having too many friends, most of the time follow the right path–well, except for my weight, which I started to leave behind after my last breakup because the guy whom I was with was completely obsessed about my physical appearance, so I just couldn't resist the pressure. But with you now is different because I know you do it as a healthy habit and not as an exterior obsession. I'm really glad, Mario, seeing all those changes and above all I'm completely happy that you want to replicate the environment and maintain over time the results that you experienced. So count me in for your suggestions and I'll be happy to abide by our new routines as a couple, taking care of how we eat, exercise, and of course, I believe we can start practicing meditation although sometimes I might fall asleep while doing them, but eventually when Vilma starts sleeping more hours, I'll be better!"

"I'm not surprised that you were shocked with my suggestions, Betty, as I have given you more a bad image of myself than the healthy version of me that I now want to cultivate and become, and how can I complain about your obsessions or structure if I never had that? What I also learned in the clinic is that having a structure, having sort of rituals, helps you to follow a healthier path, to acquire habits, and of course to maintain them.

"During my sessions at the clinic, I probably never told you, but we had at least one talk per month with some of the wisest monks in a congregation. They give support to the clinic with meditation guidance and Buddhist principles to make your mind stronger and be able to avoid the temptations of falling into drugs again, so I really remember what those monks said about their activities, about giving the mind direction, and they are all structured in what they do in their days. I believe we all need that. Resistance to that is just a bad habit that we have acquired due to media and bad marketing that wants us to be more 'relaxed' or 'light' because in that way, most of the people will fall for the shortcut and the easy way out, which is what they really want! And I'm guessing that even with all your structure or obsessive behaviors, you like to have fun and we have had plenty of fun too! So, I'm okay with your 'issue'!"

Betty and Mario were really happy, and they completely bonded again. They closed the talk and continued with their lives and attending to Vilma's needs.

The next morning, Sunday, they were trying to agree on where and how to do the baby shower party that they'd postponed due to all the issues they both were dealing during Betty's pregnancy. So, they started a short list of close people that they wanted to invite; they wanted to keep it small, as they didn't have many friends and they both wanted to also clean their social network with people that could help them instead of just making a toxic environment. Therefore, they invited their parents and some friends from work of Betty's and, of course, their "healing partners" Karen and Liam.

The party was set for the next weekend. As a strategy, Betty invited her boss so he could also meet Mario and to also have him still on her side, as Betty was a little bit worried that after the party, the next week, she was going back to work.

The rest of the week went by pretty much without any highlights; everything was pretty common routines, with the only added stress that they had to get supplies for the party and Betty's stress level was rising due to the closeness of returning to her job and worrying about the schedules that they were going to have, but fortunately for her, Mario had been looking for a safe nursery where Vilma could stay and without Betty noticing he was really aware of the dates and how things were going to change.

The baby shower was ready, and finally they ended up having some help from Karen that had a party room where she lived that she could reserve, so everything was ready. Mario was a little nervous in meeting Betty's work friends and her boss and a little tense for Vilma's behavior, but people were already arriving. Betty was stressing out too much, and she was passing that stress to Vilma, who was inconsolably crying and giving Betty a hard time too. So Mario took Vilma and held her and took her out of the room to the garden. He tried to distract her with the trees, a little fountain that had lights on and off, and some of the nature around the party room. Vilma, after some minutes, calmed down, and Mario was also feeling better about meeting Betty's friends and boss, so they came back to the party.

Karen and Liam were helping Betty with serving people some snacks, and they also organized some simple games to entertain people. Betty was definitely not feeling well. She approached Mario and told him that she was a little dizzy. Mario took her out to the garden and stayed with her for some minutes while she took some deep breaths and started to feel a little better. Mario asked her, "What's happening, Betty? Why are you so stressed?"

She was going to answer when she couldn't contain her emotions and started to cry. "I really don't know, Mario. I just feel overwhelmed for everything that's happening too fast–Vilma, us living together, me getting back to my job and knowing my boss expects a lot from me, as he should remember our last talk where he opened up to me and told me that he really trusts in me. I'm also afraid of not being able to handle everything so I guess it's a mixed cocktail of emotions that I have inside. I'm really sorry that it happened today. We're supposed to be the hosts of this party, and we're all here in the garden, haha." Betty just started laughing at how everyone was having fun with games inside while the three main people of the party were outside having their first family breakdown!

"Well, Betty, it's really funny now that we see everyone there in our party and us here, so just be patient, be kind to yourself, it's completely normal what you're feeling. Everything will change for us, for you, for me, for Vilma. But guess what, you're not alone, we're a family, we will support each other, we will understand each other, even if it means sometimes being grumpy or overwhelmed. We're humans and sometimes we don't realize that we do need some break from everything and some pause in our lives. After being in the clinic during those months, I definitely understood the concept of having a pause, of grounding with yourself, and letting your feelings regain homeostasis again, so don't worry that the others are having fun inside because we're here fixing our family!

"During this months with you, after I left the clinic, I have also felt a lot of pressure, a lot of overwhelm, more because I don't feel that I am contributing as you are, but I'm also amazingly happy because I have a family of my own, something that I could never have experienced because even as having both of my parents with me, they were not physically there most of my life, they were not emotionally with me, they just believed their role with me, maybe providing me with the material aspect and fulfilling those needs, which I'm really grateful, but they left a huge space in terms of my emotional health and the sense of belonging to a family. I've always felt as a loner, excluded from many settings or events because I felt strange in social interactions, and I know now that it's due to all the past experiences I lived! So, it's time for us as a family to change our concepts and beliefs, even though sometimes we will feel social pressure, such as in these days."

"Thanks, Mario, I feel much better now. I'm amazed each day on how you've changed, your words now, and how you are handling the situation. It's completely different from the Mario I met before the rehab time, and of course, you're right—we are now a family, and we should start understanding each other with our ups and downs and allowing ourselves to have these kind of feelings where everything seems fuzzy, but in fact is just the speed of things happening and the lack of having pauses for us."

Vilma felt the vibes of her parents, and she started to feel really happy, even having a huge smile and asking to be held by her mom. That was the best indicator to know that they could change a stressful situation into a positive experience and generate a different kind of vibe!

Therefore, they returned to the party and started to interact with people. Betty took Mario by the hand and led him to where her boss was. She interrupted the talk he was having with some friends at work and said, "Charlie, I want to introduce you to Mario. He's my partner and the father of Vilma."

Charlie said, "Nice to meet you, Mario, it's a pleasure to finally have a face of the man that Betty talks about."

"Nice to meet you, Charlie, also my pleasure to know you, and I take the chance now to tell you that I really appreciate your understanding with Betty in all these series of events that certainly came very quickly, and for trusting her as a model employee."

"Nothing to thank, Mario. She earned her way in the company, worked exceptionally professional when we were having our first audit, and really proved to be a valuable asset for me and for the team during stressful moments. In fact, we're eager for her comeback next week!"

"Thanks, Charlie, she's also eager to come back to the office, and I assure you she will have my support to handle her new responsibilities in the future."

Betty was expressing a really comforting smile after seeing Charlie's face and the way he interacted with Mario. She was enjoying now the party and also introducing Vilma to everyone. So far, everything looked fine; however, there was a surprise planned by Karen and Liam. They had prepared a dance for the family, playing a song that Karen knew Betty loved since high school. That was something unusual for that kind of party, but ironically, it was a very good moment for the three of them to bond and be seen as the family they always wanted to have and be.

After the dance, everyone started to say goodbye. Karen had fixed for a person from the building to clean up the mess so Betty and Mario didn't have anything else to do. Betty and Mario gathered with Karen and Liam. They thanked them deeply and took the chance to tell them if they wanted to be godparents of Vilma. Of course, they very happy to have that responsibility for Vilma and were happy to accept.

So far, everything came out just right. Betty and Mario also said goodbye, and they left with Vilma deeply asleep. Betty and Mario were feeling strong, more confident that the next steps in terms of new activities for everyone in the family the next week were going to work. Now they were going to be faced with a more hectic, busy life together with the challenges that Vilma was going to bring to them.

Thought Takeaways

After witnessing another chapter in Mario and Betty's life, there are some very juicy takeaways that we can extract from the story:

I. How does parental emotions affect children?

II. How do you avoid family interference in your new family?

III. What are the characteristics and challenges when raising indigo or gifted children?

IV. How can you design a space for you as a couple to talk and process emotions?

V. What important factors influence new parenting duties and your life as a couple?

Let's dive in.

←——————————————————————————————→

I. How does parental emotions affect children?

Previously, in chapter 1, we discussed how your stress, discussions, and anger can affect the baby in terms of the hormone profile that moms generate when the baby is in the womb; however, now what to do after she's born, and how can you allow yourself to process your emotions without filling your child with them?

Everyday life, as it is lived currently, except for calm and quiet towns, has the challenge of being influenced, stressed, and many times triggered toward having a pretty good amount of emotional load, which of course children are more sensitive to react, to feel it, and even to transpire it, affecting their mood and, in more extreme cases, affecting their emotional or neural development.

Dunsmore and Halberstadt (1997) proposed that parents' beliefs about emotions and their emotionally expressive behavior work together to help children create their own self and world schemas about emotion. Gottman and colleagues similarly proposed that parents' beliefs and behaviors regarding emotion, that is, their "meta-emotion theories and coaching," affect important life outcomes for children (Dunsmore 2009).

Children at a certain age, such as below three years old and probably more, imitate a lot of emotions and reflect the behaviors of their parents. Emotions in the end are the chemical transpired reaction of our hormones inside the body; therefore, all those substances are in our skin, breath, and children are more sensible in their touch and olfactory sensations than we are. Their skin also is a lot thinner, and they immediately sense how we feel–if we're stressed, nervous, fearful, any type of feeling that we're coping with will be able to be perceived by them. That's why children of that age are more prone to be crying and are difficult to control when we as parents are not in the best mood and without noticing we're filling our surroundings with those kind of stress hormonal profiles.

How might hormones affect behavior? In terms of their behavior, one can think of humans and other animals conceptually as comprised of three interacting components: (1) input systems (sensory systems), (2) integrators (the central nervous system), and (3) output systems or effectors (e.g., muscles). Hormones do not cause behavioral changes. Rather, hormones influence these three systems so that specific stimuli are more likely to elicit certain responses in the appropriate behavioral or social context. In other words, hormones change the probability that a particular behavior will be emitted in the appropriate situation (Nelson 2011).

As stated by research, we don't change our behavior due to the hormones per se; however, if we start developing a profile, a buildup of certain hormones, we will be more likely to react differently to certain stimuli, and this phenomenon can certainly be witnessed in everyday life when we start watching an emotional, dramatic movie and afterward we are exposed to a certain kind of scene where the same feelings are elicited. We react very emotionally; we might even cry or become emotional in certain events that if we hadn't watched that movie, we wouldn't have been triggered by them.

If that happens to us as adults, imagine what happens to children that are constantly exposed to environments where certain types of emotional profiles are generated, such as stressed households, places where aggressive behavior is witnessed, or even as mentioned before, movies where you're not supposed to bring your baby inside, such as horror, sexual, or violent movies.

The environment is more important than we give credit for; moreover, nowadays, a lot of research studies are validating that we need to be aware of the environment we create in our lives and even more the surroundings we want to have for our children.

The more we want to engage in creating a new environment for them, the easier it will be for them to identify their emotions, to know how to process them, to learn a new path toward feeling complete and whole without the anxious need for approval or without the emotional denial where we grew up.

As depicted before in our story, whatever our parents did or didn't do when we were children, now is the opportunity to create a different future for our children, start being more informed about our own lacks and emotional needs, recognizing that we need to work on many issues and allow ourselves to make mistakes but also recognizing that correcting them will create a completely different setting for our children to grow.

II. How do you avoid family interference in your new family?

This is such a complicated and polemic issue that will most of the time be present in every relationship as the couple's parents are certainly involved in raising children; however, there should be a clear distinction between the newly formed family and the original family involvement. Moreover, establishing boundaries between the family's involvement and interaction with children is of paramount importance to avoid conflict between the couple, as depicted in our story with Betty and Mario; the political aunt that starts giving advice to Betty as well as judging how she takes care of Vilma clearly shows why those boundaries should be enforced and discussed between the couple.

As developed in the story, Betty does a very good job by perceiving Mario's mood and asking him to go talk to another room to discuss those issues. Those kind of interactions, opinions, and even sometimes gossips, as also depicted in the story, are real examples of what can happen in a snoopy family that discuss the life of the couple as a way to entertain themselves and also daring to declare judgments on the job the young couple is doing or trying to bias or influence certain types of decisions, such as the name of the baby that was previously discussed between them and it was not an issue to be given an opinion, much less to be done as the in-laws wanted.

Many conflicts can arise in a couple due to this kind of behaviors from the political families; that is why, there has to be a clear discussion between the couple to establish ground rules in terms of the type of comments, behaviors, or even judgment the political family can express and how tolerant they will be of them. Every couple should be supportive with each other about their opinions, thoughts, values, and way of educating their children so that they don't create a bigger issue during a family reunion or in any other setting.

It is also important to pinpoint that the relation that parents show with each other even in the presence of in-laws or any other member of the political family will be very important for the child's emotions or perception because if children see that the presence of certain members of the family causes stress between the couple, he or she will certainly react negatively toward them in future events, and that will create tension for more members of the family.

It is also important that privacy of the couple's arguments, problems, and discussions be clearly stated before any kind of future conflict arises. It is many times common that couples need some kind of outlet for their discussions or disagreements. However, involving in-laws is not often the best decision; or if it is done, there should also be discussed between the couple openly and establishing probably a boundary with each of the in-laws. Meaning that if Betty, for instance, talks about her problems with Mario with his mom, Betty should be able to establish a trust bond with his mother that any information they discuss stays between them and is not to be shared to anyone else.

This, of course, is to keep any other member of the political family to start meddling in the couple's issues and a small discussion or problem between the couple starts to be in the political family's public domain, coming from one of its members to the couple's knowledge and raising a much bigger conflict.

It's completely healthy for our children to interact with the family; it's okay to have support from them and to share also important moments and interaction. It's also good for them in terms of the emotional bonds that the child is building. However, it's not healthy for them to have opposed messages of what their parents think. It's not healthy to allow things that parents wouldn't allow, and of course, it's not healthy to try to permeate values, traditions, or patterns that go against their parents' will, as all of these contradictory messages will only create confusion, a poor image of boundaries, and most likely will foster in the children to become rebellious and look for the easy way out when obtaining things or create a tantrum out of nothing just to call attention and to obtain what they want even at the risk of humiliating their parents.

Therefore, deep discussion, clear intentions, and boundaries should be established with any member of the political family as well as with friends that want to meddle in your child's education or set of values if they go against yours.

III. *What are the characteristics and challenges when raising indigo or gifted children?*

It's of paramount importance that you are aware of your children's needs, reactions, and how he or she behaves as depicted in our story. Those "simple" reactions or "strange" behaviors that children manifest sometimes very early might give us a sign that our child is different, and of course, that doesn't mean he or she might have any type of deficiency or problem. However, it means that for sure, she will need your support to understand those differences.

Several children that have a different set of abilities and often labeled as gifted, indigo, or genius present some characteristics that unfortunately make them difficult to adapt sometimes to the general population and they're also isolated as many times they don't share the same likes, tastes, or speak or act too direct or straight compared to others, so their education, social interactions, and sometimes even simple tasks become more challenging than they are for the average children.

In fact, as most of the time they have a more enhanced perception set of skills, they can become more emotional, reactive, or totally the opposite withdrawn from experiences, which for them seem risky or present some sort of excessive social interaction, noisy environments, or simply places that they don't find attractive as all the rest of children.

As depicted in the story of Vilma, from a very early age, she is starting to show a very heightened sense of perception, which in fact is showing that she's more sensitive to emotional-loaded environments or she will show her emotions without even reflecting if they can hurt some sensibilities of people or if they are diplomatically correct.

Many of these reactions from gifted or indigo children can be confused with ADHD or autism, which, if not correctly diagnosed, might make them end up being medicated and, of course, that can damage them in terms of their neural, emotional, and even metabolic abilities. Parents from these types of children should pay a lot of attention to the signs, emotions, and how their children start interacting in a totally normal environment. Moreover, if these challenges are not assertively handled, parents without noticing can easily end up pushing their children toward interests that are being chosen for them due to their intellectual and emotional differences. This fact can lead them to present symptoms of anxiety, depression, or something even worse.

As societies are evolving toward trying to be more inclusive for different types of children, it is still a challenge, a mystery, and certainly a critical task for parents, educators, and counselors to identify the correct set of skills that the child is presenting in order to be able to either explain or at least to suit up their needs.

Being gifted is something with which you are just born. A corollary to this is that things come easily when you are gifted or being gifted, which means never having to study or to try hard in school. This naïve notion of giftedness, while intuitively proper, can be debilitating to gifted students' development. Many teachers, parents, administrators, and gifted students hold this belief. It is not gathered, however, by research on talent development and development in general. Moving from an entity notion of giftedness to an incremental notion, wherein talent is developed with hard work and some failure, is a much healthier and more nurturing experience of being a gifted student. This change in understanding of giftedness is of particular importance before age ten or so (Cross 2002).

The terms *gifted*, *different*, or any other kind of labels simply starts biasing your child into a more challenging situation where they might develop other kind of symptoms such as anxiety, fear of failure, or fear of rejection, which in turn will make their lives more complicated than they are for other children.

In addition to these new endeavors and challenges, as they move from one type of environment to the other, meaning simply scaling their way through the different educational levels, such as kindergarten to elementary, high school, and college, they will have to sort with these types of "threats" as they are more prone to develop routines, certain type of rituals, and even the getting used to new classmates will represent a challenge for them.

Many parents, teachers, and administrators believe that it is their role to ensure that gifted students are perfectly well-rounded. To that end, they will encourage, prod, goad, push, threaten, and yell at gifted students to get them to spend less time engaged in their passion areas so they can engage in something the adult wishes them to do. A very common example is that of an introverted gifted student who has great facility with computers. Adults will drag the child away from her passion to get her to participate in something she may loathe (Cross 2002).

Trying to make your gifted child normal when they are clearly passionate about certain tasks, skills, or even just for not interacting as much as other children do will not only have the opposite effect in your child, but actually it will give him or her the message that something is wrong with him or her, and this fact will most likely have the opposite effect and might even trigger more anxiety and fear of not belonging in them.

However, trying to engage your child in a program where they have more interaction, a complete change of environment such as a summer trip, even if at the beginning, seems like a very risky activity or behavior that might end up giving them more confidence in their social skills, adaptation abilities, and who knows it might end up taking away the anxiety that they were feeling for having to move forward in the educational level hierarchy.

In general, gifted children should be understood as any other type of children without assigning a "difference" to others, but being very careful of those special behaviors they will have and trying for them to see it as completely normal even when other people don't understand them like that. This, of course, has a huge advantage for you as a parent—you will become along the way a more aware person, a more connected adult with your own emotions as you see their growth and development, and will take you into a world that might be more resembled to a real picture, which, of course, will be rejected, not understood, or even judged by many others, who usually live disconnected from their emotions, disconnected from other human beings, and of course disconnected of nature.

These gifted children usually present a special attraction to nature environments where they can freely express their sensibility to the signals, to rituals, to patterns that "normal" people are not able to perceive.

IV. How can you design a space for you as a couple to talk and process emotions?

Nowadays, couples, whether they're seriously engaged or just dating, keep falling for the same trivial issues or repeated patterns because most of the times, both of them are being programmed by society, marketing, and media messages that promote selfish behavior, competitive advantages, gender differences (which, of course, they exist, they are real) but shouldn't be pointed out just to create separateness or toxic competition.

Instead of really evolving those gender breaches as we should be doing, many times it seems that the inclusiveness and biased behaviors pointed by branding, marketing, and the media are so self-immersed in creating a culture where every difference is seen as a threat. We are completely different persons, as if we were different human beings that should be treated "specially," which in fact, that message promotes the competition between genders or now between different sexual preferences.

With so many labels, acronyms, and categories of "people," there's a sea of distractions that are just designed to create more boundaries, even when the message is to become more inclusive. The more we label, the more we categorize; the more we even classify people into a certain pattern of behaviors, the more we're separating them, creating differences and distracting them to the core of the issues when relating among each other.

That's why relationships have become more complicated nowadays because everyone wants to look for their own benefit. Everyone wants to strive without even seeing that we need others for that. Moreover, without seeing that the more we are supported, bounded by love, and allowed to be the most sublime expression of soul connection is the easiest way to start thriving, the easiest way it is also to start also realizing that we live in one shared home, and we need to take care of each other.

Therefore, designing a strategy to help you cope with those emotions, with those triggers, with the fact that interacting with other humans will for sure have some complications, but they don't have to grow, they don't have to be hurtful; they are just there because we were raised by different environments by a completely different set of values, priorities, routines, and even rituals, and all of those differences are the ones that sometimes collapse with each other.

However, talking to them, allowing other persons to know your story, trusting that you're with someone with whom you can open up will, in fact, promote that you become bound by your stories; you will probably realize that you share some wounds, and then healing those wounds becomes a priority for each one and then shared experiences. Shared knowledge makes you grow, allows you to have empathy, allows you to understand from where does pain come from when it is triggered, when it is expressed, and you're more able to be compassionate with your partner, you're more open to listen, to embrace the person as he or she is, and you enrolled in a cycle of healing, which, in fact, if you happen to have kids, they will be very grateful, will grow healthier, and will be able to relate better with people. Whether it is socially or romantically, always remember that now you're the example, now you become the starting point to begin a completely different environment for your new family and you will be the reference for your children either to do or to avoid some things that they resonate with or they just don't like to repeat or to adopt.

Conflicts in intimate relationships are often accidental, occasional, and unique; yet they are also systemic, repetitive, and alike, both in form and content, to conflicts that have occurred countless times in the past and will occur over and over again in the future until they are resolved. Why? Because they are initiated, organized, and brought to fruition by deeper, far more important, unresolved issues that are simultaneously heartfelt and systemic, vulnerable and fundamental to the relationship (Cloke 2015).

These systemic issues are often difficult and dangerous to address because they lie at the center of what holds the relationship together. Simply discussing, let alone negotiating or resolving them, contains the possibility of even greater divergence, separation, or loss and, with them, the experience of grief, loss, and pain. Yet also contained within these issues is the possibility of deeper understanding, renewal, reconnection, and transcendence and an intense experience of joy, love, and freedom (Cloke 2015).

As proposed by clinical psychology and, of course, several types of counselors, the best way to dissolve conflicts is by healing the deeper wounds that we have. This particular issue was also depicted and explained in our story with Mario and Betty. Designing a schedule to deal with possible misunderstandings or appreciations that each partner feels like is something that can become threatening is of paramount relevance so every "small" conflict or appreciation gets to be addressed as it is raised, as it is being also treated in a space of dialogue, and not with emotional load as it would be during a bigger discussion. Oftentimes, many of the couple's discussions end up being more an emotional storm when they are rather like a glass of water spilling off, which can be fixed simply by stopping pouring water on it. However, when emotions are ruling any type of discussion, perception, or defensiveness, denial is going to be present; and usually, ego is going to be get on the way of solving something that in other moment, with more peace of mind will be solved quicker and easier.

That's why the proposed scheduling of talking between couples should be a tool that is completely used up by as many couples as possible. It can also become an activity where if there are no issues present, then it can be used as space to plan projects together, to design activities for the weekend, to have a more ordered life, even though for many people it looks tedious or boring. In the end, this tool can save your relationship and also allow your children to have a much better emotional outcome than the one you had.

This type of tool can be compared to cleaning your house of clothes, paper, and every accumulations of stuff every six months rather than doing it every time you move to another place or until you don't have space in your house, and just like in relationships, your stress for having to clean everything and get rid of clutter will drain your energy and affect your mood.

Remember that we are not built to stand large amounts of stress without having an impact in our health and emotions, so the more you take care of every aspect that might trigger, build up or raise your stress levels the easier your life will be.

V. What important factors influence new parenting duties and your couple's life?

As mentioned before during the story of Mario and Betty, new parenting responsibilities require that ideally, of course, you have a pretty good and stable relationship with your partner, that all the issues between the couple and most of the deep emotional wounds have been addressed by each person; otherwise, you might fall into those wounds to a deeper level and adopt one of two mind-sets, the one that starts creating distance in the relationship or the other the ones that starts, of course, having a lot more conflicts when the first child arrives.

Why does this happen? Simple, because the responsibility of becoming a mother/father will demand a lot more of your time, your energy, and financial resources; therefore, if you add to those demands, the fact that you're still arguing for past emotional issues that were not healed before, that's when you will start noticing that you really need some time off or, worse, you will start hurting your partner, creating grudges, emotional pain. That is going to be mirrored in your child; he will start most likely to take all that emotional vibration, energy, and probably all the display of discussions or fights will start going deeper in his/her mind and body. Therefore, children, as they don't know yet how to cope with that amount of emotional burden, start having physiological and physical ailments, such as dermatitis, intestinal issues, respiratory infections, or maybe much worse. That will all depend, of course, on the epigenetic marks and inheritance that also their parents have already left in them. In fewer words, you will start creating a very toxic cycle of disease and emotional blame that will permeate all the members of the family, and of course, it will start disrupting the love and care that should rule in the new family.

Marital dissatisfaction can be a source of stress for parents, affecting daily interactions and relationships. Presumably, parents who are dissatisfied with their marital relationship are more likely to display negative affect and less able to be emotionally available to their children. Previous research has suggested that families that have more negative marital relationships also have more negative parent-child relationships, and that marital conflict is linked with most dimensions of parenting, especially harsh discipline and lack of acceptance. In addition, there is evidence of gender differences in the relation between marital quality and parent-child interactions with fathers being more likely than mothers to show spillover of negative affect from marital distress to their interactions with children (Nelson 2009).

Reaffirming what was mentioned before, if you're reckless with your marital problems and you didn't take some time to fix them before you had children, it's not too late to do it still; otherwise, the only effect or consequence that is going to be produced would be the spillover of frustration in your child that as mentioned before will start to create first emotional imprints in him/ her as well as physical ailments.

Moreover, this spillover behavior presents more in fathers due to perception of them feeling displaced by the child, which of course is a total misinterpretation. However, mothers when having marital issues tend to look for refuge and emotional comfort in their children, reinforcing the perception hypothesis of fathers that they are no longer needed and they're "useless" in the dynamic of the family, which little by little tends to take them more from the nuclear family environment.

Perceptions of home chaos may be dependent on other cognitive acuities about relationships in the home or on individual characteristics such as depression. Researchers have demonstrated that home chaos is distinct from other social and psychological variables, such as socioeconomic status and anxiety and is associated with less effective parental discipline. Valiente and others (2007) tested the relation between perceptions of home chaos and parental responses to children's negative emotions, finding that high levels of chaos predicted low levels of supportive responses (Nelson 2009).

Another aspect that impacts or disrupts parental behaviors is having a mess in your home. Allowing chaotic behavior and lack of routine most of all for the home chores will produce anxiety or depression mostly in women as they're the ones that stay and have more time in charge of children and the house; however, as the roles have been changing, this effect can also be perceived now in men who are in charge of the house. Whatever the case may be in your couple dynamic, you have to pay attention to these effects as they will also have a spillover effect in the child that can be reflected as a poor supportive environment for the child and then start again a toxic emotional cycle between mom and child.

Your mood in general is, of course, a disruptive factor for the family environment; mostly depression has been evaluated between parents, which is really a consequence of some misunderstood emotional wound that was not worked before or there is very poor communication between the couple. Therefore, it is very important that as mentioned before in bullet point number 3, there needs to be a space for the couple to have time to talk and address all those issues that are in the way, which might seem small, or things that you said didn't affect you, but when you dig a little deeper, it turns out that it has been a buildup of many of those small behaviors that you have left unattended. And now you have developed a sad mood that has been there at least for a few months, and exactly, that sequence is the one that can take you to a depressive state, which will definitely make things worse for all the members of the family.

When parents experience fatigue, a loss of interest, and an overall negative mood, they are likely to be less responsive toward children. In a review of the association between maternal depression and parenting, researchers found depressive symptoms to relate to numerous parenting behaviors, although the strongest associations were evident for such negative interactions as irritability and hostility toward the child, which are likely to be linked to nonsupportive parental responses to children's negative emotions (Lovejoy 2000).

Researchers also found that paternal depression was positively associated with more impaired father-child communication, characterized by less positivity and congeniality. The authors even found that communication between the child and the nondepressed parent was less positive in homes in which the other parent was depressed (Jacob 1997).

Fatigue, stress, excessive work either at home or at your office will have a toll on your mood and will eventually lead you to develop a more severe depressive behavior that sometimes gets in the background of a hectic life where there's no space to ventilate your emotions, where the lifestyle is just focused on obligations from many sources that seem to leave no space to even do some kind of physical activity, where also your eating patterns start to pay the cost of the "busy" life that you are creating. All these small toxic cycles are feeding a bigger toxic cycle that is already permeating your family, and your child is paying the consequence. Your partner also absorbing all those emotions, and that is why, it is even difficult for the child and the "healthy" member, which sometimes is the father, simply because he spends more time outside than in the trenches. However, there's a snowball that is growing by the time, and it will blow up in everyone's face. Sadly, due to the early age of the child, he or she is receiving all those messages and will imprint those memories stronger, which can last for a good while even to his or her adulthood if they're not stopped, not processed, and there's the responsibility of finding an outlet for them.

One very simple advice, though it sounds as usual easier said than done, is that the healthy partner starts creating some type of healing routine such as physical activity, with variety and novelty, designing a space to talk with the other partner, of course without forcing anything, trying to make it seem very casual, just to break the toxic pattern.

Meanwhile, the partner that suffers the depression can start to install a habit of journaling the ruminating thoughts, trying to let the emotions flow in paper, or record the voice with all the things he or she wants to say to at least have some type of outlet that helps the emotional burden start losing power, and also to have a more objective perspective.

Journaling about what happens in your mind has been proven to help your neurotransmitter and stress hormones to be reduced and actually change the profile into a healthier outlook, which will eventually help your whole body to process those emotions and allow you to start feeling better. If you start doing that together with the first attempts of doing something physical, all these activities will start to act together to give you more strength, to allow more space in your mind, to have a different perspective, and in turn to start getting out from that emotional hole.

It is well known that to end depression symptoms, you have to be scaling your emotions toward a new outlook and paradigm that sometimes or many times will move slowly through several stages, such as finding more security. You might feel guilty yourself for being in that place and not being able to help, which stimulates a sense of unworthiness. Don't be disappointed if during the journey you find yourself feeling with rage because that means you're moving forward; just be careful with whom you're feeling hateful because this emotion is particularly dangerous as you might end up blaming or taking all your frustration out either with your partner or, in the worst-case scenario, with your child.

However, as you scale up this emotional ladder, you'll start finding yourself less and less frustrated, with less rage, until you start feeling some sense of worth, little by little, which will lead to feeling more contentment and probably you find yourself now feeling also bored of the repetitive things you're doing, which ironically is now the moment to install novelty and those new activities that will push your mood though some of the levels of the emotional ladder (Abraham 2007).

Finally, your job and your career satisfaction will also affect the emotional state that you have, and of course, this as well have a profound impact in your family and in the emotional environment that you're creating. Many times, all those work-related emotions or frustration of not finding the right place or the right path toward what you want to achieve will lead you to feel overwhelm, to build up a considerable amount of stress, and to take all those emotions and spill them over with your family.

There is also evidence for crossover of work stress to family life with high occupational stress in husbands being linked to psychological stress in wives (Jones 1993).

Not unexpectedly, husbands in this case are more stressed due to the amount of time they spend at the office, the economic pressure, and the society paradigms that they ought to be the providers of the home. However, nowadays, this role is changing and work stress is also reflected in mothers. Again, whatever the case might be, all those emotions are also transferred into the family environment.

Lastly, it is important to make a distinction between parenting styles and qualities for mothers and father so that we can recognize and understand how relationships are constructed between the mother, father, and the child.

Fathering is qualitatively different from mothering, and fathers provide unique contributions to their children's development. Some evidence for such qualitative differences comes from attachment research, in which investigators have suggested that fathers provide emotional support to their children through encouraging independence and exploration, whereas mothers provide emotional support by responding sensitively to child distress (Nelson 2009).

That small paragraph, as brief as it seems, explains pretty much the ability of mothers to sense more the emotions of the child during all their growth and how fathers take the practical physical side of encouraging activities, challenging their children, and promoting that they become responsible for their own emotions in order to learn how to cope with future challenges in life.

To summarize this bullet, which was lengthier on purpose due to its impact on the overall environment for the family, we can state that all the sources described here have to be taken into account when sensing that the family environment is moving toward a toxic cycle, when you have had several calls of attention from your child's health, when you are also perceiving that your partner is stepping away from home on purpose, paying attention to all those signals will eventually help you to figure out a possible solution that will start addressing the issue(s) of the toxicity and start a healing process. Sooner rather than later, we are now in a much more enlightened time, with a lot more information and resources for help, so there's no justification to keep sinking your emotional environment and start repeating another cycle of children's emotional neglect or damage, which will backfire for you when they grow up and sadly will end up probably being repeated until one generation stops the cycle. Let it be your generation that stops the damage. Let your intuition and inner signals awake you to a more responsible and healed pathway.

CHAPTER 8

Building Your Relationship Day by Day

D OING A QUICK recap from our last chapter, we left everything with Betty and Mario bonding after the stress and anxiety episode. They were successful to overcome the anxiety and frustration they had at the baby shower party and now they'll have to face new chores, finding their rhythm and adapting to busy schedules in addition to dealing with Vilma's demands. Thus, let's move on with the story.

It was already Monday; everything was supposed to return to normal, but now with the small addition of one new member, Vilma, Betty's morning started really early. She woke up at 5:00 a.m. to feed Vilma then prepare all her things for work. Although she had a very big mixed feelings about leaving

Vilma at a new nursery, with a new environment, Mario was also feeling a little stressed. He was already taking some subjects for his career in the mornings, and after the meal, he was supposed to work two to three hours in the Uber, pick up Vilma, and then go back home to feed her, bathe her, and put her to sleep. Nothing so challenging so far, but handling everything was going to start triggering some emotional issues in Mario's character.

The Hamster Wheel Effects

Betty was supposed to be as "normal" as she could be at the office; however, she had a pretty challenging first day after returning, as they had a very important meeting with a new vice president for the company, which by the way was going to complicate Charlie's life, which in turn would have some stressful changes for Betty and the whole team as well.

Moreover, Betty had still three months of her breastfeeding schedule, which was supposed to allow her to go out one hour earlier than usual. Nevertheless, she was not using that schedule as she should have; she was more concerned about picking up her rhythm as fast as she could. Thus, as you can imagine this excess of work right at the beginning of her pregnancy as well as the new schedules that they now were both handling was going to quickly send them off to a very dangerous emotional struggle due to the amount of stress that they submitted their bodies right after finishing the maternity leave.

Vilma was just a very careful observer of how her parents were struggling, and she was already sensing some stress between them as well, as symptoms of exhaustion in facing those new challenges were being obvious. Betty was arriving pretty late the whole week, leaving Mario only four to five hours to work in the evening/night shift in the Uber, which quickly almost without noticing was going to push him to also have a shorter time for sleep.

They were both eating as they could, sometimes forgetting what they have learned from Mario's rehab clinic recommendations; therefore, this fully stressed lifestyle that started so quickly from where they were coming also had a strong effect on their mood, which first started to appear in Betty's patience; she was demanding more and more household chores and support from Mario as the days went by. Mario, on the other hand, without noticing so much, was also having less patience with Vilma, as she just wanted a slower rhythm for her food, the bath, and all the things she was supposed to do with her dad.

The only more awakened observer of that kind of stress, emotional load, and bad mood from the family as you can imagine was Vilma.

All of this busy schedules, hectic life, and poor care of their health, as they were eating pretty bad, leaving exercise out of the equation and just trying to sleep during the weekend without being able to really rest, was already provoking some consequences in the overall health of the family.

Mario was on the verge of exhaustion, as he had to get up early also in order to have time for him to get ready, leave Vilma at the nursery, and go to school. He was having a very hard time at his school trying to stay awake, as you can imagine; he was not having his best grades as he would have liked.

Betty was starting to have some memory issues at her job, forgetting important information, meetings, and was really close to having problems with her boss due to her constant distractions and forgetfulness.

On top of it all, and to close the full toxic circle, Vilma was very sensitive, crying more than usual, having some skin issues, atopic dermatitis, and she was also having a hard time adapting to formula milk, as she had to start taking some of her feeding bottles with formula. Therefore, Betty and Mario were also spending their weekends busy with pediatrician's appointments, testing new formulas, and trying to keep Vilma's skin with care so she could recover. Due to all these symptoms, her sleeping schedules were also pretty messed up, which, by the way, were adding some consequences to all the sleeping schedules from the family.

As we all know, lack of sleep is one of the main causes to start changing hormonal patterns, increasing stress as well as deteriorating the memory. That's why they were all having a very bad temper, problems with their responsibilities, and without being able to see it building a snowball effect.

Luckily, as we have mentioned in previous chapters, Betty and Mario were very lucky to be in touch with Liam and Karen, their amazing "health supporters," so the first one to scream for help was Mario. He did it first because he was really afraid of all the stress he was already building up, the lack of patience that he had with Vilma, and the poor communication that he was having now with Betty, as they didn't even have time to think about themselves with all the new activities and hectic schedules that they were handling. Mario touched base with Liam. He went to see him at his place on one of the days that he was supposed to be working in the Uber.

Liam was a little bit surprised of Mario's visit, as he thought that everything was fine as six months had already passed after their last encounter. However, when he started to speak with Mario, he noticed that he was very anxious, worried, and really looked exhausted. So, he asked, "What happened, Mario? Is everything okay?"

A Social-Supported Life Model

Mario just took a deep breath and said, "No, Liam, actually I'm feeling really overwhelmed, tired, and on the verge of falling again for some drug or something that makes my pain go away and have more energy. I've been trying to do my best with house chores schedules, my school, Vilma, but Betty and I are crossing a very rough patch together as a couple. We don't seem to agree on many things. She doesn't seem happy at all, she's been really grumpy, upset, and even rude with me and sometimes also with Vilma. I myself have not been having very healthy habits, sort of saying. I'm sleeping very few hours, working and studying a lot, also trying to help with chores at the house and taking care of Vilma, but I have been having a really explosive mood with Betty as well, sometimes very few patience with Vilma, and I think I just won't be able to hold it for much longer through this rough season. That's why before doing something stupid, I decided to visit you and talk, as you've been the only reliable person whom I can talk to, and of course you've been there for me and indirectly for Betty too."

"Thanks, Mario, I feel again grateful for the compliments. I'll do my best effort to guide you in what I can or at least point you again in a healthier direction. We've all passed through those times, and I'm sure these moments will pass soon.

"For what you've said to me, it seems that both of you are having a big burden of responsibilities that neither of you had ever handled, am I right?"

"Yes, Liam, we're both young, we both previously lived with our parents, though in my case I had a lot of independence and time by myself, but I had all the household chores always taken care for me, so I never experienced what it was like to do them on my own. You know pretty much my past. I used to do as little as possible to really make progress in myself because I thought that was the best way to get even with my parents for emotionally neglecting me so much time, first of all because my father was always worried about his business and all his social/business life that in turn led my mom to start developing a low self-esteem that dragged her to alcohol, so she wasn't even so conscious of what I was doing as well or if I ever needed her. Therefore, I was practically abandoned by them. During this time, I've felt something similar with Betty due to all the things we both had to do, the little experience we had, and practically with no help with Vilma. We don't seem to find moments to support each other, we are most of the time busy, stressed, both not sleeping well due to all that stress, in addition to Vilma's weird schedules to sleep or sometimes wake up.

"I feel we've created a snowball effect that I always felt with my parents, therefore, I was really afraid that I could start doing something stupid again and fall for some easy fix, such as alcohol or drugs."

"Okay, Mario, I'm listening and I can also notice by the way you look that you're overwhelmed, you look really tired, worried, and stressed. I can also imagine that Betty is just as you are, actually maybe she might feel worse due to all the hormonal changes that women have right after they give birth!

"Moreover, I guess that all these feelings are also growing and feeling as that snowball is constantly growing, and soon it will explode on all of you, as you mentioned, mainly because of all the routines and things you're doing. There seems to be no space or time to do something to balance them out, such as exercise, meditating, talking to each other as you used to do or at least taking some walks outside to clear your mind and release some stress. It's strange that after all that you went through and you also learned at the rehab clinic, you're not applying any of those tools, which now is the time to use them as outlets.

"But as ironic as it sounds, I completely understand you. When we just had our daughter, we also experienced a lot of challenges. However, Linda, as you know her, was very careful with all her health care, from sleep to eating very healthy, maintaining the exercise, and she picked up the meditation rituals from me as well, which worked pretty well for her too, right before she was going into labor and pretty much all the next three months after pregnancy. Even with all those healthy and outlet tools, we faced some discussions, some arguments for little things, which in those moments seemed just 'important' issues. However, as you move past those first three years of your child, everything starts to fall into place again.

"I particularly attribute all that seesaw effect to the difference that each partner had in the education, different kinds of values, different kinds of patterns to live, which of course collide in one place. And then even if you planned your child's birth and everything was according to what both of you desired, things get in the way–differences and each other's patterns and beliefs start to clash. And suddenly, you both find yourself arguing about the most stupid things that in a moment of peace wouldn't even be relevant to anyone of you.

"Additionally, your child is also an individual on her own that comes with a mix of both of you, that inherited probably some character traits from you and of course some from the mom too. Therefore, you will feel that reflection of emotions or character from her many times. Additionally, when children don't know how to talk yet, they express all their emotions through crying or sometimes if they are not able to find an outlet, they start developing some diseases that are not to be very concerned about, but they do call the attention of parents as you probably have already noticed. Children are developing their character; they're already sensing the world and finding ways to express what they feel.

"So, I'm just guessing that Vilma has also been having some health issues or, as you say, problems to fall sleep or stay sleep. Well, all those issues that you can see in her are attention calls for both of you so you can be more mindful about your emotions, the way you interact. Even if she doesn't witness discussions or fights, she is able to perceive an emotional tense environment that both of you are generating."

"Wow, Liam, I knew that I had to come to talk with you about this before I did something stupid that for sure I would have regretted for a long time. You're right, actually now I remember one of my first talks with Mike, my emotional coach at the clinic. The first sessions were more like a training in emotions that he gave us to understand how we even from the utero absorb many emotions from our parents, which later will start to be transformed into a physical symptom."

"That's right, Mario, so it is no surprise that you and Betty are just creating an emotional time bomb that might spill all of its contents over your family, and of course, it will get to Vilma more deeply than you think. So, you did the right choice, and you're perfectly on time to stop those emotions to grow. It is pretty obvious that many things will change from the way you both lived before. That's not something negotiable anymore. However, creating a team between Betty and you is the only healthy option that I myself experienced with Linda.

"So, my suggestions for you to have some emotional and mental peace, and you find more balance in your life is that you request a space to talk with Betty. I can offer myself to take care of Vilma, and actually it would be nice for Stephanie to interact with her. Steph is already five years old and loves babies. She is very affectionate and tender with them, so Vilma won't be the exception. Leave Vilma with us, have the whole Friday afternoon for you guys, take Betty to a nice restaurant, tell her to excuse herself from work by saying she has a doctor appointment, and be careful how you start telling her the things.

"You can begin by saying at least five things she does well and why you really appreciate her support. Also try to compliment her about how she takes care of Vilma. Then try to express what you feel is wrong with your emotions, pretty similar to what you explain to me, just leaving out the part that she has been grumpy and stressed for now. Just keep it very personal, narrate all the issues that you talked to me about the environment with your parents, and be specific on how the environment that you're perceiving from both of you resembles to what you lived.

"Finally, offer solutions, remind her about the learnings you had at the clinic, and of course, I don't think there is gonna be any problem if you also mention that we have talked about this already, but be careful not to compare Betty and you with us. Women hate comparisons, and that will shut her down. Just mention that you and I were reflecting on all the patterns and busy schedules that you both have and propose her to have some kind of division of tasks, which of course should include that you both support each other and be alert for toxic emotions or behaviors.

"You can even name the whole experience as a newcomer detox period for both of you, which actually is what every couple that starts to have children should have. It is so common to hear that couples with newborn babies have problems or sometimes even without babies–they just start having problems right away by living together. Nevertheless, you sort those issues out, which mainly are due to clashing of patterns and the way both were raised. Most of the time we are all raised very differently in terms of values, traditions, patterns to live our lives, even to do the simple things such as the house chores, but when you share a space with another human being, all the learnings and backgrounds start to collide. Usually what clashes more are the emotional wounds, beliefs, and behavior tendencies that you witnessed and learned by replicating them as an adult."

"Well, Liam, that sequence of steps to start talking with Betty was the best advice on how to begin to unfold a solution. It should start to work pretty well."

"Yes, Mario, just be careful to have patience to implement it, and little by little, you will both start healing again. Now you both need to commit to a new outlook for a renewed course of action as a team. And as we mention it before, Mario, many couples don't seem to yet understand that it's not about winning an argument, it's not about counting who does more household chores or who earns more or who's more successful between the couple. Supposedly when you join your life with a person, it is to come together and support each other through the good times and bad times, more than the paper, the party, or all the show that is performed. The concept of couple, or let's call it love partnership, should be the key element for two people to live together, which will sustain a marriage and more importantly will help you to raise a baby together.

"If we were more conscious about all those emotional wounds–definitely, I dare to say that more than 80 percent of couples have not yet healed before they get engaged or compromised to live together–then we wouldn't have such high rates of divorces, separations, or toxic emotional environments for children. And we would all be more successful to avoid so much pain that is witnessed at such an early age and many times just gets imprinted in our mind or, worse, in our hearts."

"I completely agree, Liam, and now that I have lived both sides of the coin, I can attest to the amazing difference that makes living with a more conscious behavior, living with a purpose of being better, without having to compete with anyone, and also now I can verify that having a social environment that is supportive, such as you and Karen for Betty, makes also a huge difference.

"You know my story when I was having drugs, just living to survive and make my parents pay for the emotional pain they caused me. My social network was so poor that I couldn't rely on anyone to talk about serious things. Actually, I myself didn't even had the clarity in my brain to see that I needed help or to see other things that could make a difference in my life because I was immersed in self-pity, in revenge to my parents, in toxic emotions that also permeated through me and didn't allow me to attract a different kind of people."

Your Five-Core Inner Healing to Save Your Relationship

"Now that you mention all that responsibility, I also can relate that to what I see in many people when I have them in my Uber, how they're immersed in social media or toxic news environments, which in my humble opinion pretty much resembles a pharmaceutical or recreational drug because it "'distracts' them, takes them out of their meaningless or painful lives, that they see with no interest, that they see as boring or monotonous, that they need to find escape from, and their mind is not able to clearly see that the distraction, advertisement, or 'information' in all these outlets is not the best way to start opening up their mind. And recognize or see more clearly that you really need to start having a connection with you, not with anything that is outside.

"So it really looks like a never-ending loop that many of us are creating, and if we add to that mixture, the fact that many people don't have a reliable source for help or they're just trying to find a quick fix, then the emotional snowball seems to be bigger than what you can handle, which is all the reflection that we are now seeing in most societies that are suffering in many health areas.

"No wonder we are at such high rates of chronic diseases, mental illnesses, as well as immunological deficits that generate clients for many of the big pharmaceutical companies and they also become easy targets for all the cheap and hollow marketing that you can find at all media outlets. They are ready to sell you, to enroll you in something that will give you a quick boost of emotion. They are just palliative measures, but then in a few days or weeks (if it was not that useless), it will lead you to a lower valley where you feel even worse than before getting that help you thought you needed."

"Exactly, Mario. Now I feel that you're back, I feel that I'm talking again with the Mario that came back from the clinic. You see, it's all about finding that space, grounding yourself in the emotions, recognizing that you are feeling overwhelmed, but trying to see them from another perspective, seeing them pretty much as an observer, and it is okay to ask for help as you did this time.

"That's the other key element. Drowning yourself, or drowning together as a couple, in your own emotional pain will only take things more quickly to grow in terms of the emotional load that both of you are generating. So please always feel free to come here and talk to me or you also have your friend from the clinic, Mike. Whoever you decide to choose, we'll try to help you in whatever way we can.

"Thanks, Liam. I really feel much better, optimistic that we'll get this obstacle out and move on to the next challenges. Thank you also for taking care of Vilma, we really will make that time be worthy for us!"

"No problem, man, now just go and set your date with Betty for this Friday before she makes another commitment at her job."

Mario felt totally revved up and ready to reclaim their emotional health and also protect Vilma from their reckless behavior, which was very important now for him as he didn't want to cause the same story of his parents at all!

Therefore, Mario called Betty. It was a Wednesday afternoon, and Betty was a little bit concerned she didn't receive calls from Mario at those times so she immediately thought about Vilma. She answered the phone abruptly, asking what happened without even letting Mario talk at the beginning; therefore, Mario just told her to relax and affirmed that Vilma was okay.

"By the way, I'm okay too, nothing bad happened. I'm just calling you to ask you for a big favor, and I'm not going to take no for an answer."

"Okay," said Betty with a calmer voice, but still curious about the topic of the call. "Tell me, Mario, what is it?"

"Well, I want you to have a date with me this Friday at 4:00 p.m. I'll pick you up from work, and we are going out for the whole afternoon. I already set up everything for Vilma—Liam and Linda will take care of her, so there's no rush or need to worry about her. You better tell Charlie that you have a doctor's appointment about some skin rash of Vilma. You can tell him that you haven't said anything because the doctor hasn't confirmed the appointment yet."

"Okay, Mario, I'm still intrigued, but I definitely need an afternoon to relax and do something different so your plan sounds good so far."

The next days before the date, Betty tried to take something out from Mario's mouth about that Friday, but his lips were sealed. "It's a surprise," that was all he said to Betty. So she took that as a good sign and just took the expectation of doing something different, of having some time for themselves, and that was enough to already have a smile on her face for those couple of days, as well as feeling glad to be able to reconnect with him. Therefore, those two days flew by. Vilma was even starting to sleep a little better those two days, and they all had better nights to rest and recharge batteries!

The day of the dinner arrived. Mario picked Betty up at her work as they discussed it; he even had the good gesture of buying her a small bag of heart chocolates, which Betty loved, so everything was going pretty well. When they were approaching the place, Betty immediately recognized it—it was their favorite restaurant, the one where they got engaged. Betty was very emotional, so she started to cry and thanked Mario for all the details he already had with her so far. And the date had not even started yet! Mario felt really appreciated and recognized by Betty, so all those positive emotions also did a good effect on him.

Mario had everything planned, so once they arrived, they gave them the same table where they got engaged. Everything was falling into place; it was an autumn afternoon with a very warm weather, clear skies, and Mario even ordered some wine to celebrate!

As soon as they got seated, Mario started saying, "Well, Betty, the mystery is over. As you have noticed, this date was requested by me and settled so that we could have time together and talk about how we feel and, of course, smooth some emotional issues that I have been having. So please try to relax, forget about everything for this couple of hours, and let's enjoy this time." Betty, with her eyes still red and watery from the emotions she just had, thanked Mario again for all the attention and details he already had with her. Mario just replied, "There's no need to thank me, Betty. It is my pleasure to have this time with you as well, and I feel that we both needed this time apart from the routines and from everything that may distract us or stress us!"

"Yes, Mario, indeed we needed a break from everything. Even if for now it is just this afternoon, I promise you my phone is going off and I'm planning to have full attention and pleasure with you!"

"Thanks, Betty, I really appreciate that. My phone is off too, so we can both fully enjoy the moment. I completely trust Liam, and I know that Vilma is in good hands. Just so you'd be aware, I already sent him a message telling him that we are here and we are not going to answer any calls, so if there is something wrong with Vilma, I gave him the phone of the restaurant. But of course, nothing will be wrong, so don't worry!

"Well, Betty, I set this date on purpose because I wanted to talk about all the series of events that have been happening for both of us. I've been feeling really overwhelmed between the school, responsibilities to Vilma, household chores, and pretty much all the things that have been extremely stressful for me. I have been feeling that I'm not sleeping well, I'm eating pretty lousy, and in general, I feel that I needed some kind of outlet as my primary craving was to find a quick outlet such as alcohol or drugs. I started to really worry, and that's why I contacted Liam and went to talk with him because I really felt that I was on the verge of falling back to consuming alcohol or some kind of drug in order to be able to disconnect from all the stress and the pain.

"As you probably noticed during these past few months, all the interaction that we've had has been completely to speak, arrange, or discuss something about work, Vilma's issues or needs, and I really felt that if we continued like that, we would quickly arrive at becoming like my parents, starting to create distance between us, holding grudges toward each other or some emotional pain. And also, we would be even more predisposed to have a big fight or discussion that could end pretty bad. Therefore, I started thinking that I really don't want that kind of relationship for me, for us, and of course, for Vilma.

"In fact, I have noticed that she's been having a lot of problems to remain asleep. She's been also upset with her skin issues, which reflect that she's already absorbing some of our emotional pain, and I think that if we don't start changing our behavior and organizing better between us, everything is going to be very difficult, and I don't think we will be able to overcome whatever challenge we might have ahead.

"So, I propose to you that we start working as a team. We can start dividing the responsibilities that we have and being more conscious to find time to do some exercise, to eat better, and take care of each other to sleep more. I guess that you still remember all the strategies and lifestyle that I learned when I was in the clinic, right?"

"Of course, I do remember all the things that you wrote me in the letters, and you were very specific and detailed about the routines and schedules."

"Well, now is a good time to take those learnings and to start trying to analyze and choose the things that we can, or if we're able to do them all, start at least the implementation of the ones that can take us out of this unhealthy patch and toxic environment that we ourselves have been generating. We can start shifting our schedules to sleep either earlier one of us and getting up with Vilma, trying to help her sleep more and more continuously, as well as finding at least thirty minutes to do some kind of exercise, at least for the time that Vilma starts picking up a different time pattern of sleep."

"I completely agree, Mario. I'm sorry that I've been so stressed, grumpy, and just focusing on Vilma. I once told you that I didn't want us to be that kind of couple that is just concerned with child issues or household chores and forgetting about you because I also saw those kinds of examples in my family, and the end result was not positive, of course. I just feel that everything has happened so fast. We had very different stories when we grew up, and it's been difficult to take a pause and just accept that we needed to talk to settle things up and to find some peace among the chaos. It is clear for me, and I'm guessing for you as well that Vilma is not being an easy 'package' to handle, and we will have many challenges still to face. So, the stronger we become as a couple, the better we'll really work as a team like you propose will always be a good example for her.

"Moreover, I'm feeling that if we're able to set things up between us and develop a good strategy to have blocks of time assigned for all the things we need and we want to do, we will start to feel better, and in turn, that will help Vilma with her sleep patterns as well as that dermatitis that she's been having lately."

"Exactly, Betty. There's no one to blame here, at least speaking for me. It will never be a matter of blaming you or looking for someone to be guilty. It's more about saying how we feel, trying to find solutions, and implementing everything for our own sake and Vilma's too, of course."

"I'm really thankful with you, Mario. If you haven't made this pause, as you said, we would probably end up having a big argument, a fight, and just damaging Vilma more with all our emotional issues and stress. As we witnessed some months ago, Vilma is a child that is extremely sensitive about all the vibrations and all the mood changes that people around her might have, so we ought to be careful with our emotions. We can make our talks that we started doing when we just began living together. Even if things seem tight or urgent, we are the priority, and our emotional and physical health comes first."

"Perfect, Betty. Now that we agreed on that, can we please also add a day off to be with each other? Can we make a commitment to find either Liam, Karen, or someone else to take care of Vilma so that we will be able to enjoy afternoons like this?"

"Yes, Mario, that sounds pretty good to me. I'm thinking that my cousin, who is now twenty years old, might be interested in earning a little money by taking care of Vilma during a weekend and help us."

"Would she be doing that by herself?"

"No, of course, my mom might help us too, with the condition that my aunt doesn't show up while Vilma is at the house."

"If we are able to set that baby care up, then that sounds even better to start having a trip together, which can be some kind of routine that we might do once or even twice a year. Do you like the idea, Betty?"

"Of course, Mario, that would be amazing, and that would definitely help us interact more as a couple and reclaim our emotional health together, rest, and completely recharge the batteries up."

"Well, I'm surer now than ever that we needed a neutral place, a break. We're thinking a lot clearer now, I really feel that we can work this through together and install these healthy practices as a new lifestyle for us, which, by the way, Vilma can see and grow up much better than watching us drain our lives or feel constantly overwhelmed."

"Actually, I was just thinking, Mario, about at least three of my friends from work who warned me about what was just happening to us, and I completely remember them saying with a very sad face and disgust for their husbands that marriage was really an awful routine, that it was as if they've lost all the passion and romance with their partners and now it is clear for me that's very easy to fall into the trap of everyday life. It's so easy to justify that there's no time to do things, that sometimes also there's no money to get something or to achieve something, when in fact all that you need is one sane person in the relationship to see things from another perspective or sometimes even one of your friends and people around you that can help you find solutions, such as what you did with Liam.

"However, there are so many prejudices, so many beliefs and hypocrisy among people to accept that they need help. It is as if you were in a race to become the parents of the year, and by accepting that you're stressed, that you might be sometimes angry or whatever emotion that you're feeling, is seen as bad points as parents as well as a sign of weakness, a sign that you're failing or not doing a good job, allowing other people to be able to judge or to criticize you, when, in fact, recognizing that you need help is the first step toward sanity, toward finding a bond again with your partner, and being able to come together. Sharing what each other thinks, feels, and wants to do is the only path to heal first as an individual, also helping your partner to join and finally repair any damage done to children!

"And as you also mentioned, we need to be able to look for spaces, to reconnect with ourselves, to find outlets to all the stress and emotions that we have inside. It's almost impossible that if you live in a society with so many sources of information, with so much variety in cultural terms, backgrounds, values you don't absorb, some of the emotions from people that surround you, either at work, or family members, or even your own partner brings some kind of emotional burden and is not able to release it. Now it all seems so obvious that couples first start to build up emotions. However, as it happened to us, when you let too much time to pass, when it is the 'common' thing to do, to swallow your feelings, you start creating a variable mood, a dumb game of competition to blame each other or to want to win arguments. Eventually, everything ends up permeating all that emotional burden to other members in the family until the whole house is, let's say, 'infected' with the emotional toxic load. The next step would be to explode, and someone will be the first to do something that he or she might regret. And as it happened in our case, children are the first ones to show the damage, either with some slight health issues such as sleep patterns, nightmares, some skin rash, or frequent respiratory diseases.

"In many cases, all these slight health changes in them are just a mirror of the toxic environment that we as parents are creating for them. We don't seem to see it, and then what happens is that we take children at such a short age to physicians that sometimes unconsciously, I prefer to think, prescribe antibiotics or other kind of drugs that start damaging their organs, their immune systems, to finally predispose them as adults to develop a much more chronic or serious disease. Moreover, those more complex diseases now are a mixture of all the emotional issues that children witnessed, that they perceived and absorbed, plus the amount of drugs that they received since they were one, two, or three years old."

"Exactly, Betty. We are now witnessing in every society what happens to many families that engage in the hamster wheel of life. More now than ever with hectic lifestyles, the toxic amount of information that we're having from so many sources, and the creation and perpetuation of unconscious people that acquire power in political spheres and use it to manipulate more the system, to intoxicate people and practically doze them up with alarming news, scandals, and all series of attracting and distracting events that keep them paralyzed to be able to turn to their inner tools, their inner wisdom, and power.

"Nevertheless, as we did it, the solution has been and will always will be in your hands, connecting with your inner self first, then trying to connect with your partner to wake him or her up without blaming anyone, just trying to find a common ground to work as a team.

"So many promises are made when you join your life with another person, so much attention is placed on external things such as the ring, the party, the religious beliefs, and so little attention is placed on the compromise to really commit from a soul level, from a real love connection, to learn how to cope with emotions, to learn how to develop outlets for each other, to heal together, to upgrade awareness that there are so many 'simple' and most of the times 'free' solutions, such as exercise, what we are eating, the things we are seeing on TV or social media, the people we're surrounding ourselves with, and of course, the time and spaces that we are no longer looking for to be at peace, to be in stillness, in quiet, and contact our thoughts and feelings to finally start feeling more alive, connected, and grounded with our divine essence.

"Now, Betty, if you ask me what would be the most important step to become a couple, to become a healthy family, I can say without hesitation that all the emotional and physical learning I received during my recovery should be a must for many young people that is either starting a relationship or is already in one because there's no excuse for anyone, and there shouldn't be regrets later, even if they're just trying to have a relationship to have 'fun.' Sometimes the fun ends up with a baby that was not planned or ends up with a person that is deeply hurt and will unconsciously save that pain and take it on to the next person, just as a virus that spreads from one coughing person to the next."

"Wow, Mario, I could have not said things better, as we came here when we got engaged with a ring and now, we repeat the spot and pretty much the encounter is also about healing. I make today a commitment to compromise with you from my soul, from my heart, and with a true free love that has no boundaries, that is not looking to be complimented, justified, or be competing with you in any aspect of our lives.

"I believe in us, I believe in healing couples, and I believe we have the power to help more individuals in this journey if we set the example and spread the new vaccine–couple's love! Family love! Healing love! Straight from your soul and heart!"

The end . . . for now!

Thought Takeaways

After witnessing the closing chapter in Mario and Betty's story, you can find below the last very juicy takeaways that we can extract from the story:

I. Do you live in the hamster wheel of life? What are the signs and symptoms?

II. What are some common expressions of health issues in children that call your attention?

III. How can you build a social-supported life?

IV. How does eating, physical activities, and stress affect your overall health?

V. Are you repeating old patterns? What can you do to stop them from growing?

Let's dive in.

I. Do you live in the hamster wheel of life? What are the signs and symptoms?

As harsh as it sounds, more than 75 percent, if not more as you read, is affected by stressful situations in life. Stress per se and in certain degrees and for short periods is not bad for you; however, as we know, those "ideal" data are not followed or complied by everyday people.

Therefore, to have a clear reference of what are the "normal" and tolerable amounts of stress in a regular person, let's look at research on stress.

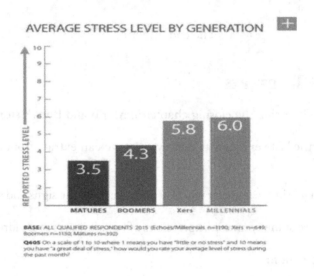

Figure 2. American Psychological Association, 2015.

As you can also see in the statistics of stress per generation, newer generations tend to present more stress than in the past, and the main causes of these increments are as follows:

Top Causes of Stress (American Institute of Stress, 2014)		
1	Job pressure	Coworker tension, bosses, work overload
2	Money	Loss of job, reduced retirement, medical expenses
3	Health	Health crisis, terminal or chronic illness
4	Relationships	Divorce, death of spouse, arguments with friends, loneliness
5	Poor nutrition	Inadequate nutrition, caffeine, processed foods, refined sugars
6	Media overload	Television, radio, internet, e-mail, social networking
7	Sleep deprivation	Inability to release adrenaline and other stress hormones

There are no updated data, but I would say that those categories seem pretty stable for five years that have passed since their last update. And as we can see, your job is the most important source of stress, which does match with the amount of time that most people spend doing it, whether it is from your house, your company, in the streets, or even when it is household chores, as this has to be considered a job for many people that perform this kind of activities every day and sometimes even in addition to the regular job. This is just a scale of categories; however, if we add to the list the stress produced by children, the level of stress can clearly be raised at least in two points, which would lead us to having a level of stress in the numbers of 7–8 according to the perceived stress scale.

_____ *1. In the last month, how often have you been upset because of something that*

   happened unexpectedly?

_____ 2. *In the last month, how often have you felt that you were unable to control the important things in your life?*

_____ 3. *In the last month, how often have you felt nervous and stressed?*

_____ 4. *In the last month, how often have you felt confident about your ability to handle your personal problems?*

_____ 5. *In the last month, how often have you felt that things were going your way?*

_____ 6. *In the last month, how often have you found that you could not cope with all the things that you had to do?*

_____ 7. *In the last month, how often have you been able to control irritations in your life?*

_____ 8. *In the last month, how often have you felt that you were on top of things?*

_____ 9. *In the last month, how often have you been angered because of things that happened that were outside of your control?*

_____ 10. *In the last month, how often have you felt difficulties were piling up so high that you could not overcome them?*

The PSS Scale is reprinted with permission of the American Sociological Association (Cohen, S., Kamarck, T., and Mermelstein, R. [1983]. A global measure of perceived stress. *Journal of Health and Social Behavior* 24, 386–396).

Important Note. The scores on the following self-assessment do not reflect any particular diagnosis or course of treatment. They are meant as a tool to help assess your level of stress.

You can determine your PSS score by following these directions:

- First, reverse your scores for questions 4, 5, 7, and 8. On these 4 questions, change the scores like this: $0 = 4, 1 = 3, 2 = 2, 3 = 1, 4 = 0$.

- Now add up your scores for each item to get a total. **My total score is** _____.

- Individual scores on the PSS can range from 0 to 40 with higher scores indicating higher perceived stress.

  ▶ Scores ranging from 0-13 would be considered low stress.

  ▶ Scores ranging from 14-26 would be considered moderate stress.

  ▶ Scores ranging from 27-40 would be considered high perceived stress.

This is a sample of a stress scale, which is based on perceived stress, that can become practical and handy when you want to perform a self-evaluation and start working toward some type of outlet to allow your body and mind to arrive at a more homeostatic (balanced) level.

Some of the most relevant symptoms that you can start perceiving in your life as part of a high amount of stress are the following:

- ⊙ Headaches. Increased or intensified level.

- ⊙ Heartburn. Increments of production in the stomach acid can lead to heartburn or increase it.

- Rapid breathing. When stressed, the muscles that help you breathe tense up, which can leave you short of breath.

- Risk of heart attack. Over time, an increased heart rate and high blood pressure damage your arteries, which can lead to heart attack.

- Pounding heart. Stress hormones make your heart pump faster so that blood can quickly reach your vital organs and limbs.

- Fertility problems. Stress interferes with the reproductive system in both men and women and may make it harder to conceive.

- Erectile dysfunction. Your brain plays an important part in the process of getting an erection. Stress can interfere with this process.

- Missed periods. Fluctuating hormones can throw your menstrual cycles off or, in severe cases, stop it altogether.

- Increased depression. Chronic stress can wear you down emotionally and lead to depression.

- Insomnia. Stress makes it harder to fall asleep and stay asleep, which can lead to insomnia.

- Weakened immune system. Long-term stress can weaken your immune system's defenses, leaving you more vulnerable to infections.

- High blood sugar. Stress causes your liver to release extra sugar (glucose) into your bloodstream, which over time puts you at risk for type 2 diabetes.

⊙ High blood pressure. Stress hormones tighten blood vessels, which can raise your blood pressure.

⊙ Stomachache. Stress affects your body's digestive system, which can lead to stomachaches, nausea, and other tummy troubles.

⊙ Low sex drive. Stress, and the fatigue that often comes with it, can take a toll on your libido.

⊙ Tense muscles. Stress makes muscles tense up, and chronic stress can lead to tension-related headaches and backaches.

If that is not enough in terms of the physical damage that you're doing to your body, and you keep the tendency to allow yourself to feel overstressed, perhaps these other symptoms will allow you to be more aware that you need to stop:

⊙ Irritability

⊙ Anxiety

⊙ Depression

⊙ Headaches

⊙ Insomnia

Many times in our lives we really don't consider that also stress can lead to generate epigenetic marks, which we have been mentioning throughout previous chapters, and these stains to your DNA will start to build up and moreover will pass on to the next generation, which kind of explains why each generation has a higher score in stress levels.

Finally, the stress that you're producing internally is an incoherent and chaotic wave of energy vibration in your body that emanates and permeates to your children even if you try to hide it, even if you try to fake or use a mask so no one can notice that you're stressed. Just by reading the huge list of physical symptoms, I'm guessing it will now be more obvious for you to understand that having any of them will lead you to feel more emotional, being triggered by small things, and also reduce a lot your levels of patience, tolerance, and compassion toward the ones that surround you.

Therefore, I really wish that you pay more attention to your internal signals and to your inner voice that you need to pause before you have lost control and it's too late to fix a problem that could be minor and easily treatable, instead of being stubborn or trying to be oblivious to all the messages to stop, release, and recharge your energy.

There's nothing wrong with stopping in your life, with making the necessary pauses that you need to do, to be concerned about you in order to give your best energy to anyone around you and more importantly to your loved ones.

II. What are the common expressions of health issues in children that call your attention?

Before they learn to speak, small children do have forms of expressing their stress caused by an unhealthy family environment, which, as we have mentioned previously, permeates the child with toxic emotions.

Stress, as reviewed above, has many ways of propagating among people, whenever parents are having an unhealthy relationship first with themselves, then with their partners; and they bring that energy into the house, into the core of the family. Then the emotions, the stress, and the negativity starts to spread, sort of an airborne virus. The fact that we don't want to see the effects doesn't help to allow the healing.

However, infants have a wiser way of expressing that although it is a more louder voice, and it is the way they first start to cry, apparently for everything, their sensitivity starts to rise, then if not listened, sleep problems start to come, uneasiness, and also an irritable mood, followed by probably a skin issue, respiratory, and more dangerous intestinal disorder.

Why is the scale of disease expressed like that? Well, if you think deeper crying is a very graphical way that we should understand, it would be like screaming in adults or older boys.

Then sleeping issues is the next "symptom" of emotional stress for them, as they need more than adults and is the time they use to repair and is also something that is deeply affected by emotional load and negativity!

This is followed by the same reflection of irritability in them, uneasiness to stay at peace, or doing some "strange" things to call the attention, such as being rude, throwing things or tantrums, or behaving "bad" at nursery or when they're older at school. Children are just trying to imitate what they see, and if they see irritability in you, impatience, intolerance, they will act the same way, reflecting how you feel and act, not at all with the intention to make your life more difficult but in a harder way to call your attention to begin to recognize that you've been stressed and with a bad mood! That not only is harmful to you but is also dangerous for people around you.

In addition to that, the pattern of toxic chemicals that is triggering you to react is will be permeated to your child through the incoherent pattern that you're developing and some small particles that can literally travel through the air and be perceived by others.

I believe that during your life, you have had the opportunity to encounter or run into places that have a strong smell, that doesn't even make you want to get inside, whether they are food places, museums, libraries, people's houses. If you dare to enter but stay for a longer time (let's say more than thirty minutes), you'll be experiencing a different mood, and most likely you'll become more irritable and sensitive to small things and feel drained of energy and also kind of grumpy.

Smell, as one of the chemical senses, is critical for the sampling of the environment and to elicit information about it. Aside from its recognition and warning functions, the olfactory system serves other purposes and may be influenced in turn by many factors at the central nervous system or CNS level. Olfaction facilitates the identification of food, partners, predators, and serves both sensual pleasure as well as warnings against danger. It thus remains one of the most important means of communication with the environment. The process, however, is complex. Following the initial sensory process, axons from the thousands of cells expressing the odor receptor converge in the olfactory bulb. From there, odor signals are relayed to higher cortex regions, handling conscious thought processes, and to the limbic system, generating emotional context. These include a multitude of projections including the amygdala, septal nuclei, pre-pyriform cortex, the entorhinal cortex, hippocampus and the subiculum, many of which form the limbic system, and are thus concerned with motivation, emotion and memory (Strous 2006).

Body odor in general is processed by brain structures outside the olfactory cortex (anterior and posterior cingulate cortex, occipital cortex), and smelling the body odor of significant others (body odors from strangers or relatives) activates brain structures involved in emotional and attentional stimulus processing, such as the insula and the precuneus (area of the brain related to conscious experiences, episodic memory, visuospatial processing, reflections upon self, and aspects of consciousness). Another study, investigating the perception of the body odor of emotionally stressed odor donors (skydivers), focused on the amygdala's involvement in stress perception (Prehn-Kristensen 2009).

Chemosensory signals of anxiety activate brain areas involved in the processing of social anxiety signals (fusiform gyrus) and structures, which mediate the internal representation of the emotional state of others (insula, precuneus, cingulate cortex) (Prehn-Kristensen 2009).

As reviewed and stated by research, many of the processes involved in olfactory perception as one of our five senses allows us to perceive stress signals to warn us of danger, to allow us to be prepared for any kind of threat.

However, as we were referring to a stressful household environment– that is, fed by parents that many times arrive from work carrying all the emotional baggage from work and all the stressful interactions that they had through their day–this kind of unconsciousness events will start to produce a toxic environment within the family, which for infants will be translated into a certain type of psychosomatic diseases as they are absorbing and introducing all the stressful chemicals through their olfactory systems, which are more developed for obvious reasons: to defend themselves from threats. Additionally, they are also perceiving them through their skin, which is the other huge sensory organ that has a lot of layers of tissue, which cover up our entire body.

Therefore, these two powerful receptors of the environment will amplify the stress signals sent by parents and build up a wide range of stressful neurotransmitters and hormones that are constantly accumulating inside their home.

Moreover, it is not uncommon that children at an infancy stage mainly develop three types of "common diseases." The first type would be the ones related to respiratory airways, the second type would be skin rashes or atopic dermatitis, and if things are even worse at their home, the third type would be to develop gastrointestinal issues, such as lactose intolerance, food allergies, or even worse, chronic diarrheas or intussusception (medical condition in which a part of the intestine folds into the section immediately ahead of it; it typically involves the small bowel and less commonly the large bowel, symptoms of which include abdominal pain that may come and go, vomiting, abdominal bloating, and bloody stool).

As explained above, all the sensory organs in children will have a direct encounter with the stressful events that parents have, that they allowed to increase, that many times they were blind to see, because of the same hectic rhythm of living their lives.

It is so common nowadays to find pediatric doctor's offices full of children that have any kind of these illnesses that are just a product of the poor attention they have at home; of the polluted environment they are exposed to every day.

If we add to that, that many of the main cities around the world have a very fair amount of toxic pollutants flying around in the air, then it is not hard at all to see all the symptoms and consequences rising up like crazy!

This is all a background, these are all the results, but what can parents do to avoid these toxic environments?

Well, throughout the story, we've let you see that there some simple free tools that you can always use to start lowering the volume of your stress and helping your family to live in a healthier environment in addition to give you a much better outlook for your relationships and interactions with them and even with the people at your job:

- ⊙ Start by first accepting you're overwhelmed and stressed. As obvious as it sounds, people don't seem to find a solution for the stress because they're not even capable of accepting they're stressed; they're still in the denial phase.

- ⊙ Realize that the way you feel only depends on you. No one else has the power to "stress you" unless you release that power to them. They can assign you things, they can disagree with you, etc., but they can't stress you. That is a choice that you're making by yourself.

- ⊙ In line with owning your choices, and as we are on a path of choosing a healthier path, look for time and space to write down at least 5–10 issues that quickly come to your mind and you feel stressed about.

- ⊙ Start identifying the real things that are stressing because many times our brain, past emotions, patterns and programmed beliefs play a very important role in creating things that are not even real or will not happen unless you really call them to happen!

- ⊙ Make yourself a priority for you to have at least 2–3 periods of 5–10 minutes during the day, where you completely isolate from everyone, where you find yourself a quiet space or use some relaxing music (nature sounds or classical music). During that time, close your eyes and start thinking 2–3 things that you're grateful for. Savor the feeling of gratitude and add details to the events, persons, or things that you're grateful for and just breathe. Take deep breaths, and every time you exhale, let all the negative things or unreal things out! Every time you inhale, savor the things you're grateful for and say thank you from your heart!

⊙ Take a short walk before you have contact either with your family or with someone at your job that you need to interact and you want to have a pleasant, healthy interaction. If you have some more time during days, allow yourself to exercise your body at least 20–30 minutes, four days per week. This will allow you to self-regulate your mood for the whole week as well as handling stress more gracefully to develop more patience and resilience to sudden changes.

⊙ Right before you have the interaction or encounter with your family, try to picture in your mind, how you want things to be before meeting them, and think of some small phrase or grateful comment to them to allow a more positive interaction.

⊙ Before going to sleep, allow yourself 5–10 minutes to write down and let go of stressful thoughts, emotions, or discussions. Create a personal diary where you just put emotions in the paper and let them out from you. By the way, sleep at least 6–8 hours, as a poor routine of sleep will build up cortisol during the night and predispose you to feel tired in the morning.

⊙ The last one is to be mindful of what you eat. Sugary or processed food will trigger your hormones and some stressful signals in your body that will also raise stress and cortisol in your body.

III. How can you build a social-supported life?

Oftentimes in our lives, we will have moments where we will really need some help from people that might be more experienced or have lived through similar kind of situations, and having a network of right-minded people will always be a very valuable asset, more in terms of parenting issues as you will be understood, listened, and empathized, which is something that many parents and more first-time parents need whenever they find themselves trapped in the "busy lives" wheel or the parenting routine.

There are many strategies that you could implement in order to have a solid, mature, and objective community of parents that can feel supported and that can have a space to talk and many times to let all the stressful things out as well as giving advice to one another.

It might be utopic to think that we could create a community wherein three to five parents are willing to share some of the struggles or difficulties they've had and even address what happened to them in childhood without having to expose themselves. Just being specific in the topic and the objective of the dialogue could make a huge difference in their lives.

As depicted in our story, in the case of Mario and Liam, talking and discussing some disturbing events as well as relating to past experiences and struggles narrated by Liam and how he and his wife solved them, trying to set a frame for Mario, was very helpful for him to become more aware that he actually had the tools to address many of the issues that he was suffering from. However, he didn't have the right perspective, or he was too immersed in the stressful events that it was difficult for him to realize that he and Betty had to take a hard deviation and a more determining decision on how to stop the stress wheel and start focusing more on their basic needs. These basic needs could be having time for themselves to do other things different than talking about work or worrying about any kind of parent issue, giving also some time for themselves to be alone and quiet, and relax at least some minutes during the day, treating their bodies differently regarding what they were eating and doing of physical activities. This is such a big issue with many couples that start their journey as parents. All the demanding child-related issues take away a lot of energy and time; however, there is a possibility of squeezing some time to exercise even if it means taking turns in taking care of the children.

All of those choices explained as strategies in the last bullet will be very important in terms of regulating the emotional load and changing the internal chemistry of substances that are being generated within you to start shifting your predisposed or triggered state, toward a more resilient and stable one that will allow you to handle more the everyday stressful events, household issues or chores, and even help you to be perceived and received with a better attitude by your spouse/husband and your children.

Chronic exposure to adverse childhood experiences (ACEs), including abuse, neglect, and household dysfunction can damage long-term physical and mental health. The effects of ACEs on neural circuitry are particularly salient during sensitive developmental periods and highlights the need for effective intervention during infancy and early childhood (Woods-Jaeger 2018).

Parents with multiple ACEs are at risk for mental health and substance use problems, disrupted social networks, and limited educational attainment. The weight of these problems, combined with the stresses of economic disadvantage, make it difficult for families to provide a supportive, nurturing environment for their children, which can lead to an intergenerational cycle of ACEs and chronic stress (Woods-Jaeger 2018).

As found by research, we are just in time to stop the cyclical repetition of events in many families. We're facing a turning point to cultivate in our children a healthier, deeper, and richer environment than the one we had. We are able to detach from those painful experiences, from those shameful situations that many of us have lived when we were children, and deliver our children a more aware and conscious way of living life.

During the course of the story, we mention that children will be a reflection of the parent's character, behavior, and attitudes in the early stages of development, taking that as a punch line to address the shifting the new generation toward a different stage and a more coherent, congruent, and healthier choice that would mean that as we are the example to them, we ought to be more responsible of the kind of attitudes, behaviors, and patterns we want them to see in ourselves. Because you might be skeptic or you might want to remain in the denial phase, but your children are for sure seeing everything that surrounds them, they're evaluating, they have a more clearer picture of the things and events happening all around them, even as they missed "maturity" or "learnings"; ironically, that is what makes them more aware of things and how they're much simpler than they seem to you.

All of us as parents have experienced more than once when our children see us worried, anxious, stressed, or angry; and they come closer to us and ask us very humbly and also naturally, "Why are you crying, Mom/Dad? Why are you angry?" Once you gave them the reason, they turn to you and the first thing they do is hug you, grab your hand or face, and tell you, "I don't like it when you cry or when you're angry." Depending on their awareness and sensitivity, they can also tell you, "Don't be sad or angry, everything will be fine."

For them, everything is as simple as it should be for us; they don't yet understand why we give up our right for being happy and at peace due to some external event or person that literally stole our joy and happiness to live. And I'm guessing you've also witnessed that when they are angry, sad, or even when you yell at them or scold them for doing something they shouldn't have done, after a few minutes, they just forget everything. They are as loving as they usually are, and their lives return to the happiness they most of the time have.

We have to be more open to see the world of lessons that they are here to teach us; we think we are the ones that have to instruct, educate, or develop them when in fact they chose us for the simple reason that they also needed to teach us a lot of things. Therefore, remain open to see things with more simplicity, with more detachment, and focusing on the obvious messages that they see will be the key to developing also a team relationship with them and allow a more peaceful, sharing and loving environment for all the family, which will in turn start automatically healing plenty, if not all the physical ailments that could have been already developed by any of the members of the family.

The stronger we allow ourselves to develop tools, healthy routines, network support with other parents, spaces to share, and strong bonds with our children, the easier it will be for every member of the family to grow in resilience, inner strength, and of course in building a richer, healthier lifestyle that will be picked up by them, allowing families to close the toxic circle of inheriting toxic patterns.

IV. How are eating and physical activities affecting your overall health?

Though it seems a broad question in terms of the huge amount of information, we are going to focus just on main metabolic and emotional issues and how they're influenced by those three aspects in a very summarized but practical way to see them.

Therefore, let's start with eating or your nutrition!

The categories of your nutrients pretty much are covered by three main groups that many people have heard of–carbohydrates, lipids/fats, and proteins. Two minor groups compose the vitamins and minerals. So, everything you eat will fall under those categories. Even when nowadays we have very synthetic and artificial foods, they at least have some mixture of any of those components!

However, here is where the good metabolic and biochemical journey will enlighten you at least so you can distinguish how your body processes all food. Your carbohydrates are divided in two main categories (to simplify all): simple and complex. Simple means all sugars in any kind of form–glucose, fructose, sucrose, etc., and of course, synthetic sugars such as aspartame, saccharin, dextrin, sucralose or sucrose, high fructose syrup, neotame, stevia leaf, sorbitol, mannitol, etc. All those count as simple sugars although the synthetic or artificial sweetener category wants to be labeled as healthier; in fact, they are the most toxic than natural sugars!

These simple carbohydrates are the ones to be reduced at least to the levels of 30–50 grams (max) per day (7 to 12 teaspoons) for adults. Children and teenagers from two to eighteen years of age should consume a maximum of 25 grams per day (6 teaspoons).

Complex carbohydrates are the ones that are longer than three subunits of sugar, meaning they are a chain of sugar units bound like a pearl necklace that can take many shapes, depending on the function and type of bonds. Therefore, as they are longer and more complex in structure, these are the ones that will be processed slowly by your metabolism because they have to be broken down unit by unit in order to be able to give us energy or material to produce other chemical molecules essential for your body!

As such, they are necessary not only because they will release some sugar units if needed for energy but also because these kinds of carbohydrates will allow the maintenance of essential molecules within your body such as your nucleotides, which are your DNA block units. They will allow the assembly of complex proteins named generally glycoproteins, which are in your membranes and serve the function of a receptor (antennae to receive signals). They process the nutritional signals and maintain a proper homeostasis; also, you will need them to form transporter channels that are also structures that provide an important access to nutrients, such as minerals, and even to some essential molecules that are needed for your metabolism to function and your enzymes (metabolic helpers) to perform your inner reactions!

That is why they should be under the range of 20–25 percent maximum of your overall diet. Earlier, the percentages said 30–35 percent; now we know that our bodies don't need as much, pretty much what happened with the simple sugars.

Having an excess of these carbohydrates will only lead your metabolism to produce more fat, your brain to be foggy, and your main metabolic and hunger hormones to be dysregulated and give you a hard time in terms of your emotions, as well as leading you to become anxious, compulsive, reactive, and in an ambivalent mood due to the internal imbalance!

Fats or lipids is a category of macronutrient, whose subunits are known as fatty acids; they're also essential and now very popular in reducing the amount of carbohydrates and used as an alternative source of fuel and energy for your body!

In addition to giving you a lot more energy than sugars, fats are essential to replenish your membrane components, which are used in most of your cells and organelles (your inner cities that have specific functions to produce your building materials and allow your metabolism to be functional). They also mix with proteins, forming a mixture named lipoproteins, which mainly are in charge of cleaning and moving the fatty acids (smaller molecules of fat) to the place where they're needed although some of them interfere with the movement of fat such as the low density lipoproteins (LDLs), and very low density lipoproteins (VLDLs). But we also have the good ones, high density lipoproteins (HDLs); these in particular are the ones that will move the cholesterol and triglycerides to the place where they should be either burned for energy or used to assemble something else that your body needs!

When we have an excess of saturated fats, this leads to the accumulation of general white adipose tissue, which is the one that raises your risk of several metabolic and chronic diseases, such as obesity and cardiovascular and metabolic syndrome, in addition to the well-known dyslipidemias, which are the accumulation of triglycerides and the bad lipoproteins (VLDL and LDL).

Arriving at the proteins, this macronutrient category is composed of subunits named amino acids, which allow your body to construct all the essential structural components that enable you to perform pretty much all your physiology and metabolic functions. They are part of many essential molecules, such as neurotransmitters, hormones, immune messengers and defense systems, structural and muscle functions, and to end with one of the most important functions they are needed to assemble the nucleus and core of your nucleotides needed to form DNA (your internal hardware) and RNA (your internal software) that will allow the production and main control of everything in your body! And without forgetting that proteins or the subunits amino acids are needed to produce the nucleus of the heme group, which is needed to assembly your blood.

In excess, they can also become toxic due to the high amount of nitrogen that can have harmful effects inside your body; that's why your liver and kidneys allow the cleaning process of this nitrogen, taking it out in the urea and creatinine expelled in your urine! And of course, in your feces.

As you could see and read, all the three main categories of macronutrients are essential for you, and even if there are popular "diets" that tell you that you don't need one of them, it is just popular and marketing strategies for you to buy something or to engage in something "miraculous," which so far doesn't exist and

I just think never will! Therefore, if you want to save time, effort, and energy by consuming miraculous products, you might end up finding later that the downsize of that is much more expensive for your health and your internal pathways!

Let's summarize as well the micronutrients, such as vitamins and minerals. Those two categories are still very broad and powerful, as they're sort of like the password to your enzymes to be activated and to start degrading or synthesizing practically all your essential molecules. Therefore, without even one single mineral or vitamin that turns out to be essential for some enzymes, you could end up having a very serious disease and might end up being dead if not detected at the proper time!

To finally end up with this summary of food and how they can impact your health, the difference between minerals and vitamins is that minerals are inorganic ions or metals and vitamins are organic in nature (meaning they contain carbon) as they usually act as coenzymes, thus the nickname of "passwords." When they attach to a specific site in the enzyme, they activate a change in their shape that allow the enzyme to start working and either degrade or synthesize a molecule.

Your emotional, mental, and of course, your physical health are influenced by how well you balanced the five groups of nutrients mentioned above. Therefore, you'd better think twice when you want to sacrifice your business or practicality over the nutrients that you give to your body. Additionally, the cleaner you eat and the less frequently, the healthier you'll become. Eat real food, natural mostly without preservatives or additional chemicals, and practice fasting for a period of twelve to sixteen hours, which most people can get used to. Allowing your body to have three meals and no snacks in between will clean your overall internal machinery and will increase your energy and clarity.

Moving on to what are the effects of your physical activity, as we all have heard of as well, exercise or physical activity is not just an aesthetic aid for your body or external outlook as many marketing campaigns seem to be eager to install in your mind. Exercise is the most powerful tool you can use to detoxify your body, boost your brain and cognitive abilities, in addition to extending your life by reducing the amount of oxidation and inflammation in your body, and finally increasing the length of your telomeres (small caps that cover the end of your chromosomes, sort of like the plastic ends of your shoelaces in simpler words); these structures measure the age of your cells, meaning how young you are internally.

Moreover, exercise has been proven effectively to contribute to the balance of neurotransmitters, immune messengers, and hormonal balance, which control your mental health, immune system strength, and your mood swings or changes regarding your emotional health.

So, as you can see, your eating and activity behaviors have a tremendous impact in many aspects of your internal health, whether you want to acknowledge or whether you want to keep looking for shortcuts or hacking ways to avoid the effort.

Just always keep in mind that your body, which include your brain and heart, perform an amazing number of functions and processes for you without complaining, without trying to look for shortcuts or hacking ways in order to deliver you complete and ultimate health! They were designed to give you that and more, so at least be reciprocal with them.

V. Are you repeating old patterns? What can you do to stop them from growing?

We were all subjected to some kind of programming and biased beliefs, which fortunately or unfortunately took many of our own best qualities as children. And sadly, many of those scenarios that we witnessed in our houses and/or environments had already permeated some part of our psyche, designed some of our personality traits, and even were installed as epigenetic memory in our genes even before we were born. That is why we start swiping some behaviors that are very similar to both of our parents since we're very small. I'm guessing you clearly remember that Vilma was showing some behaviors of her dad like twisting her feet exactly as he did it as a sign of comfort and feeling secure or at peace. When Mario witnessed those small gestures, it was an eye-opener that some innate behaviors totally bring about by the memory conserved in our body through the imprinting of the DNA. And like those behaviors, we are now in an era where we are witnessing a lot more coming out in the realm of epigenetic science that is linking what happens in the environment to what will start developing inside of you!

Well, emotionally, I'm sure that you have witnessed a lot of repeated expressions, character traits, and personality resemblance to both of your parents although we usually develop a stronger attachment to one of them, which is with the one we interact more and from the one we perceive more things as we grow up. Nevertheless, our character, our personality, and the way we behave as adults is pretty much shaped by the programmed images and behaviors, we witnessed in our first seven years.

Although that doesn't mean that you're doomed to anything, neither does it mean that you're just a reflection of them. Moreover, this is the key point to start creating a focused mind into those negative patterns and actually having the awareness to first detect them then accept that you're doing the same and last find a coherent reason that allows in your consciousness to stop repeating the cycle. Even if you course correct, once you've done or said something, you can still be able to change the end result.

And in the worst-case scenario, making a mistake or falling again in the pattern shouldn't also push you to perform to give up and become again identified with the label that you have given yourself. The power of your words is so amazing to change the result of things that sometimes you think are just "habits" and that you're just "that kind of person."

Our higher ability of the brain located in our prefrontal cortex allows us to laser our attention, instruct, and direct the actions of our mind; we just have to train more in order to be able to do it as a habit.

Normative strategies for emotion regulation are predicated on reappraising aversive events in a more positive narrative-based context or on behavioral strategies for the suppression of emotionally expressive behavior. However, mood disorders are broadly characterized by a failure to adaptively regulate emotion, owing to heightened emotional reactivity and increased self-focus. These reactions can reduce a patient's cognitive resources for positively reappraising stressful stimuli. In such situations, mindful emotion regulation may be of service, offering a nonevaluative means by which to attend to negative emotional experience (Farb 2012).

As verified by research and proved by several clinical trials, developing an ability to be less self-centered, less judgmental, and increase the attention to what we're doing to why we're doing it, to become detectives of our own emotions, and to dig more in our past memories is a technique that will work for you because many of the thoughts and behaviors that we're repeatedly allowing are simply not ours. They were imprinted in us since childhood, and they have become our truth because we keep reinforcing them without even paying attention to why we engage with them and many times even use them to identify us, to generate a label, and of course, to make the cycle a lot stronger. When we just get curious with yourself with the naïve mind-set of a child to look for the "treasure" without even expecting anything, the meaning of that emotion, the source, and most likely the event when it happened will just pop out in your mind. Thus, with this new perspective, you will be able to find out answers, to understand meaning, and above all, you will suddenly find out that now it makes no sense to repeat those behaviors. Whenever you're doing them, you'll be able to simply see them as "an invitation" that now you're able to reject and to instead act from a much more conscious standpoint than the one that you were before.

All of these sequence of becoming more curious, more introspective, sets the ground so that you liberate a lot of the emotional load and power that those emotions had in you, something that will give you more freedom, confidence, and will allow you to regain your energy from a process that was just draining you, that was labeling you, and that most likely was predisposing yourself to become a replica from what you said many times you didn't want to do or someone you repeatedly said you didn't want to become.

Your life was given to you to get creative, to write your own script, not to unconsciously copy and replay an old version with new actors.

What makes all this process harder to see it simply as it is, is the fact that we're overwhelmed with stress, distractions, and a pile of to-do's that unconsciously blocks the strategy area of the brain (prefrontal cortex) and activates the primitive area, creating confusion, more stress, and anxiety to simply react, exert a response, and keep reaffirming the victim identity that you have created, where you, of course, feel powerless and don't even have the energy and clarity to see any kind of solution.

FINAL REMARKS

A New Generation to Heal Our Earth

*A*S WE WITNESS *our life using our amazing ability to integrate our five senses, which give us the capacity to embrace a small bite of the world that we were given to enjoy, to savor, to expand, to heal, to create, to help, to guide, and to love, we cannot fall in the misleading promise that many decades ago was started, was initiated, thinking that we're the only ones that matter in this earth, placing all of our attention just in an ego-driven society that has been programmed many times to consume, divide, and apparently thrive to some created standards.*

We are so much more than a bunch of cells and bacteria (within). We are evolved creatures with consciousness, with awareness, with a prefrontal cortex able to allow us to rise, to become independent thinkers, to become more conscious, to become more awake!

Just as when we were born and everything was a beautiful spectacle of surprises and discoveries.

We should do our best efforts to disengage from distractions, digital influences, biased information, and political manipulation that just want a society that perpetuates disease and produces an income for a small group of "investors" that have a monopoly disguised in many platforms—the food industry, the pharmaceutical industry, media platforms, education systems, and of course, many irresponsible governments that inevitably get inside the equation to maintain the majority of the population "under control" dependent on external aids, individuals, or products to sustain the leftovers of the earth. Sadly, we have become accomplices by being manipulated, unconscious and reactive to everything that has been fed to us.

We are now in a strategic standpoint that can turn around the course of our humanity, to probably still make a difference, to still be able to rescue the direction toward depleting all of our essential natural resources.

We are more than capable to turn around, to go inward, and to create the most powerful connection and energy field with our beautiful planet if we just let our heart guide us with its infinite wisdom, if we unite in one common front toward compassion, empathy, and love. I humbly and firmly believe we will succeed in the only endeavor that probably was given to us—live, love, create, and expand!

ENDNOTES

Chapter 1

Anxiety Centre. "Anxiety Symptoms, Disorders, Explained". (2020), https://www.anxietycentre.com/anxiety-symptoms.shtml.

Tartakovsky, M. (2018). 9 Ways to Reduce Anxiety Right Here, Right Now. Psych Central. Retrieved on November 1, 2018, from https://psychcentral.com/lib/9-ways-to-reduce-anxiety-right-here-right-now/

Vaish, A., Grossmann, T., & Woodward, A. (2008). Not all emotions are created equal: The negativity bias in social-emotional development. Psychological Bulletin, 134(3), 383-403. doi:10.1037/0033-2909.134.3.383

Ainsworth, M.D. (1969). "Object Relations, Dependency, and Attachment: A Theoretical Review of the Infant-Mother Relationship," Child Development 40, 969-1025.

Chapter 2

Feinberg, M. E., Jones, D. E., Granger, D. A., & Bontempo, D. E. (2012). Anxiety and chronic couple relationship stress moderate adrenocortical response to couple interaction in expectant parents. British Journal of Psychology

Suzuki, A., Poon, L., Papadopoulos, A. S., Kumari, V., & Cleare, A. J. (2014). Long term effects of childhood trauma on cortisol stress reactivity in adulthood and relationship to the occurrence of depression. Psychoneuroendocrinology, 50, 289-299.

Davis, E. P., & Sandman, C. A. (2010). The timing of prenatal exposure to maternal cortisol and psychosocial stress is associated with human infant cognitive development. Child development, 81(1), 131-148.

Laurent, H. K., Powers, S. I., Laws, H., Gunlicks-Stoessel, M., Bent, E., & Balaban, S. (2013). HPA regulation and dating couples' behaviors during conflict: Gender-specific associations and cross-partner interactions. Physiology & behavior, 118, 218-226.

Calmes, C. A., & Roberts, J. E. (2008). Rumination in interpersonal relationships: Does co-rumination explain gender differences in emotional distress and relationship satisfaction among college students? Cognitive Therapy and Research, 32(4), 577-590.

Nolen-Hoeksema, S. (2012). Emotion regulation and psychopathology: The role of gender. Annual review of clinical psychology, 8, 161-187.

McRae K, Ochsner KN, Mauss IB, Gabrieli JJD, Gross JJ. 2008. Gender differences in emotion regulation: an fMRI study of cognitive reappraisal. Group Process. Intergroup Relat. 11:143–62

Mauss IB, Evers C, Wilhelm FH, Gross JJ. 2006. How to bite your tongue without blowing your top: Implicit evaluation of emotion regulation predicts affective responding to anger provocation. Personal. Soc. Psychol. Bull. 32:589–602

Firestone, L. "Healing from Attachment Issues". Psychology Today. (Feb 28, 2018), https://www.psychologytoday.com/us/blog/compassion-matters/201802/healing-attachment-issues

Steinberg, Neely. "He Said, She Said: Are Men Intimidated By Strong, Smart and Successful Women?". Huffington Post. (Dec 31, 2012), https://www.huffingtonpost.com/neely-steinberg/dating-advice_b_2043795.html

Morgan, M. J. (2000). Ecstasy (MDMA): a review of its possible persistent psychological effects. Psychopharmacology;

Gordon M. S. (2001). What are the effects of the drug ecstasy? Scientific American.

Chapter 3

Turban, D. B., Moake, T. R., Wu, S. Y. H., & Cheung, Y. H. (2017). Linking extroversion and proactive personality to career success: The role of mentoring received and knowledge. Journal of Career Development, 44(1), 20-33.

Ratliff, K. A., & Oishi, S. (2013). Gender differences in implicit self-esteem following a romantic partner's success or failure. Journal of Personality and Social Psychology, 105(4), 688.

Chapter 4

Mishra, K. K., et al. (2007) A clinical study on cortisol and certain metabolites in some chronic psychosomatic disorders. Indian J Clin Biochem., 22:2, 41–43.

McIlwain, D. (2010). Living strangely in time: Emotions, masks and morals in psychopathically-inclined people. European journal of analytic philosophy, 6(1), 75-94.

McEwen, B. S. (2017). Integrative medicine: Breaking down silos of knowledge and practice an epigenetic approach. Metabolism, 69, S21-S29.

Young-Eisendrath, P. (2008). The transformation of human suffering: A perspective from psychotherapy and Buddhism. Psychoanalytic Inquiry, 28(5), 541-549.

Chapter 5

Young, J., & Schrodt, P. (2016). Family Communication Patterns, Parental Modeling, and Confirmation in Romantic Relationships. Communication Quarterly, 64(4), 454–475.

Feldman, R. (2015). Mutual influences between child emotion regulation and parent-child reciprocity support development across the first 10 years of life: implications for developmental psychopathology. Development and psychopathology, 27(4pt1), 1007-1023

Fricker, M., 2016. What's the point of blame? A paradigm based explanation. Noûs, 50(1), pp.165-183.

Larkin, K. T., Goulet, C., & Cavanagh, C. (2015). Forgiveness and physiological concomitants and outcomes. In Forgiveness and Health (pp. 61-76). Springer, Dordrecht.

Mullet, E., Neto, F., & Riviere, S. (2005). Personality and its effects on resentment, revenge, forgiveness, and self-forgiveness. Handbook of forgiveness, 159-81

Alicke, M. D. (2000). Culpable control and the psychology of blame. Psychological Bulletin, 126(4), 556–574

Kafka, H. (2008). The Man Who Could Not Cry and the Psychoanalyst Who Could: Mutual Healing in the Maternal Transference/Countertransference. The American Journal of Psychoanalysis, 68(2), 156–168.

Pribram, K., & Rozman, D. (1997, April). What New Research on the Heart and Brain Tells Us about Our Youngest Children. San Francisco: Whire House Conference on Early Childhood Development and Learning.

Childre, D.L., Martin, H.H., & Beech, D. (1999). The HeartMath Solution.p.33

Dispenza, Joe. Becoming Supernatural. Hay House. p. 331

Caldwell, J. G., & Shaver, P. R. (2012). Exploring the Cognitive-Emotional Pathways between Adult Attachment and Ego-Resiliency. Individual Differences Research, 10(3).

Chapter 6

Davis, D. E., Hook, J. N., Van Tongeren, D. R., DeBlaere, C., Rice, K. G., & Worthington, E. L. (2015). *Making a decision to forgive. Journal of Counseling Psychology, 62(2), 280–288*

Ripley, J. S., Garthe, R. C., Perkins, A., Worthington, E. L., Davis, D. E., Hook, J. N., ... Eaves, D. (2016). *Perceived partner humility predicts subjective stress during transition to parenthood. Couple and Family Psychology: Research and Practice, 5(3), 157–167.*

Cloke, K. (2015). *Designing Heart-Based Systems to Encourage Forgiveness and Reconciliation in Divorcing Families. Family Court Review, 53(3), 418–426.*

Ferriby, M., Kotila, L., Kamp Dush, C., & Schoppe- Sullivan, S. (2015). Dimensions of attachment and commitment across the transition to parenthood. *Journal of Family Psychology, 29,* 938–944.

Childre, D.L., Martin, H.H., & Beech, D. (1999). The HeartMath Solution. p. 41.

Gambrel, L. E., & Piercy, F. P. (2014). Mindfulness-Based Relationship Education For Couples Expecting Their First Child-Part 1: A Randomized Mixed-Methods Program Evaluation. Journal of Marital and Family Therapy, 41(1), 5–24.

Chapter 7

Pollak, S. D. (2008). Mechanisms linking early experience and the emergence of emotions: Illustrations from the study of maltreated children. *Current directions in psychological science, 17(6),* 370-375.

Nancy Eisenberg, Amanda Cumberland & Tracy L. Spinrad (1998) Parental Socialization of Emotion, Psychological Inquiry: An International Journal for the Advancement of Psychological Theory, 9:4, 241-273

Dunsmore, J. C., Her, P., Halberstadt, A. G., & Perez-Rivera, M. B. (2009). Parents' beliefs about emotions and children's recognition of parents' emotions. *Journal of nonverbal behavior, 33*(2), 121-140.

Nelson, J. A., O'Brien, M., Blankson, A. N., Calkins, S. D., & Keane, S. P. (2009). *Family stress and parental responses to children's negative emotions: Tests of the spillover, crossover, and compensatory hypotheses. Journal of Family Psychology, 23(5), 671–679.*

Denham, S. A. (2007). Dealing with feelings: How children negotiate the worlds of emotions and social relationships. *Cognition, Brain, Behavior, 11*(1), 1.

Nelson, R. J. (2019). Hormones & behavior. In R. Biswas-Diener & E. Diener (Eds), *Noba textbook series: Psychology*. Champaign, IL: DEF publishers.

Cross, T. L. (2002). Social/emotional needs: Competing with myths about the social and emotional development of gifted students. Gifted Child Today, 25(3), 44-45.

Cloke, K. (2015). *Designing Heart-Based Systems to Encourage Forgiveness and Reconciliation in Divorcing Families. Family Court Review, 53(3), 418–426.*

Lovejoy MC, Graczyk PA, O'Hare E, Neuman G. Maternal depression and parenting behavior: So A meta-analytic review. Clinical Psychology Review 2000; 20:561–592.

Abraham (Spirit), Esther Hicks, Jerry Hicks. The Astonishing Power of Emotions: Let Your Feelings be Your Guide. HayHouse. (2007)

Chapter 8

Daily Life. The American Institute of Stress. "The good stress: How eustress helps you grow". (October 21, 2019), https://www.stress.org/the-good-stress-how-eustress-helps-you-grow

The PSS Scale is reprinted with permission of the American Sociological Association, from Cohen, S., Kamarck, T., and Mermelstein, R. (1983). A global measure of perceived stress. Journal of Health and Social Behavior, 24, 386-396.

Strous, R. D., & Shoenfeld, Y. (2006). To smell the immune system: olfaction, autoimmunity and brain involvement. *Autoimmunity reviews*, *6*(1), 54-60.

Prehn-Kristensen, A., Wiesner, C., Bergmann, T. O., Wolff, S., Jansen, O., Mehdorn, H. M., ... & Pause, B. M. (2009). Induction of empathy by the smell of anxiety. *PloS one*, *4*(6), e5987.

Farb, N. A., Anderson, A. K., & Segal, Z. V. (2012). The mindful brain and emotion regulation in mood disorders. *The Canadian Journal of Psychiatry*, *57*(2), 70-77.

INDEX

A

Abraham (spirit) 285, 352
Adaptive 38, 176
Adaptation 175, 215, 273
Adrenal 175, 182,
Adrenaline 2, 3, 17, 22, 27, 28, 29, 30, 37,
    68, 69, 136, 182, 315
Adversity 145, 146
Analytic 52, 348, 343
Anger 10, 16, 27, 47, 49, 53, 135, 150-152,
    169, 181, 183, 201, 214, 225, 264,
    347
Anxiety xiv, 20, 37-38, 41, 47, 49, 52-53,
    101, 113, 124, 147, 169, 181, 187,
    191, 201, 205, 216, 218, 241, 271-
    274, 281, 288, 319, 323, 342, 345-
    346, 353
Artificial xii, 333
Autoimmune 29, 137, 147, 182
Autonomic 145, 174, 182
Autonomous Metropolitan University
    (AMU) 3, 15, 204-205
Awake xiv, 9, 36, 287, 290, 343

Awareness xv, 19, 33, 36-37, 79, 102, 153,
    155, 170, 178, 189, 218, 222-223,
    246, 312, 331, 340, 343

B

Biology 66, 68, 72,
Blessed 170
Blame 78, 144-145, 155, 166, 168-170,
    173-174, 178-181, 183-184, 187,
    227, 244, 280, 307, 310, 349
Bold 138
Brain xii, 17, 28, 29, 36, 38, 45, 101, 112-
    114, 126, 145, 154, 175, 183-187,
    201, 215, 222, 235-236, 300, 318,
    323, 326, 334, 338-340, 342, 350,
    352-353
Breathe 50, 101, 125, 153-154, 164-165,
    221, 318, 327
Buddhism 349

C

Carbohydrates 333-335
Cardiovascular 38, 112, 146-147, 182, 335

Cases 20, 70, 104, 111, 113, 140, 187, 265, 310, 318
Centers 38, 125
Central 113, 188, 221, 266, 322, 345
Change xii, 12, 36, 53, 58, 61, 75, 91, 145, 155, 158, 173, 178, 193, 213, 252, 259-262, 266, 272-273, 284, 296, 317, 337, 340,
Chronic 20, 31, 113, 134, 141, 182, 301, 311, 315, 318-319, 325, 330, 335, 346, 348,
Clever 13, 21, 83, 136
Clinical 277, 341, 347-348, 353
Clinging 178
Coherence 126, 154, 180, 184-185, 187, 194, 215, 237
Collapse 276
Collide 295, 298
Conditioning 66, 70, 169, 196
Confidence 14, 26, 41, 76, 87, 109-110, 128, 133, 138, 141, 143, 156, 161, 192-193, 200, 202, 205, 209, 212, 227-228, 231, 237, 245, 273, 342
Connection 37, 121, 155, 187, 238, 250, 275, 300, 312, 344
Contribute 104, 188, 338
Conscious and consciousness xv, 24, 26-27, 34-36, 39-40, 79, 125, 142, 147, 156, 160, 170, 184, 197, 227, 232-234, 293, 299, 306, 323, 330, 340, 342-343
Constructs 18, 87, 188
Cortisol 17, 27-29, 37, 68-70, 136, 175, 182, 328, 346, 348
Creation and creations xii, 311
Creative 136, 342
Criticize 55, 166, 309
Cultivate xi, 111, 233, 257, 330,
Cycle and cycles 16, 26, 34, 38, 40, 41, 126, 147, 163, 156, 180, 184, 276, 280, 282-283, 287, 318, 330, 340, 341,

D

Depression 20, 30, 41, 76, 87, 97, 101, 113, 124, 145, 147, 175, 181, 187, 235, 271, 281-284, 318-319, 346, 353
Depressive 74, 282-283
Desperation 95, 181, 191
Destructive 63, 93
Diarrheas 325
Dimensions 280, 351
Digestive 319
Directly 105, 177, 229, 244
Disease and diseases xii, 20, 23, 29, 31-32, 38, 122, 137, 146-147, 182, 280, 295, 301, 310-311, 321, 324, 335, 337, 344,
Distraction and distractions 34, 126, 180, 275, 291, 300, 342, 344,
Divine xii, 102, 172, 312
Dreams 49, 232
Dysfunction 38, 134, 182, 318, 330

E

Earth xi, 198, 343-344
Ecstasy 94, 95-97, 99, 111-114, 118, 120, 348
Electrical 185-186
Elevated 186
Emotion see also
  Emotion regulation 174, 183, 236, 340-341, 347, 349, 353
Emotional abuse 136, 138, 145, 149, 151, 214, 224
Emotional development 230, 345, 352
Emotional health 147, 261, 302, 308, 338
Emotional experience 41, 140, 341
Emotional memory 42
Emotional needs 267, 352
Emotional resonance 236
Emotional state 37, 185, 231, 233, 285, 324
Emotional vibration 279

Emotional wound(s) 8, 32, 34, 37, 159,
    162, 193, 232, 279, 282, 298-299,
    Negative emotions 24, 74, 132, 142,
        176, 281, 283, 352,
    Process emotions 69, 79, 264, 274
    Toxic emotions xiv, 27, 140, 149,
        155, 184, 298, 300, 321
Empathy 45-46, 80, 108, 110, 140, 152,
    154, 183-184, 219, 223-225, 227,
    236, 276, 344, 353
Encourage 150, 188, 273, 351-352
Energy see also
    Heart's energy 154
    Healing energy 173, 184, 187
    Inner energy xv, 155
    Negative energy 151, 163, 172, 180
    Powerful energy 154
    Positive energy 163,
    Toxic energy 102
    Vibration energy 279
    Wave of energy 186, 320
Engage see also
    Engage in suppression 73
    Engage in impulsive 74
Environment see also
    Family environment 231, 233, 281-
        282, 286-287, 321
    Toxic environment 2, 30, 73, 146,
        246, 258, 306, 310, 324
Epigenetic and epigenetics 30, 125, 146-
    147, 175, 280, 319, 339, 349
External see also
    External aid 156
    External circumstances 170
    External slavery 155
    External stimuli 177, 179
    External trigger 125
    External influence 178

F

Fat 29, 38, 206, 334-335,
Fatty acids 29, 335
Fantasy 9

Fear 16, 25, 44, 49, 53, 63, 83, 87, 108,
    118, 142, 156, 171, 183, 272-273
Fearful 116, 190, 265
Fight 23, 29, 32, 45-46, 68, 130, 136, 144,
    225, 305, 307
Fill 22, 31-33, 47, 102, 104
Five core 300
Flight 28-29, 45-46, 68, 136, 142
Flow 12, 29, 103, 215, 284
Freedom xv, 85, 155, 205, 225, 227, 277,
    342
Frequent infections 137
Frequent respiratory diseases 310
Frequency 169
Future see also
    Future challenges 287
    Future decisions 249
    Future generations 178
    Future life 2
    Future relationships 42, 133-134
        Healthier future 131-132

G

Gain 19, 89, 137, 245
Genes 20, 23, 30-31, 125, 146, 339
Global 316, 353
Goal xiv, 107, 170
Gratitude xii, 7, 103, 180, 193, 214,
    216, 327,
Grateful xiv, 45, 59, 64, 85, 91, 153, 155-
    156, 162, 166, 172, 207, 214, 217-
    218, 252, 261, 276, 293, 327,
Grudge 32, 72, 238
Grumpy 261, 292, 297, 306, 322
Guilt 13, 47, 220
Guilty 54, 132, 164, 174, 285, 307

H

Habit and habits 2, 9, 20, 23, 159, 232,
    252, 257-258, 284, 292, 340
Happiness 44, 98-99, 196, 216, 331-332
Heart coherence 194, 215

HeartMath 350-351
Heart rate 29-30, 318
Heart rhythm 185
HRV (Heart Rate Variability) 186
Heart and brain 184, 350
Homeostasis 101, 175, 261, 334

I

Ideal 57-58, 139, 314
Identity 342
Identified 40, 102, 340
Identification 322
Image see also
    Ego image 176
    Self-image 111
Immune messengers 336, 338
Immune response 68
Immune system 28-29, 38, 103, 182, 318,
    338, 353
Induction 353
Integral 102, 196
Integrate 343
Integration 235
Intention 220, 322

J

Journal and Journaling 75, 191, 201, 284
Joy 44, 103, 192, 198, 240, 277, 331
Joyful 170
Junk food 125

K

Knowledge see also
    Self-knowledge 189

L

Light up xii
Light and energy 173

Loved 10, 45, 48, 98, 129, 153, 162, 197,
    209, 213, 217, 263, 303, 320
Lured 9, 21, 95

M

Marketing 258, 274-275, 301, 336, 338
Medical 242, 315, 325
Meditation 77, 101, 103, 191, 201, 233,
    256-258, 294
Memory see also
    Memory of your body 17, 19, 35
    Epigenetic memory 339
Mental 47, 77, 87, 111, 134-135, 215, 297,
    301, 330, 337-338
Metabolic see also
    Metabolic abilities 271
    Metabolic effects 29
    Metabolic functions 175, 336
    Metabolic helpers 334
    Metabolic hormones 175, 182
    Metabolic responses 145
Metabolism 38, 103, 112-113, 125, 334-
    335, 349
Metabolites 348
Mind see also
    Dependent mind 101
    Mind-altering 111
    State of mind 186
Mirror and mirrored 149, 185, 220, 237,
    239, 279, 310
Music, see also
    Relaxing music 153, 164-165, 326
Mystical 171

N

Nervous system 113, 136, 141, 174, 182,
    186, 266, 322
Neural 134, 176-177, 185, 230-232, 235,
    265, 271, 330
Noise 169
Nutrition 101, 256, 315, 333

O

Observer 24, 28, 55, 59, 125, 149, 154-155, 162, 289-290, 301
Open up 34, 76, 139, 209-210, 276
Oxytocin 174, 230

P

Pattern see also
    Attachment pattern(s) 227, 229, 235
    Incoherent pattern 322
    Isolation pattern 229
    Repetitive pattern 189
    Toxic pattern(s) 33, 133, 143, 189, 197, 332, 284
    Upbringing pattern 82
    Withdrawn pattern 72
Peace, at peace
    Mental peace 77, 297
Peace of mind 77, 183, 278
Perception see also
    Clear perception 236
    Heightened perception 248
    Olfactory perception 324
    Stress perception 323

Q

Qualitative 186
Qualities 12, 87, 95, 110, 133, 139, 141, 197, 286, 339
Quality 280

R

Reactive 234, 271, 335, 344
Recognition 11, 14, 20, 37, 142, 155, 230, 322, 352
Recognized 40, 139, 303
Recognizing xii, 16, 25, 36, 91-92, 96, 267, 301, 309
Reconciliation 60, 79, 81-82, 191, 214, 219-220, 221-222, 249, 351-352

Recovery 70, 105-106, 132, 143, 158, 173-174, 189-193, 214, 218, 222, 312
Reflect 18, 22, 156, 158, 176, 180, 236, 265, 305, 316
Resentment 14, 25, 32, 35, 135, 151-153, 159, 163, 173, 180-183, 187, 225, 238, 349,
Responses 72, 137, 141, 145, 266, 281, 283, 352

S

Sensitive 134, 136, 187-188, 221, 236, 265, 271, 291, 307, 322, 330
Sensitive 145
Sensitively 235, 286
Sensing 75, 287, 289, 296
Sensory 266, 324-325
Suicidal see also
    Suicidal thoughts 50
    Suicidal rate 76
Surpass 165
Survive 5-7, 167, 197, 299

T

Talent 122
Tapping 102
Telomeres 338
Tolerance 27, 33, 320
Tolerate 56, 195
Traditions 45, 202, 206, 208, 209, 269, 298
Transcendence 277
Transgressions 226
Transferred 135, 286
Transformation 3, 158, 349
Transformed 14, 197, 297
Transition 2, 228-229, 231, 234, 351
Trigger 20, 26, 69, 125, 134, 137, 139, 168, 177, 225, 273, 279, 328
Trust 14, 24, 26, 40, 71, 76, 78, 89-91, 123, 126-128, 133, 137, 141, 156-157, 191, 193, 195, 198, 210, 254-255, 269, 304

U

Undervalued 69, 92
Unhappy 235
Unique 90, 140, 171, 177, 217, 277, 286
United 201
Universe 51, 57, 100, 179-180,
Upbringing 22, 44, 49, 82, 83
Unravel 82, 174
Unresolved 34, 277
Unrecognized 189

V

Value(s) and valued 19, 48, 51-53, 62, 78,
    86, 88, 103, 111, 198, 202, 208-
    209, 255, 268-270, 276, 295, 298,
    310 see also Self-valued 72
Victim 22, 66, 83-84, 155-156, 159, 165,
    169, 183, 194, 342
Vision 225, 64
Visualize 38-39, 165, 201, 214,
Void(s) 8, 32, 36, 102, 104

W

Wake 23, 104, 251, 294, 311
Wellness 102, 125, 245
Wheel see also
    "Busy lives" wheel 328
    Hamster wheel 289,
    Stress wheel 329
Wheel of life 311, 313-314
Whole (as a state of being) 102, 267
Wonder (as an emotion) xii

Y

Yell 69, 150, 273, 331
Yelling 28, 69, 151, 164
Yoga 77

Printed in the United States
By Bookmasters